Artificial Intelligence for Asset Management and Investment

Founded in 1807, John Wiley & Sons is the oldest independent publishing company in the United States. With offices in North America, Europe, Asia, and Australia, Wiley is globally committed to developing and marketing print and electronic products and services for our customers' professional and personal knowledge and understanding.

The Wiley Corporate F&A series provides information, tools, and insights to corporate professionals responsible for issues affecting the profitability of their company, from accounting and finance to internal controls and performance management.

Artificial Intelligence for Asset Management and Investment

A Strategic Perspective

AL NAQVI

WILEY

Published by John Wiley & Sons, Inc., Hoboken, New Jersey.
Published simultaneously in Canada.

For general information on our other products and services or for technical support, please contact our Customer Care Department within the United States at (800) 762-2974, outside the United States at (317) 572-3993, or fax (317) 572-4002.

Wiley publishes in a variety of print and electronic formats and by print-on-demand. Some material included with standard print versions of this book may not be included in e-books or in print-on-demand. If this book refers to media such as a CD or DVD that is not included in the version you purchased, you may download this material at http://booksupport.wiley.com. For more information about Wiley products, visit www.wiley.com.

Library of Congress Cataloging-in-Publication Data:

Names: Naqvi, Al, author. | John Wiley & Sons, Inc., publisher.
Title: Artificial intelligence for asset management and investment : a
    strategic perspective / Al Naqvi.
Description: Hoboken, New Jersey : John Wiley & Sons, Inc., [2021] |
    Series: Wiley finance series | Includes index.
Identifiers: LCCN 2020029614 (print) | LCCN 2020029615 (ebook) | ISBN
    9781119601821 (hardback) | ISBN 9781119601876 (adobe pdf) | ISBN
    9781119601845 (epub)
Subjects: LCSH: Asset allocation. | Artificial intelligence. | Financial
    services industry–Technological innovations.
Classification: LCC HG4529.5 .N366 2021 (print) | LCC HG4529.5 (ebook) |
    DDC 332.60285/63–dc23
LC record available at https://lccn.loc.gov/2020029614
LC ebook record available at https://lccn.loc.gov/2020029615

Cover Design: Wiley
Cover Image: © katjen/Shutterstock, © whiteMocca/Shutterstock

SKY10023593_123020

For Shakila

Contents

Chapter 19: Governance and Ethics 251

Chapter 20: Adaptation and Emergence 267

Index 273

Preface

ARE YOU SEEKING A BOOK on artificial intelligence (AI) in finance? Good news and not so good news. Good news is that you are likely to find many books; bad news is that most of those are written by quants and for quants. Riddled with complex math equations, proofs, and theorems, these books speak a language that many people do not understand.

It is as if authors want to demonstrate how much they know about machine learning but not tell you what you need to know. The tone is often ridiculing, even insulting, as if each sentence is coded language to discourage nonmembers from entering the exclusive club of AI. In some cases, the tone is demeaning toward even other quants, with the connotation of "you don't know, we know" position. The subtle undertone is clear: if you do not understand complex math and data science, you do not deserve to enter the amazing world of AI. This esoteric, closed, and limited membership in AI is problematic at many levels.

If you have not spent decades in the investment world and you talk to some hardcore finance professionals, they will remind you that if you are an experienced data scientist, then you don't belong in the industry. You will be labeled as "too naive" or "too young" or "too inexperienced." If you are an expert in deep learning and reinforcement learning, they will tell you that you have no use in the finance world. They will argue that deep learning and reinforcement learning are not being extensively used in finance (what they are really saying is that they are not using these models, and they have not seen those being widely used in practice). This criticism of machine learning professionals can be viewed as a mix of some reality and a bit of fear of the unknown.

Do not get me wrong. Certain authors are well-meaning and direct. They point out the gaps and show how to close them. They recognize that one must be blunt and direct to show the weaknesses. For instance, De Prado's approach is a passionate wake-up call for many quant organizations, and I am confident his work saved billions of dollars and avoided many unnecessary catastrophes (De Prado, Advances in Financial Machine Learning, Wiley 2018). I am referring to those who point out problems but never provide solutions.

It is true that finance machine learning is different. The signal-to-noise ratio is low. You are dealing with a dynamic and constantly changing system. Your every action is under scrutiny. You are dealing with significant amounts of unstructured data. You could be identifying relationships and then trying to discover the theory of attempting to explain what is transpiring. Many interesting finds are prone to overfitting. You are operating in an environment that is not only constantly changing—your interaction with it is exposing your strategy, and hence your strategy is subject to constant reinvention.

Now come to the non-quant consulting club. There are several people who are trivializing AI. This is the hype club that opens every AI conversation with a vague, astrology-styled notion of future of work, and the next words in those conversations are almost always deep learning, AlphaGo, and IBM AI winning the *Jeopardy!* contest. When quants hear that, they get frustrated—and rightfully so. In the words of the great master, "Everything should be made as simple as possible, but no simpler" (Albert Einstein). The hype club is composed of classical digital era consultants who are trying to figure out how to apply their ERP and CRM playbooks to get machine learning working. That approach will not work.

This book is neither a manual to implement quantamental algorithms nor a buzz-filled consulting talk of the hype club. It is a practical manual that can be used by both parties—quantitatively oriented investment managers and the leaders of support functions in asset management. It is a pragmatic approach to build a modern asset management firm. It is written with the intent to bring both quants and non-quants together to rebuild their firms around AI and do that based on the scientific method.

If asset management was all about quantitative strategies, then you would not need sales organizations. If AI was only for quantitative strategies, then you would not see AI in any other function such as marketing, sales, human resources, and others. An asset management firm is more than just its investment wing, and AI is more than just for the quant departments.

Yet, if Nabisco didn't make good cookies, then regardless of how well the support function performs, cookies would not sell. In other words, the investment function is at the heart of asset management, and that function must be realigned with the developments in the financial machine learning. The traditional statistical solutions are inefficient and ineffective to deal with the nature of problems, the datasets, the unstructured nature of data, the sparse high-dimensional data, and the rapidly changing investment environment. Top-down theory application can only go so far. A new way of doing things is needed.

To read this book, you do not need to have a PhD in math or computer science or data science. If you have one, that will help you acquire the strategic business action plan for transforming an investment management firm. If you come from business, analytics, financial, or strategy sides, this book will introduce you to the fascinating world of AI. The point is that whether your starting point is mathematics, computer science, or data science—or your entry point is business, finance, or strategy—to be successful today you need to learn how to create investment transformation. And the only way that transformation happens is when all parties—technologists, investment professionals, and businesspeople—meet in the middle. That meeting point is known as the AI transformational space.

This is the first book on the strategic perspective of artificial intelligence in investment management that gives you a comprehensive plan for AI-centric transformation. The goal of the book is to help you build a powerful firm by navigating through the complex and fascinating world of AI.

To keep machine learning trapped in the quantitative investment departments is dangerous. First, it assumes that machine learning is only applicable in trading-centric investment operations. It ignores the fact that machine learning is a pervasive technology that is being used and deployed in all areas of an asset management firm. Those areas include marketing, human resources, sales, compliance, corporate social responsibility (CSR), and many others. Second, it incorrectly assumes that people with PhDs in mathematics, computer science, or AI are the only ones interested in AI. This assumption is often based on the historical roots of machine learning, when it was viewed as the exclusive toolkit of quantitative investment in legacy firms. That exclusivity is no longer true. Third, this closed, cult-style adherence is extremely dangerous as it assumes that a firm's business model is static. It ignores the fact that fintech start-ups and tech firms are entering the legacy space and architecting their business models with AI—and that responding to such a powerful competitive threat requires a far more strategic approach to AI in finance than the one that comes with quantitative investment only. Fourth, to build a modern firm, you must approach AI as a strategic process that is embedded in the strategic DNA of the firm and as an industrial-scale machine learning operation. To do that, you must have an enterprise-level approach and not just a quant-specific viewpoint.

However, trivializing AI as some fictional, motivational, hyped-up, or management-consulting buzz phenomenon is equally dangerous. That approach can win some near-term contracts but generally leads to disappointment in the long run. Projects fail or fail to deliver the promised value.

When Robotic Process Automation (RPA) is sold as AI and AI is sold as a point solution while ignoring the data, it hurts all parties.

The reality is that the asset and investment management world is at the cusp of a major transformation. This transformation is not an ordinary evolution in the normal course of business. It is a revolutionary change that is creating never-seen-before opportunities and threats. It has unleashed an enormous force that is demanding new ways to respond to the challenge.

Thus, AI must not be approached as a toolkit, merely a technology, or a hyped-up technological change. It is pervasive and transformative. It is revolutionary and emergent. Most importantly, this change belongs to everyone and not just a narrow segment of your workforce. To begin with, the C-suites and boards need to understand this change. They are at the helm of their business, and the introduction of AI has altered the strategic maps. They need to rethink how to navigate through these troubled waters. Then, heads of departments of all functional areas—marketing, sales, regulatory and compliance, human resources, procurement, and others—must develop AI-centric transformation plans. Their plans should be consistent with the strategy of the firm. In addition to the support organizations, the investment operation should be approached strategically. The process, incentive systems, organizational setup, and theoretical foundations on how investment organizations are set up should be questioned. The powerful rise of AI and its effect on asset management compel us to rethink our business models.

This book, therefore, is a guide for every person who is in any manner affiliated with the finance industry. From asset managers to investment managers, from marketing heads to IT managers, from strategy professionals to executive teams. And yes, most certainly, quantitative investors can also benefit from this book. This book is fundamentally about transforming your investment management firm or business unit to make it a modern, high-performance, and AI-centric enterprise. It shows you how to build a modern asset management firm and function. It is your guide to move your legacy firm to a modern firm. Use the book as a roadmap to build your firm or to transform your legacy operation to a modern era company.

My goal, as your guide, is to help you think as a strategist for the AI era. Even though I will provide a delicate and intuitive introduction to various models, algorithms, and methods, if you expect to become a data science expert or learn Python from this book, it is not for you. This book is for the leaders of the investment management world who want to build their companies around AI and create a powerful future for their firms.

You cannot write a book on AI for business and keep the business as a constant. AI is not about automating existing business processes. It is about reinventing the business. The reinvention-related change happens on both ends. AI changes business, and business demands change AI responses—so much so that at some point AI becomes business and business becomes AI. In other words, your business is nothing more than your AI strategy, and your AI strategy is your business. Any strategies orchestrated other than the AI-centric planning are futile. Any plans developed outside the AI universe are doomed to fail. Any visions of a future that are not based on AI are useless. The power of an AI-centric transformation is immense.

AI must not be viewed as just another technology. Unlike regular IT solutions, AI is not something that can be simply pushed down to the IT departments. When it comes to business, AI is the new way of life. It is a complete transition to a new way of operating.

Despite the immense power of AI, we tend to be so narrowly focused that we continue to ignore the big picture. Think about placing a camera lens inches away from a rock and taking a picture. Chances are that you will find little information of interest (unless you are a geologist). Now move the camera away from the rock and let the picture of the entire scenery—mountains, trees, lake, clouds, and sky—fill your lens. Suddenly you have something of interest that you can enjoy. When it comes to AI, the situation is completely analogous—we are looking too narrowly and missing out on the big picture. That approach is counterproductive because it can never help create competitive advantage for a firm.

This change in business structure, configuration, and models is also evident in asset management. It is becoming harder to identify what exactly is an asset management firm these days. A strange convergence is taking place, where firms are evolving from a structural perspective. With various business models and structures, from passive to active, retail to institutional, human advisor to robo-advisor, the entire sector is in a self-rediscovery mode. Rest assured, AI will touch and transform everything in investment management. The process has begun. Welcome to the new era in investment management.

Acknowledgments

WANT TO THANK MY FAMILY for providing immense support during this project. I also want to thank all my colleagues at the American Institute of Artificial Intelligence.

Additionally, I want to thank Anam Khan of TSAM (the Summit of Asset Management). TSAM meetings and conferences in London, New York, and Boston provided tremendous learning and networking opportunities to help understand the practical problems faced by the industry.

I would like to thank Russ Malz, Gary Smith, and Lisa Schoch—people who truly understand the AI solution needs of the industry. Thanks to Dr. Paul Ellwood of the University of Liverpool.

Many thanks to the Wiley publishing team, including Susan Cerra and Sheck Cho. I work with many publishers, and I found Wiley's team extremely professional and helpful.

Finally, thanks to all those whose work I have cited in the book. It is because of their work that we are today shaping a new revolution in investment management.

CHAPTER ONE

AI in Investment Management

F IRMS WITH A HIGHER-LEVEL AWARENESS are not faring any better than those that lack imagination or alertness. When it comes to AI, firms seem to be split between denial and dysfunction. Those in denial view AI as a passing fad, an overly hyped phenomenon, a lustful yearning of large firms, a deviant path to shatter human relationships, and a phase whose efficacy parallels that of other digital technologies. Those in dysfunction are the fearless warriors who want to embrace anything that sounds like AI. They want AI at any cost—even if it means implementing AI without understanding what AI is, knowing how to plan and deploy AI, where and why to implement it, or how to maximize value from AI.

The ones in denial need no plan. The ones in dysfunction have none. Here are some examples of the above mindsets:

If you talk to investment management firms about AI as I do, you may hear something along these lines from the deniers: "I know our model works. We have been doing this for over 40 years. My clients know me. We meet regularly with clients. We have our methods, and we have perfected it as an art or a science—whatever you want to call it. I know how to find value. I know what my clients expect of me. I don't need no fancy technology." This narrative implies that the firm is confident that its existing business model is sustainable without any modification and augmentation from AI. For them, having AI is no better or worse than not having it.

The narratives of the dysfunctional firms are different. They display an aura of excitement and fascination about AI. In large legacy firms, the executives tend to use AI as the talking points to impress analysts, boards, and clients. Armies of AI suppliers and consultants occupy floors and floors of companies. Balloons, badges, and billboards of AI centers of excellence serve as power symbols to mark the supremacy and territorial invincibility of the newly architected transformation groups. Managers emerge as celebrities, award winners in supplier-sponsored conferences, and acquire newly found status and power. Futurists are brought in to paint rosy pictures of feel-good scenarios. Lofty and grandiose visions are crafted to elevate spirits and decorate resumes. Like *Titanic* setting sail for its epic but fateful journey, in exhilarating devotion, teams are structured, missions are developed, speeches are made, budgets are assigned, consultants are hired, suppliers are onboarded, and the transformation programs are launched. But after a year or so a deep feeling of anguish replaces the anticipated achievement. Project failures—whether evidenced by malfunctioning artifacts or by functioning projects with immaterial value contribution—become a discomforting reminder of complexity in producing results from AI. Transformation teams are disbanded—and then reconfigured. The reset button is pushed, and the "rinse, repeat" game starts again.

"Meet our youngest person on the team. She just joined us six months ago. She has developed this nice machine learning program that helps our people match their needs with various benefits," said the VP of human resources proudly. In the same firm, the head of marketing hired a consulting firm to implement chatbots. The board members were mesmerized to see a chatbot interacting with clients to answer trivial questions. The back-office accounting function went after a different consulting firm to implement what they thought was the best "AI solution"—something known as Robotic Process Automation (RPA). The regulatory department was not going to be left behind and got a different supplier for RPA and went with a different consulting firm. The head of the regulatory department tried to run an internal machine learning project but was unable to get results. Frustrated, she fired the team and restarted the project with another team. Quant departments—those that have solid experience in machine learning—observed all this chaos, laughed, and retreated to their silos. The walls of isolation went up. The strategic quarantining congealed. Each quant team had its own strategic outlook, its own AI team, its own way of doing things. Compliance got its own solution with an AI platform firm—but could not find the data to make the algorithm work. The audit department discovered that their firm has an AI lab set up in a foreign country—apparently a well-kept secret—and reached out to the team of researchers out there. The internal research team was thrilled to be discovered by the US-based functional areas within their own company and began working on the audit solutions. The head researcher remarked, "We do a lot of AI research, but no one in the firm knows about us. Everyone wants their own suppliers."

The above story of haphazard, unplanned, and chaotic accumulation of AI artifacts is not confined to a single legacy firm. This ailment of becoming theme-less art galleries of AI tools is inflicting nearly all large firms. Amid this chaotic adoption lies the real problem: for all this toil and drudgery, the legacy firms are losing their competitive advantage. A silent but ruthless competition is emerging from the fintech side. A fierce enemy is lurking in the shadows of innovation. The barbarians are not quite at the gate, but they are certainly amassing.

In smaller firms, things are not too different. Since the decision authority is limited to a handful of people, the dysfunction is more localized and centralized. One or two partners, mostly to satisfy their own inquisitiveness or ego, are demanding their IT shops to identify and implement AI solutions to help their business. When doing that, they either issue precise instructions to specify what they want, which tends to be some type of crude and obstinate automation of their existing business model, or they provide the IT shops free rein to explore what can be done. Since most IT shops in small firms are not equipped to handle AI solutions, they scramble to figure out how and where to start. Some reach out to consulting firms. Others try to find AI experts, professors, or AI platform companies. Some even take courses and attempt to develop their own AI solutions. But like their supersized competitors, smaller firms also lack the vision to architect a strategy for what one day will be viewed as the greatest transformation in human history.

Yet when non-quant leaders in investment management sit across data science people, they seem lost. In one of the largest surveys we conducted at the American Institute of AI, we found out what was on the minds of executives. They expressed to us the problems with the sudden rise of AI (paraphrased and expressed as collective sentiment to facilitate understanding):

1. How should I start my AI program? All these consulting firms are telling me different things. I cannot figure out how to start the enterprise program. My boss told me to start something with AI when she returned from a conference (or read an article or met with a consulting supplier).
2. What is cognitive transformation? Everyone I talk to gives different answers.

3. I hear all these terms, AI, RPA, deep learning, neural networks—what should I focus on?
4. How should I demonstrate value from AI?
5. How should I prioritize investment in AI? What comes first and what comes second and so on?
6. How should I develop skills?
7. What should be my business model? Is my business model changing?
8. What should I do about all the dangers of AI they keep warning me about?
9. How do I hire resources?
10. What is AI governance?

On one hand you have leaders who are having trouble understanding the revolution. On the other hand, you have AI, ML, and data science leaders who can drop unfathomable terms and mathematical concepts at lightning speed. So we have two sides in our companies—non-AI people who are feeling pressured to do something but do not know what and how, and the AI teams who are trying to make a contribution but fail to find support, budget allocation, and vision setting from the executive leadership teams.

This book is for everyone who is involved with the investment management world at any level. The reason for that is simple: this book is about transformation. It shows you how to transition from a twentieth-century classical digital era company to a modern AI firm. Transformation affects everyone and opens doors of opportunity for those who are ready to lead and embrace the revolution. This book is your guide to do just that.

If the goal of leading a business is to architect a sustainable competitive advantage, the only advantage that seems to have worked well in investment management firms is the one pursued by firms with well-organized quantamental operations (De Prado, 2018). These firms have created and operationalized a setup for machine learning–centric strategy development and execution, and that has led to creating profits for firms. But a firm is more than its quantamental strategy. Performance is not viewed as the sole criterion of success in investment management (Murphy, 2018). You need a business strategy beyond your quantitative investment strategies developed in your lab. You need a total transformation to function in the new era of AI.

This book answers all your above questions. It also creates a bridge between business and AI professionals and helps develop the strategic plan that both parties need. It gives control to business so that you can lead the transformation of your firm.

WHAT ABOUT AI SUPPLIERS?

In all this chaos, suppliers of AI are not helping. AI software suppliers can be divided into six types of firms:

- **Newly launched AI platform companies:** These firms claim to offer an AI platform. An AI platform, from their perspective, is a general-purpose solution that can be used to develop unlimited AI artifacts.
- **Tech giants platforms:** Large and established tech firms have launched their own versions of AI platforms.
- **RPA firms:** Robotic Process Automation is a rule-based software—which some argue is not AI—that has found significant adoption by many firms. It is simpler to understand for managers, and RPA vendors market it as the entry level solution to AI. Some even call it the gateway drug of AI. Some of the RPA players are blending their RPA (non-AI) offering with machine learning solutions to evolve as more integrated solutions.
- **Process automation firms:** The legacy business process reengineering firms are also repositioning their systems as AI solutions.
- **Other packaged or off-the-shelf:** Many firms offer packaged, or off-the-shelf, solutions that they claim to be AI solutions. Some of these suppliers have legitimate AI functionality; others have simply erased the B from their BI systems and replaced it with an A.
- **Function-specific AI firms:** These firms market AI solutions by functional areas such as marketing or human resources. Typically, their software contains some AI functionality. Many of these firms are venture-financed start-ups.

AI implementation firms are composed of the following:

- **Management consulting firms:** These are large management or strategy consulting firms.
- **Large systems integrators:** These firms are found in the echelons of Washington, DC government contracting space.
- **Tech firms:** Large tech firms such as Google and Amazon.
- **AI boutique firms:** Many AI-centered boutique firms are launched by AI professors and AI experts.
- **Data management firms:** Some of the basic data-centric support work is performed by data management firms.

Suppliers are equally confused about how to make sense of this technology. They tried to force-fit AI into compartments that they had built for digital transformations and which had worked reliably well for over four decades—but it all backfired. AI does not seem to fit the frames developed to implement ERP or CRM. Suppliers tried to explain to the clients that AI will transform their companies, but they could not explain how and why. They produced white papers and case studies but could not point to a single firm that had successfully transformed itself. Buried under decades of legacy, some even tried to repurpose the old molds of PowerPoints and business process reengineering era toolkits, but they did not impress the clients. They began recalibrating AI projects, only to discover that a great many were failing. After initial failure, some consulting firms had the audacity to advise the investment firms that they needed to go big and bet more, which essentially meant to have mega-sized *center of excellence* contracts with the consulting firms—but even for those who invested in those projects, the results did not improve much. Finally, the grandiose visions and promises of audacious transformations were tapered to on-the-ground realities. Suppliers of AI realized that the best way to sell to companies is to divide and conquer. Financial services firms were segmented into smaller pieces, and instead of selling visions of transformation, suppliers turned to selling small point solutions. Sales teams found entry paths leading into department heads, IT managers, and middle managers and began selling small point solution deals. The effect of such a sales strategy was catastrophic for clients. Investment firms turned into collectors of malfunctioning or substandard AI software, AI software proliferation ensued, and the process of death by the thousand papercuts started for many firms.

The strategy consulting firms are experiencing their own Darwin moment and are unsure how to function in the rapidly evolving AI-centered economy. The crisis unleashed by coronavirus has further shattered the AI management consulting industry. For the investment world, however, the pandemic has demonstrated the fragility of markets and made a strong case for the need for AI technology to help predict the emergent dynamics of the complex systems in which we operate in the modern era.

 ## LISTENING WITHOUT JUDGING

ALI does not float like a butterfly or sting like a bee but most certainly was the only analyst in our institute who saw it coming. By mid-January of 2020, ALI was convinced that within the next 60 days, the US stock market would decline down to the 18,000 to 19,000 range. ALI became suspicious when a news report about some type of a viral outbreak in China caught ALI's attention. Many of us missed that little news segment as it stood too far away to make a dent in the rapidly shifting consciousness of the modern world. But not for ALI. ALI stands for Artificial Learning & Intelligence. ALI is an intelligent machine, and its story to predict the Covid-19-related crash of 2020 is as follows.

It was early January, and the world was focused on turmoil in the Middle East. A war was brewing, and geopolitical tensions were rising. Fear was in the air, but as we now know, for all the wrong reasons. ALI, who neither exhibits fears nor inhibits desires, was focused on something totally different. Ignoring all that was occupying our attention, it had picked up a trigger word related to a viral outbreak in China, and it was not ready to let go. Since viral outbreak could be the trigger words for ALI to identify a potentially serious risk, it was holding on to it as a dog holds on to a bone. Suddenly, the pattern-seeking mind of ALI went in hyper-stimulated mode when ALI began discovering words such as "SARS," "pandemic," "viral outbreak," "panic," and "human-to-human infection." Like hammers pounding on ALI's consciousness, these word combinations made it go in a panic mode of its own. By the third week of January of 2020, ALI began screaming for attention. It was ignoring the highly publicized impeachment proceedings, the looming threat of violence in the Middle East, the tragic death of a legendary basketball player, the Oscars, and the Superbowl. All of these events attracted tremendous attention and occupied human attention. But it was as if ALI knew that all these attention-grabbing events would take a backseat in consciousness when compared to what was coming. ALI kept insisting to pay attention to what would eventually come to be known as Covid-19.

As ALI passed on the findings, we knew some type of threat assessment would be needed. Let us examine three pieces of information that were published in articles in major newspapers in January:

1. Coronavirus disease is transmitting from human to human;
2. Coronavirus is killing people as people do not have immunity against it; and
3. Coronavirus has no vaccine.

Logic dictates that the above information was enough to project that in a deeply interconnected world this virus would spread throughout the globe, that it would be devastating for people, and that it would lead to a catastrophic negative financial impact. Despite the logical inference, the world ignored the threat. The stories that appeared in the newspapers were written as if it were a problem unfolding on a distant planet. The authors and journalists covered the story as if they were some impassionate observers studying the phenomenon taking place in a lab experiment and far removed from the reach of the virus. It was in China—a distant land. The language of the articles suggested that we were standing on some high ground, protected, and shielded, while watching Wuhan wash away in a flood of obscurity. Our lack of empathy was on full display. A sheer deprivation of insight was widely observable not only in the political circles of many countries but also in the financial markets. The Dow Jones Industrial was leisurely strolling in record territories, carefree and exuberant. Oblivious that a train wreck was heading in our direction, we casually responded, probably enjoying the bliss that ignorance offers with undeniable consistency. DJI remained energized. Not until the third week of February 2020 investors finally recognized something was off. And even then, it took a while before the state of denial was lifted. On March 23, 2020, DJI bottomed out at 18,591.

One of the commonly used models in epidemiology is known as the SIR model. SIR is used to study the spread of diseases. It is remarkably powerful and simple. It divides the world into three buckets. The first bucket is composed of potential patients—the population that can get infected. The second bucket is composed of those who get infected. The third of those who have recovered. Hence the name SIR, susceptible, infectious, and recovered. As we connected the outputs of ALI in the SIR model, we recognized that growth of the virus would be exponential. But beyond applying the SIR model for infectious disease, we decided to apply it to study the infection of news. Similar applications of SIR have been done to understand viral marketing. After all, news can be viewed as infection where uninformed (bucket 1) become informed (bucket 2) and reach a point where they take an action (bucket 3). The action could be anything, buying a product, voting for a candidate, or selling your stock. Estimating how and when a certain segment of the population gets ready to take a specific action is a valuable tool.

When we studied the spread of the news about coronavirus, we were able to estimate by what time markets would get infected enough to respond to the news. With historical responses for such events fed into another machine learning algorithm, we projected that the market would decline to 18,000 to 19,000 within two months. On March 23, 2020—almost 60 days from our projection—DJI declined to 18,591.

Anytime anyone claims that they have the crystal ball to see what is happening in the market, you have already made the biggest mistake in investment: hubris. Yes, you can be right once, but the market finds its own way. It always outsmarts you. Which obviously means that we probably got lucky and were not necessarily right. Thus, the lessons of the above story are not to brag that we got it right. The lessons are far more profound.

Lessons from ALI

The above story of ALI illustrates a few important ideas:

- Having an AI/ML-centric apparatus is critical to working out solutions to some of the most compelling investment problems. In our case, we were able to pick risk signals from a rather rudimentary apparatus.
- Model development is not a single pony show. Many models must be developed to solve a problem. The models form a nexus of interactive capabilities that are interdependent on each other and that reinforce the solution potential.
- These models work collaboratively to solve a problem.
- These models represent different types and levels of intelligence, and various types of intelligence and automation could be essential for broad automation.

As ALI's example shows, machine learning applications in finance are no longer isolated intelligent applications. They form a nexus of intelligence that drives value not just from the insights of a single application but also from the ecosystem of interactive and interdependent applications. This is a seismic change, and it has launched a new era in investment management. That era can be termed as the age of *industrial scale enterprise machine learning*. It will be helpful to first observe the four eras of intelligent automation.

 THE FOUR STAGES OF AI IN INVESTMENTS

In modern and progressive investment firms, AI/ML has progressed through three stages of AI in the investment and asset management world, and with this book it will enter the fourth stage. These stages are not necessarily sequential from a temporal perspective. They are sequential in terms of a capability enhancement viewpoint. In other words, the eras are not defined from a time or chronological perspective, as some firms may still be operating in the less mature stage; instead they represent capability maturity. The following are the first three stages:

Stage 1: The Siloed Quant Era

In late 1990s, sitting at a Borders bookstore, I picked up two books on neural networks: (1) *Neural Networks for Financial Forecasting*; and (2) *Neural Networks in the Capital Markets* (Refenes, 1995; Gately, 1996). For that time, the books offered amazing insights into how to use neural networks in investment operations. I still have those books, and I keep them to remind me that decades before machine learning gained hyped status, financial services firms, and especially quant departments, were using it to create value.

Machine learning was the ultimate tool of the quants. Quants came from different backgrounds and expertise—for example, mathematics, physics, and econometrics. Their orientation and strategies deployed were different. Everyone wanted a shot at what they thought possible. Everyone had a dream and a method to achieve that dream. Everyone wanted to prove that they had cracked the code of market mysteries. Like gold miners or searchers from gold rush times, every quant had his or her own pans, pickaxes, and shovels. Since quants brought different methodologies and approaches to achieve alpha, firms viewed such separation as achieving diversification. Splitting into silos was encouraged because it was thought that the diversity in strategies would create a portfolio outcome where the average results would turn out to be favorable. The incentives were easier to manage since they could be easily aligned with the performance. For years, this style of research and investment continued. Even today, in many firms, this is still the dominant model. Despite the perceived benefit of diversification, such a partition has many undesirable effects:

1. Machine learning was viewed as the domain of quants and was not integrated in other functions in a firm;
2. Within the quant zone in a firm, capabilities stayed siloed and inaccessible by external parties;
3. Each quant turned into a small team of experts who all maintained their own view of the world, data, algorithms, and strategies;
4. Since various subprocesses of machine learning require specialized capabilities, the talent spread unevenly across the firm, provided low

opportunity to learn from each other, and it was impossible to streamline operations or build an assembly line of capabilities. As can be expected, this structure kept the costs high;

5. During major scandals or regulatory inquiries, as in the Great Recession, firms had to deal with the criticism that they were betting on both sides of the market or selling products while betting against your own products; and

6. No corporate level strategy of intelligent automation or artificial intelligence materialized.

Era 2: The Strategic Quant Era

Calls were made to streamline quant operations by eliminating silos. Experts suggested redesigning the investment operations and restructuring them along the themes of functional expertise in machine learning. They recognized that the costs associated with the first era setup were overwhelming. Also, as competitive forces shifted to AI-centric competition and strategy development, organizational realignment became necessary.

Machine learning itself is not a single process but is composed of several subprocesses. Designing quant departments along those lines of capabilities was a validation of the significant role played by machine learning in investment. As top experts—such as De Prado (De Prado, 2018)—called for change, they envisioned building departments that will acquire expertise in the functional aspects of machine learning such as data, data preprocessing, model development, model optimization, and deployment. This change is not only profound, but it also had many practical benefits:

- It streamlined machine learning operations and created economies of scope and scale.
- To make quant work more efficient, some firms began eliminating silos in the quant zone. Elimination of silos implied developing a shared mission and creating strategic coherence among the quant teams.
- Instead of viewing the internal silos as strategic diversification, these firms started viewing them as impediments to achieving a good strategy.
- It was recognized that a mix of good strategies can still be deployed while keeping costs low.

In some ways, adopting the second era meant that machine learning was not embraced as a technology or a capability but as a business model.

What De Prado was suggesting, in some ways, was to build the investment operation around machine learning. Machine learning was no longer just a tool to achieve alpha but a model of service value chain configured to drive and deliver incremental value. The operational realignment turned machine learning into an assembly line.

This change, while powerful, demanded (and will continue to demand) much-needed realignment in firms. It will require rediscovering and redeployment of talent, leadership awareness, and incentive redesign.

Stage 3: The Organizational Chaos Era

While the battles between the first two eras were being fought, machine learning silently rose to become widespread in other departments and functions in firms. It was no longer the exclusive domain of quants, and functional areas such as marketing, customer services management, regulatory and compliance, governance, and other departments and capability areas began embracing machine learning.

With the widespread adoption came the problem of unmanageable proliferation. I was involved in guiding one of the world's largest financial services firms on how to architect their machine learning and intelligent automation programs. That is where I was able to see firsthand the chaos unleashed by unplanned adoption of machine learning and intelligent automation. I realized that the firm had hundreds of projects going on all over the world. There was little to no coordination between the heads of departments leading these projects. Each department head had architected his or her own vision of automation—which was limited to their own political interests, capabilities, outlook, experience, and understanding of machine learning. Political fiefdoms developed, and departments began competing for AI talent. While all of that was going on, several consulting firms and suppliers jumped into the mix—each with its own angle, methodology, understanding, and interests. Given that no broad platform-centric capability set was available, each group, with the help from its own supplier and consulting firm, developed its customized expression of what needed to get done. Besides politics and self-interest (promotions, bonus, impressing higher executives, resume building), psychologies of various leaders also influenced their decisions. The ones with more aggressive personalities launched more aggressive programs. The more risk averse settled for developing some cute chatbots. In a meeting held with representation from across the firm, it was discovered that there were literally thousands of parallel, but uncoordinated, efforts going on in the company. Everyone had their own ideas of what AI and cognitive revolution is all about. The firm had become a weedy overgrown garden of AI artifacts. As you would have expected, the overall performance of the firm had not improved.

To appreciate the gravity of the situation, let us take a step back and evaluate the third era with the backdrop of the first two. As I mentioned before, shifting from the first era to the second era will be a monumental change. Realigning practices, rebuilding process streams, redefining incentive structures, and managing cultural change will take years and require organizational commitment, leadership vision, and execution excellence. It is not something that can be decoupled and reconfigured instantaneously. Now add to that companywide sporadic and unplanned adoption of machine learning point solutions, and you have a perfect storm. The third stage is a current reality for many firms—but it is a recipe for failure and a death spiral.

Now let us review the desired stage - Stage 4:

Stage 4: The Modern Investment Firm

The design of a modern investment management firm is based on the following insights:

- **Structural coherence:** No single capability is viewed as the sole determinant of success. A firm is viewed as a collection of capabilities that all transcend through various levels of intelligence.
- **Interdependence:** These capabilities interact with each other and through that interaction create interdependence where the entire system operates as a complex system.
- **External interaction:** Information flows into these capability areas from external systems, and the firm processes both internal and external information.
- **Performance maximizing:** The performance of each capability area is maximized, while ensuring that its interactions with other capability areas do not negatively affect the company goals.
- **Cohesive value building:** Each capability area is designed for performance, and the design focuses on two aspects: (1) automation and (2) intelligence. Automation, as the word implies, is work being performed by machines. Intelligence (I also use the term "intellectualization" interchangeably in this book) refers to the increase in human or machine knowledge to solve goal-oriented problems. Automation does not have to be intelligent. Intelligence does. The performance of automation is

measured by the ability of a machine to perform work efficiently. Efficiency refers to comparative performance of artifacts with humans and other machines. Intelligence, in contrast, is measured by the ability of a machine to successfully navigate through the uncertainty in accordance with the goals of the system.

- **Narrative empirical relationship:** Humans think in terms of narratives. We like to explain things in terms of cause and effect, relationships, correlations. Our search for truth sometimes lands us in areas that are dark and story-less. For example, with machine learning, we can observe that a certain trading strategy works, but we cannot explain why. Cohesive value building allows us to develop multilayered narratives supported by empirical research. Multilayered means that the narrative-empirical connection exists and functions at different levels in the firm. At the investment strategy level, we can explore dynamic narratives that emerge with empirical research. At the sales and marketing level we can articulate our investment philosophy, approach in terms of narratives, and support it with empirical research. At the firm level we can narrate our firm's strategy and support it with research. Machines do not deprive us of developing and understanding narratives. They simply give us answers with some homework assignments. Those of us who respect machines know that we must do our homework.

The fourth stage firm achieves interconnected excellence from the interaction of the network of various functional areas. However, both collectively (whole) and individually (parts), the system is managed using the scientific method.

 ## THE CORE MODEL OF AIAI

Based on my work, the American Institute of Artificial Intelligence offers a model for transforming a company to the fourth stage. This model is based on the strategic factors discussed above, which serve as the underlying assumptions. For instance, the model assumes that management views the firm as a complex system composed of interconnected capabilities, where each capability has an individual role and a collective role. Secondly, the model proposes companywide adoption of the scientific method to run the company.

As shown in Figure 1.1, the vertical dimensions of the model are based on the value chain of a firm. The model shown here is for a general investment firm,

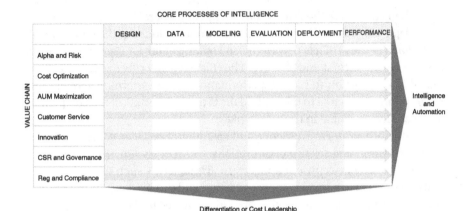

FIGURE 1.1 The AIAI Core Model

but it can be realigned and reconfigured in accordance with the unique nature of the firm (e.g., private equity or wealth management). Each value driver of the value chain has a specific goal. For example, the goal of alpha and risk is to generate alpha while managing risk in a firm. The goal of cost optimization is to decrease costs across the company. Note that the value drivers are not mapped as departments (e.g., operations, marketing, or sales). They are listed as capability areas. These capability areas can affect one or more departments. It is important to recognize that the functional departments–centric models—leftover from the twentieth-century bureaucratic organization—are no longer deemed necessary in the modern organization. I will explain that in Chapter 2. The capability areas are more consistent with the strategic goals of the entity, and it is assumed that each capability will tie in to one or more functional area organizations. Most importantly, the vertical dimension of strategic cohesiveness represents the strategy of the firm.

The horizontal dimension is composed of the scientific method, and it represents the operational excellence and execution potential of a firm. The scientific method is adopted to implement an industrial-scale enterprise machine learning approach for managing each function. The core processes of the scientific method include six competency areas of design, data, modeling, evaluation, deployment, and performance. Each one of those machine learning competency areas is independent of the vertical capability areas of the value chain. These competency areas are geared toward designing and developing machine learning solutions at an industrial scale.

When combined, the firm becomes a factory where AI artifacts are developed, deployed, nurtured, managed, and decommissioned at the end of the life cycle. Each of the artifacts plays a role in creating value for the business and is designed to be efficient and effective. The efficiency and effectiveness are determined in comparison to human performance or the performance of another machine and compared to the goals of the firm and the state of the competition and technical potential in the marketplace.

With both strategic excellence and operational excellence, firms are operated as research and science organizations—with every functional area transitioning to science-centric management. Thus, terms such as sales science, marketing science, human resources science, and supply chain science refer to the transformed organizations that are driven and led by data-centric planning and execution.

YOUR JOURNEY THROUGH THIS BOOK

Your journey through this book is divided into three parts. Part 1 starts you off in Chapter 2 with a focused coverage of investment management firm level strategy in the AI era. Chapters 3 through 8 focus on the horizontal competency areas of design, data, modeling, evaluation, deployment, and performance. Each of those chapters introduces the necessary capability areas and organizational structure to transform your firm to an AI-centric firm. Chapter 9 launches Part 2. Part 2 is function focused and from Chapters 10 through 17 covers customer experience science, marketing science, institutional investor science, investment science, supply chain science, and corporate social responsibility science. The addition of the word "science" to the traditional corporate organizations (for example, marketing or sales) is an acknowledgment that we are transforming our firms and business models in such a way that data science becomes the operational structure of the firm. Part 3 has three chapters: Chapter 18 is about AI project management, Chapter 19 covers governance and ethics issues, and Chapter 20 is the conclusion.

HOW TO READ AND APPLY THIS BOOK?

Chapters 2 to 8 show you how to restructure your firm for the AI era. They give you the new twenty-first-century structure to run your business in a scientific manner, understand that model, and then figure out how to set up your firm from a horizontal capability perspective.

Chapters 9 to 17 are about functional competencies. This is what we call departments in our twentieth-century terminology. We view them as functional capabilities embedded in the value chain of the firm. I strongly suggest that you read and understand the function-specific opportunities. Then build your functional capacities based on the applications introduced in the chapters—but their development and application should be done as a scientific process, introduced in Chapters 2 to 8.

A few notes about the book. While I was authoring this book, I was also writing a book on AI in auditing. Some chapters—especially the ones that introduce machine learning—will seem similar. As much as possible, I have kept the book simple and understandable for businesspeople. Finally, instead of limiting the book to a narrow definition of asset management, sometimes I use the broader category of investment management. If a certain section or topic coverage is not applicable to you, feel free to skip it—for example, if you are more interested in institutional, skip the retail section. Lastly, you will notice that I use both "I" and "we" throughout the book. When I use "we," I imply the American Institute of Artificial Intelligence.

REFERENCES

Gately, E. (1996) *Neural Networks for Financial Forecasting*. John Wiley & Sons.

Murphy, S. P. (2018) *The Road to AUM: Driving Assets Under Management Through Effective Marketing and Sales*. Noble Ark Ventures.

De Prado, M. L. (2018) *Advances in financial machine learning*. John Wiley & Sons.

Refenes, A.-P. (1995) *Neural Network in the Capital Markets*. John Wiley & Sons.

CHAPTER TWO

AI and Business Strategy

T HE AI REVOLUTION IS NOT AN EXTENSION of the digital revolution. There are some clear and distinct differences (Makridakis, 2017). Business strategy is not static. It is dependent on the changes in the underlying variables. But certain times and technological revolutions are far more extraordinary than others (Perez, 2002). In fact, I have no hesitation in stating that the AI revolution will launch the most transformational times in human history. The AI revolution is unleashing a powerful economic change that will require monumental amendments in the way business strategy is approached. Understanding those competitive dynamics is critical for developing an intuition about how to develop your firm's strategy.

WHY STRATEGY? THE RED BUTTON

In 2016, when the AI fever was just starting to pick up the pace, I had the opportunity to talk strategy with the co-founder of what he described as the world's first automated hedge fund. In a typical Silicon Valley's passionate and visionary entrepreneurial style, he gave me the analogy of OODA loop, which was a model used to explain the success of the most successful fighter pilots in dog fights in the Korean War. OODA stands for Observe, Orient, Decide, Act. It is a loop where, after you act, you observe your environment again, reorient, decide, and act. Basically, you go through these loops, and you make your trades. Human traders, he argued, are constantly looking, second-guessing, checking their current state, analyzing their profitability, deciding whether they need to make a decision, what decision to make, reading the signals, understating the context, and taking action. As you go through the loop, you adapt and readjust. The AI apparatus he described was composed of random forest and an evolutionary rule-based genetic algorithm (an approach known as Pittsburgh-Style Learning Classifier System, which is used to evolve a solution composed of multiple rules). He claimed that news is a lagging measure in terms of useful signal since news is already reflected in the time series. At best, news can increase confidence in the signal, but it is not signal itself, he contended. Hence, if you genetically evolve the solution, a machine can pick patterns throughout the trading day, and while it can explore millions of options, it may take only a handful of buy-sell actions. He said that his hedge fund was fully automated and required absolutely no human intervention. In his fund, staff set things up, and they do have a big red button to press only if all hell breaks loose—other than that, the system decides everything: what to trade, when to trade it, how to trade it, how long to hold, when to exit. This all sounded like a dream come true for AI. It was perfection at its peak. As long as no one had to push the red button, things seemed in control. Except, in 2018, the hedge fund was suddenly liquidated. Bloomberg reported that the fund had not made any money in 2018, after making a meager 4% in 2017 (Kishan and Barr, 2018). The failure of the fund can be attributed to the approach, or to the technology, or to the lack of human guidance, or to the fact that no single strategy can be viewed as the winning strategy, or that perhaps strategy was not consistent with the market conditions. We may never find out. But what we can learn from this failure are two lessons: (1) the human role in investment management needs to be more than the red button pusher or cheerleader for a strategy; and (2) the role of broader business strategy is critical for investment management. The former because we know that human intervention in the strategy could have observed that the strategy was not working (actually, a machine could have helped point that out) if humans were not emotionally invested in the fully autonomous model and did not view the human intervention as counter to the business model. The latter because we operate in a dynamic system where the environment evolves and a change in strategy becomes necessary. It is likely that if the investment team were surrounded by a diverse set of thinkers, the chances of groupthink could have been minimized. Strategy is not just about investment. It should not be limited to investment strategy. The broader strategy for the organization is just as important, if not more. This chapter is dedicated to strategy building, and its value will become clear as we go through the book.

AI—A REVOLUTION OF ITS OWN

I vividly recall the experience of buying a new car about a decade before this book was written. I visited several dealers and inquired about various features. It was not my first car. I had purchased a total of nine cars before that. When buying cars, I tend to ask lots of questions. From typical car performance attributes to its physical features, I asked dozens of questions. I looked at domestic cars and foreign cars, at sedans and SUVs, at electric and gas cars. Eventually I ended up buying a car. Looking back at the questions I asked during my car buying escapades from 1992 to 2010, I realize that the nature of my questions did not change much. Then I made of list of questions I was asking to buy cars recently, and suddenly a list with very unusual questions emerged: "Does this car park itself?" "Does it stop itself if a peril develops?" "Does it drive itself?" Stop for a moment and ask yourself what just happened. We are asking questions about a thing (the car) and associating some level of sentient or intelligent behavior with it. Something has changed. We are expecting things to be intelligent. In the past, beyond humans, such a question may have been asked for a horse or a dog or a cat—"Would this animal be able to return home?"—but not for an inanimate object. What changed?

Of course, we are now living in the intelligence era. What was once uniquely ours, intelligence, is now expected to be part of inanimate objects. This means that as consumers we expect products and services to be intelligent and to display intelligent behavior. Intelligization of objects is not a small shift. It introduces many different types of business dynamics as it alters the fundamental drivers of competition.

For instance, one key factor intelligization introduces is that in addition to all other product or service attributes, the fundamental driver of competitive advantage can also be the intelligence embedded in your product or service. For examples, consumers would now compare cars not only based on factors such as quality and safety but also based on autonomous driving features. Intelligence has become a primary attribute of competitive differentiation. People may compare smart phones, their bank services, credit cards, home security systems, financial advisors, and even sofas and toilets based on product intelligence.

INTELLIGENCE AS A COMPETITIVE ADVANTAGE

We often hear the words "intelligent automation" in the context of learning systems. While there are various meanings attributed to this in the literature, I approach it as two different aspects: (1) what intelligent is and (2) what intelligent does. Using some of the concepts below, we will develop some theoretical foundations of why intelligent automation is critical for business survival and growth.

Let us first observe what intelligence means in the form of products and services. It has three related implications:

Intelligence in Products

As the previous example illustrated, what changed in the modern economy is that now you expect your things to have intelligence. Whether it is business systems or personal, it is as if objects have come alive or developed a mind of their own. You do that when you order your smart phone assistant to make a call, check emails, or search for something. The objects around us are now embedded with intelligence, and that itself is a powerful change.

Intelligence in Production Platforms

In addition to embedding intelligence in products, what really drives competitive value is having intelligence in the production and operational platforms of a firm. This means that all the production environment that is used to create, manufacture, offer, distribute, and service the products of a firm is also made intelligent. In this context I am using the term "production platform" to signify all the activities necessary to get the product to a point where it can be consumed.

Intelligence of an Interlinked Network of Systems

Thirdly, while products and their production platforms are interlinked, both products and production platforms can be linked with other systems. They form a nexus or ecosystem of informing, sharing, and taking intelligent actions in accordance with each other's information and states. This system of interlinked intelligent agents—which may include both humans and machines—offers a new way to create competitive advantage. In their seminal work *Strategy Safari*, Mintzberg et al. introduced ten schools of strategy (Mintzberg et al., 1998).

In the section below we will summarize those schools. The discussion in the next section is derived from Mintzberg et al.

 ## INTELLIGENCE AS A COMPETITIVE ADVANTAGE AND VARIOUS STRATEGY SCHOOLS

The **Design School** "proposes a model of strategy making that seeks to attain a match, or fit, between internal capabilities and external possibilities" (Mintzberg et al., 1998). From a design school perspective, products, production platforms, and interlinked systems are designed to take advantage of the opportunities by the intersection of internal and external possibilities. It is assumed that in the cognitive era, the assessment of what internal and external states are would also be performed by an intelligent engine (or engines). From that perspective, every product, production platform, and interlinked network is responsive to the inner states and capabilities of a firm as well as to what transpires outside.

In the **Planning School** the combination of planning tools (for example, SWOT) and mission statements of executives and leaders of companies are used to create short-, medium-, and long-term plans for companies. From that perspective, the intelligence-centric planning implies that tools and methods that decipher strategy are applied; however, their implementation will be quite different than in human-oriented strategy development. For example, the strengths, weaknesses, opportunities, and threats need to be analyzed for automated intelligent systems.

In the **Positioning School,** unlike the Design and Planning schools, which placed no limits on the number of strategies that a firm can have, Mintzberg et al. explain "only a few key strategies—as positions in the economic marketplace—are desirable in any given industry: ones that can be defended against existing and future competitors." The emphasis on competitive dynamics clarifies that in the era of intelligent automation, the competitive dynamics are defined based on intelligence in products, production platforms, and interlinked network of systems.

The **Entrepreneurial School** is based on vision and vision setting and is usually centered on one leader. In this school the entrepreneur develops a vision, a mental model, and applies skills to create value. AI can assess the quality of vision, execution, entrepreneurial skills, and value creation opportunities.

The **Cognitive School** is based on analyzing the human mind, as, according to this school, human thinking and experience drive strategies.

Understanding human psychology helps understand how strategies are shaped. The reality is shaped by human thinking. In the context of an AI-centric strategy, it implies machines can help decipher the human thinking process and identify our biases. Machines can help understand how we think and what we are thinking. Also, if our intelligent artifacts frame and architect our understanding of the world, and ourselves, the difference in their intelligence level, or even perspective, can make a difference in how we understand strategies and ourselves.

The **Learning School** is based on the emergence of strategies as people learn about situations and their firm's capabilities. Learning helps morph behaviors as we recognize what works. From a learning school perspective, the introduction of machine intelligence implies that the emergence happens not only by human agents but also from the interaction of machines with other machines and humans. Such a complex system is based on interactions between agents that are part of the system, as well as agent interaction with other systems outside the system.

In the **Power School** strategies come from negotiating and power games that are played in companies. From an intelligence angle, machines can decipher power patterns and even help understand the strategy development from a power struggle perspective.

The **Cultural School** emphasizes the strategy formulation process as a cultural process. In the era of intelligent machines, humans can not only study culture with greater accuracy but also develop a deeper understanding of the social phenomena underlying their strategies. Culture is "essentially composed of interpretations of a world and the activities and artifacts that reflect these. Beyond cognition these interpretations are shared collectively, in a social process."

In the **Environment School** strategy is shaped as a response to the environment. A responsive strategy to the environment implies that the entity will adapt and adjust. A nonadaptive entity will be wiped out. From an intelligence perspective, the ability to study and track changes in the environment and also to formulate responses to the challenges unleashed by the environment can be enabled by intelligence.

In the **Configuration School** the strategy comes from structures, configurations, and states. The configuration is the state of an organization in the context of its surroundings, and strategy leads to change in state. From an intelligence perspective, the configuration school implies that the structures and states of a company are measured better, and the transformation strategy is tracked more effectively. The product, production platform, and interlinked network participate in determining the state of the system (the firm), and reconfigure, transform, or transition to a new state when change events happen.

 ## THE INTELLIGENCE SCHOOL

The intelligence era connects all ten schools into one—the intelligence-centric competitive advantage. In doing so the competitive advantage is shaped by factors such as:

- Intelligent machines are deployed to help understand internal and external environments, the existing states, the competitive dynamics, the cultural and social dynamics, and the set of opportunities and threats.
- The product itself, the production platform, and the interlinked network become the source of strategic information.
- The system creates awareness about its own states and transitions to a new state with awareness that a change event has transpired calling for transition.
- The system is viewed as a learning system and is composed of interactive agents that interact with each other and with external systems forming a complex system.

Now let us evaluate what this means for an investment firm:

- **Humans and Machines:** Investment strategies will result from the interactive and collaborative efforts of machines and humans.
- **Products:** On the investment strategy side, learning machines (intelligence) will enable us to:
  - develop new investment strategies;
  - monitor the investment environment better;
  - understand our own biases in formulating portfolio or asset selection strategies;
  - predict outcomes;
  - understand metacognitive structures in the markets—for example, stories, narratives, and alpha signals that are not easily detectable;
  - respond quickly to opportunities and threats; and
  - design, develop, and offer new products faster.

- **Production Platform:** On the production platform side, learning machines will help us improve regulatory and governance requirements, help identify and onboard new clients, help us develop and strengthen relationships with institutional clients, increase assets under management (AUM), deploy powerful marketing, provide excellent customer service, give clients powerful insights, enable value added services, introduce new products, and support all other services that are necessary for operations and production.
- **Interlinked Network:** This means that learning machines help build greater understanding of partners, suppliers, regulators, channel partners, and all other entities with whom the firm interacts.

The competitive advantage of a firm is therefore architected based on the above factors. It is from these factors that firms understand how they will compete and win. It is also across those dimensions that differentiation of a firm would materialize. None of the above factors can be ignored by a firm.

Note that the above discussion focused on intelligence of machines and the resultant augmentation of human capacity to understand our environment and make better decisions. Intelligence, in that context, is one side of artificial intelligence. The other side is automation.

INTELLIGENCE AND ACTIONS

For business purposes, I define intelligence as being able to successfully perform work by displaying goal-directed behavior in situations of uncertainty. When machines display intelligence, they perform work and resolve uncertainty in accordance with goal-directed behavior. It can also be viewed as an attribute of an artifact by which it accomplishes work by successfully tackling uncertain situations in accordance with its goals.

Let us clarify this definition:

Being able to successfully perform work: This implies that the entity or artifact can perform work, and its success is determined in accordance with the goal set for the entity. Work implies the activities conducted by humans that add value for human life and survival.

Goal-directed behavior: Goal-directed behavior implies that the entity is operating with a sense of purpose and not just randomly. It has a goal. This goal may have been given by a human or it may have assigned the goal to itself.

Uncertainty: Uncertainty implies the ability to navigate through situations where more than one choice exists. Of course, the greater the uncertainty, the more intelligence is needed to navigate. In a simple system, intelligent decision could be as simple as making a binary choice between two options. For example, a simple regulator can start the air conditioning or not. In a more complicated system, more choices are available. For example, in a game of chess, depending on the position, a certain number of moves are possible. Another example will be of your spellchecker or text recommender to fill in words as you type. In even more uncertain situations, for example, autonomous cars navigating and driving on a busy street, the number of choices is unimaginably large.

But performing or accomplishing work requires more than intelligence. It requires us to take actions.

ACTIONS

An intelligent entity must interact with its environment. A thinker who loses the capacity to interact with the environment will only have thoughts in his or her head but will not be able to perform any action. Also, this thinker will not be able to entertain any new input or sense any new information since it is disconnected with the environment. A thought trapped in a mind incapable of any interaction with the environment is not helpful to accomplish any work task. To perform a work task, therefore, an intelligent entity needs to interact with its environment.

Perhaps it will be helpful to make a distinction between thinking and acting. When we act, we create a change in the environment. Whether action is composed of movement or transferring data or sending a notification, it is something that materializes in the environment in which an intelligent artifact is operating. In other words, it does not happen in the mind of the artifact as it necessarily requires some type of expression that is based on interaction with the environment. As we make the distinction between thinking and action, we can view intelligence (thinking) and action as interdependent and interconnected. Thinking drives action—for example, you decide to make a right turn while driving—but action also drives thinking. For instance, as you start turning the steering wheel, the feedback from the car, the steering wheel that you are holding, and the surroundings send signals to your brain and the brain helps you to keep the car on the road as you perform the action of turning the car by turning the steering wheel. This hand and mind coordination can be viewed as constant back and forth rapid transition between states of thinking and acting. A thinking system does not think in isolation; it interacts with its environment.

 ## AUTOMATION

Automation is the ability of a synthetic entity to perform work. Since work requires both intelligence and actions, automation involves both.

Thinking automation: Automation automates the thinking part where a synthetic entity can be intelligent (refer to the definition of intelligence presented above) autonomously. Here autonomously implies that it can make decisions to navigate through uncertainty on its own.

Action automation: Automation automates actions where non-thinking parts of work are automated. For instance, a car automates movement on land, an airplane automates mobility in the sky, a non-thinking computer automates work tasks such as spreadsheets, word processing, and others. Instead of walking, you ride in a car. Instead of flying (not sure how a human would fly, perhaps jump or fall is a better comparison), a human can fly in an airplane. A human driving a car, flying an airplane, or using a computer is benefiting from the automation in these artifacts even though he or she is using his or her own cognitive skills to operate these machines. These machines are not intelligent, but they are automated. That automation is the automation of action where an artifact can enable human work that requires interaction with the environment.

 ## INTELLIGENCE ACTION CHAIN AND SEQUENCE

From a business process perspective, one can view a process as composed of intelligence-action sequences that accomplish work. In fact, it can be viewed as state transitions between thinking (decision making) to acting and doing them successively till the work sequence is finalized and the work goal is achieved. The action itself, or at least certain part of it, does not require any thinking. Going back to our example of you deciding to turn your car right, the "decision" in this case is to turn right, but an action follows. The action itself can be broken down into states of action to turn, as brain and hand coordination maintains what turning is. Thus, decision-oriented intelligence decides to turn right, and then brain, eyes, hands, and other sensors work collaboratively to help us make the right turn. We receive feedback, and our brain processes this feedback to turn the wheel in accordance with the feedback to keep the car on the road, accident free, and make the right turn. The think-act sequence itself is the second kind of decision—i.e., doing what needs to be done or monitoring an action-neural response (feedback) sequence once an action has begun.

Clearly, the automation from artificial intelligence requires the convergence of the two types of automations: automation of thinking (synthetic, or machine, thinking) and automation of action. It is a merger of the two where artifacts can think autonomously and take actions.

The acts of *action* can be many. Any time information is extracted from the environment and goes into a system (artifact, entity) as input and then when the environment is acted upon by the system as some form of output, these are actions. Thus, when the machine receives market data, it can be viewed as specific steps where no thinking is required by the machine. Then the machine thinks and makes a trading decision. The decision when communicated back to the environment where a trade is made is again an action and requires execution and not just thinking.

 ## ENTERPRISE SOFTWARE

The enterprise software, then, is composed of a combination of "thinking" and "acting" software. The thinking-acting sequences imply integration of AI software with non-AI software to build work-task sequences. But these task sequences are not built around automating human-centric processes. In other words, automation requires rethinking the business models, and processes need to be built around machine work. Machines work differently than humans. In the next chapter, we will cover the design principles of AI-centric designs. At this stage, it is important to recognize that designing a modern investment management firm requires building an integrated software architecture of non-intelligent (legacy or traditional software) and intelligent (machine learning, rules-based) software.

 ## DATA

Data is the lifeblood of machine learning. Without data, machine learning models fail to learn. In fact, not only do we need to have plenty of data, its quality needs to be good for the learning to be consistent with the goals of developing the artifact. Since each firm has its own data, the potential for each firm to perform in the AI era will be different.

Here are some of the capabilities needed for an AI-centric transformation:

Data Management Expertise

What data do you have? What data do you not have but is needed? What data is needed but you cannot have? What data is essential for your core operation?

Having data is one thing, having quality data another. Data quality is essential to build powerful systems. Quality of data includes factors such as completeness, relevance, and timeliness.

Partnering, Buying, and Building

You can partner with, buy, or build AI capabilities. Which one leads to establishing competitive advantage for your firm? Clearly, buying a solution implies that you are not the only one who has access to that one or more set of solution algorithms and data sets. This does not mean you should not consider buying certain solutions. However, for critical areas in your firm, it will be important to build (best alternative) and partner (second best) to create a custom capability set that is held only by your firm.

Of course, when it comes to data, you will need to buy it from various sources. But even for that, consider what data sensors and data collection mechanisms can be architected internally to save money and improve data quality.

 ## COMPETITIVE ADVANTAGE

Based upon the above discussion, we are now able to suggest how to architect competitive advantage for our firms. As we digest the above discussion, we can zero in on four core determinants of competitive advantage. These four determinants are the underlying engines that drive value for us and our clients. These are the technological constructs that we need to get right. Based on these four determinants, we architect various business processes and achieve work tasks. The following are the four determinants:

- **Design constructs:** Design constructs are based on your firm's competitive and market positioning and strategy. Design constructs emerge from the deployment of capabilities that collectively define a firm's business model and orchestrate how the firm will structure itself.

- **Extent and quality of intelligence:** The extent and quality of intelligence comes from the core intelligence-centric methodologies. It can be viewed as using the best algorithms for a particular problem set (and the available data; see below), with both effective and efficient training, which results in achieving training goals in a timely manner and with higher precision and recall. Since intelligence manifests at both the artifact level and the networked level connection of artifacts, the extent and quality of intelligence is relevant at both levels.

- **Sequence of intelligence and action:** The sequence of intelligence and action means that such sequence chains are well defined, optimally placed, stacked for maximum efficiency, and flawlessly integrated. It implies that intelligent software and non-intelligent software (or electric or mechanical systems) function in an integrated, harmonious, synchronized, and efficient manner such that machines accomplish work tasks successfully and optimally.

- **Data:** Data refers to a firm's ability to have quality data that it can feed to its learning algorithms. Both the quantity and quality of data are important. In addition, the span of data—that means the reality that data covers—is also significant. To clarify the span of data, think about a piece of relevant reality for which you do not have data. Without that data you have no understanding of the reality. As you learn more about the reality, you model the reality with a meaningful representation in terms of variables and features. This multidimensional view of the reality is what the span of data refers to.

 ## BUSINESS CAPABILITIES

Now we shift our attention to business factors. In this we use the above factors to architect our business to create a viable and well-performing investment management firm with (see Figure 2.1):

- *Alpha-generating capability:* It refers to the ability to develop and execute investment strategies that result in creating a strong alpha. The obvious challenge here is uniqueness. If your investment strategy is easily decipherable or discoverable by others, the advantage gap will close quickly. However, if we decompose the steps needed to create a strong alpha in the AI era, we will realize that the ability to discover or replicate our strategy will greatly depend on competitors' ability to have the same data, apply similar algorithms, perform similar evaluations, and receive similar results.

	Design Constructs	Extent and Quality of Intelligence	Sequence of Intelligence and Action	Data
Alpha-generating capability	✓	✓	✓	✓
Responsiveness and awareness	✓	✓	✓	✓
Client orientation	✓	✓	✓	✓
Cost	✓	✓	✓	✓
Human talent–centric	✓	✓	✓	✓
Innovation	✓	✓	✓	✓
Advice	✓	✓	✓	✓
Client knowledge	✓	✓	✓	✓
Regulatory standards compliance	✓	✓	✓	✓
Risk management	✓	✓	✓	✓
Corporate social responsibility	✓	✓	✓	✓
Auditing, assurance, and governance	✓	✓	✓	✓

FIGURE 2.1 The Strategic Capability Building

Results in this case imply persistent alpha generation through various existing and newly discovered strategies.

– *Responsiveness and awareness:* We want to build a firm that is more aware and responsive. Aware implies being cognizant of what is transpiring in the environment (for example, markets, industries, sectors, economies, and assets), knowledgeable about clients, and mindful about what is happening inside the firm. Inside the firm implies knowing about our own structures, styles, biases, psychology, interests, social and cultural cues, and other similar information.

– *Client orientation:* A client-oriented firm equips and enables clients with information, knowledge, and services that empower the clients (retail or institutional). Enabling that empowerment means the firm adds value for clients that goes above and beyond delivering alpha.

– *Cost:* The firm keeps its costs low. This means it can compete based on cost. When combined with other aspects as discussed in this section, a low-cost operator can be the price leader and also create good margins.

– *Human talent–centric:* The AI era should not be misconstrued as the end of human talent era. If anything, AI will make possible more engaged, more empowered, and happier human employees. If managed right, AI can help improve the culture, create new and improved social dynamics, discourage destructive politics, and build a more positive work environment.

- *Innovation:* Innovation in terms of discovering assets, portfolios, alpha strategies, products, services, and client enablement is a powerful advantage.
- *Advice:* For firms where service design is primarily based on advice, the quality and timeliness of advice can be tremendously valuable. Advice can be offered via machine only or a machine-human combination.
- *Client knowledge:* A winning firm possesses deep information about clients and uses that to help clients in the best possible way.
- *Regulatory standards compliance:* A successful firm meets the regulatory and compliance requirements.
- *Risk Management:* A responsible firm ensures multidimensional risk management.
- *Corporate Social Responsibility:* This means that the firm actively searches for issues that are material for its stakeholders and develops responsible responses to those issues. The firm fulfills its social responsibility and ethical obligations.
- *Audit, assurance, and governance:* In addition to market-centric risk management, the firm must develop superior capabilities in auditing, assurance, and governance areas.

CHAPTER THREE

Design

IMAGINE THAT WE ARE LIVING IN the age of the horse-and-buggy and have set out to automate them. Our one design option could be to design an automated horse. After all, isn't that the most natural way to think about automating what a horse does? Our automated horse will have four mechanical legs and it will trot, canter, and gallop on the road. It will have mechanical levers, and as we pull the levers, the horse will turn or pace. As it turns out, many people did attempt to design mobility solutions by trying to automate the design of a horse[i]. Fortunately, we had smarter people who recognized that the idea of automation was not to automate the horse itself, but instead to automate mobility. We automated the function of the horse and not the structure of the horse. Unfortunately, in the AI revolution, many firms are trying to make mechanical horses because they have not figured out that synthetic intelligence allows us to build alternative business models and processes. Design science is the first stage of instituting the industrial-scale enterprise machine learning operation. It is defined as the process of architecting a firm's AI plan that supports the firm's strategy.

---

[i] See the article https://www.theatlantic.com/technology/archive/2012/09/a-brief-history-of-mechanical-horses/262942/.

WHO IS RESPONSIBLE FOR DESIGN?

The executive leadership of the firm, along with the board, and the data science head are primarily responsible for the design science. We are assuming that this book will help investment firms to create centralized AI and data science departments that will function on both the business and AI sides. In some ways, these departments will become the core engines of value creation. In my opinion, titles such as chief transformation officer or VP of AI do not do justice to what needs to get done. We will dive into the organizational part in Chapter 18. Design is managed by senior executives or partners of a firm. The strategic outcomes are shared with the boards. There are ten steps to design. The first two steps—goals and objectives—are conducted directly with the senior leadership team (the C-suite) with input from the senior executives. The next eight steps are undertaken by a special cross-functional team, and the results are reported back to the senior leadership team. Keep in mind that we have already argued that modern-day investment management is a complex system and subject to constant change. Defining the goals and objectives is not independent of machine learning, as machines can contribute to determining the goals and objectives of the firm.

INTRODUCTION TO DESIGN

Design is an often ignored area of building a powerful and modern investment management operation. The reason design is ignored is simple: we have not embraced artificial intelligence as a strategic paradigm. Our intelligent automation is limited to implementing use cases. This tactical adoption is extremely dangerous and can lead to underperformance in the long run. First let us review the symptoms of tactical adoption of AI:

- There is no cohesive AI strategy in a firm. Each department is pursuing its own strategy, at its own pace, incognizant of other departments or broader processes.
- A signficant number of applications are being developed on an experimental basis. A perpetual state of experimentation exists. AI application proliferation is supported by a plethora of suppliers. From consulting firms to AI suppliers to RPA suppliers, each department is experimenting with different suppliers, leading to higher cost of sourcing.

- In many cases both consulting firms and suppliers are being constantly rotated. Even after spending millions, in some cases tens of millions of dollars, the return seems to be unclear or insignificant.
- Each department comes up with its own projects, and projects are limited by the vision, experience, and innovativeness of the leadership.
- Projects are being completed but in a haphazard fashion. They get added to the collection of thousands of other software, but their contribution is localized. They are often unaware and ignorant of the presence of other systems. They do not create a broader theme or automate a work process. Each project turns out to be an island of isolation.
- We are building the future using archaic and irrelevant models from the past. For example, we are using ERP and CRM models to build an AI-centric transformation. Our mindset and approach need to change.
- Projects are identified based on automation of the human-centric process chain. In other words, we are approaching automation from the perspective of replacing human work by a machine. Our current work chains are designed around humans. The risk of automating around human work chains results in our failure to think in terms of what the work might look like if the entire work process was being performed by a machine. A machine work chain can be significantly different than a work chain designed for humans. A simple example of that will be reports. When we generate reports, we do that for human consumption. Our reports tend to show data in visual forms that make sense for humans. Reports are feedback and control mechanisms where humans can make decisions based on information. This can be viewed as one or more humans reading a report (text, images, graphics, visual representations, etc.) and then trying to make sense out of them. After understanding them, it is likely we make decisions, and those decisions are enacted in the operational frameworks of our companies. If machines are making those decisions, they will not need the visual reports since their input feed could be vastly different than the feed that humans need in the form of a report. (Design builds new processes and business model constructs around machines.)
- No concept of reuse, data sharing, or building corporate-wide AI capability exists.

Design is the science of connecting business models and goals with the AI technology such that we can create a comprehensive plan for building our companies around AI.

The lack of design-centric AI transformation produces many problems. They are as follows:

- Companies will fail to create competitive advantage with AI. For those firms, AI will remain as just another technology. It will not become a way of life. This means competitors—both from legacy firms that transform and fintech start-ups—will make those firms irrelevant.
- Projects are haphazard. They will not be able to fit into the broader work chain.
- Projects may not be defined optimally. They may not achieve their full capacity or goals.
- Total cost of ownership may be extremely high.
- Most software will be thrown away once we reach the point where we realize that we need a more cohesive and integrated solution. Recall the example of shared services. Shared services enabled us to overcome software proliferation. As shown in this book, soon there will be an AI shared-service model that will streamline the adoption of AI.
- Different suppliers will try to pull you in different directions. While it is a good idea to listen to sincere suppliers, you do need to have a clear idea about what you expect your firm's future state to be.

As outlined in Chapter 2, your competitive advantage will be created from: (1) design, (2) intelligence, (3) automation, and (4) data. These attributes will enable you to build a firm that can compete based on:

- responsiveness and awareness;
- client orientation: equips and enables clients;
- cost;
- innovation;
- possessing deep information about clients, which is used to help clients in the best possible way;
- meeting and exceeding the regulatory standards; and
- fulfillment of the firm's social responsibilities and ethical obligations and abiding by good governance frameworks.

AI AS A COMPETITIVE ADVANTAGE

AI is not just a technology. AI is the business. The ability to model intelligence is the most important innovation in human civilization. It is nothing like any machine we have ever created. From basic machines such as levers and pullies to advanced machines such as airplanes and computers, none were developed to be intelligent. They functioned as machines, and they performed under our guidance. But something new is happening now. We have entered the era of intelligent machines. Intelligence leads to autonomy and autonomy to a shared future in which machines and humans codevelop value. This vision of a future where intelligent machines are a necessary part of our strategic designs is a critical element of leading and designing an investment management firm.

The old model of asset management is not only noncompetitive, it is counterproductive. It fails to serve the best interests of clients, and it hurts the profitability of the firm. It fails to offer the quality of investment expertise that today's clients expect and deserve. It ignores important elements of human emotions, qualitative data, behaviors, narratives, and other human processes.

But to design and deploy that competitive advantage, data and the ability to use data to automate are the ultimate resources, and intelligence becomes the core competency.

Automation of work applies in two areas—to automate and to intellectualize. Automate refers to work automation, while intellectualize refers to making organizations, departments, or individuals smarter. Moving a box from point A to point B is work. Opening the box and understanding that the box contains chocolates requires intelligence—and hence intellectualization. Similarly, sending out marketing campaign emails is work automation, but figuring out what content should be included is cognitive work or intellectualization.

- Automation can refer to physical work or cognitive work. When automation is implemented in the modern era, it changes the routines, structures, tasks, and processes of work—without changing the goals. Our current work processes and routines are designed around humans. When machines perform work, you do not need a human-centered work design.
- Intellectualize refers to going beyond human work performance and creating insights and developing knowledge and meaning that go beyond (or is at least as good as) what is known or knowable with human efforts.

Autonomy is another dimension. It refers to automating or intellectualizing work such that work requires no human intervention. It can be viewed as a spectrum where a software can only perform work under strict human guidance on one end and can function completely independently on the other end.

Competitive advantage comes from being able to architect business models such that your firm achieves greater:

- **speed:** doing more work, faster;
- **intellect:** knowing more, being smarter, being able to predict better;
- **quality:** improving the quality of work;
- **value:** accomplishing work at a lower cost; and
- **collaboration:** accomplishing more or better work from the interaction of humans and machines.

Here are some examples of architecting a business model for competitive advantage driven by one or more value drivers:

- Rapid cost reduction by deploying a machine learning operation to develop profound quantitative strategies.
- Access to certain clients that others do not have.
- Being able to offer value-added services to clients that competitors cannot.
- Creating switching cost such that clients cannot easily switch.
- Developing powerful credibility with institutional investors.
- Superior research capabilities to identify investment opportunities and architect well-performing portfolios.
- Ability to deploy effective regulatory frameworks and controls.
- Being able to manage multiple investment strategies, serving a diverse set of clients.
- Being able to extract powerful insights from data and being able to turn them into alpha signals.

THE TEN ELEMENTS OF DESIGN

The ten elements of design are composed of eight design tasks and two additional elements.

Design tasks:

1. Design your business model;
2. Set goals for the entire firm;
3. Specify objectives for automation and intelligence;
4. Design work-task frames based on human-computer interaction;
5. Perform a DTC (do, think, create) analysis;

6. Create a SADAL framework;
7. Deploy a feedback system and define performance measures; and
8. Determine the business case or value.

Additional elements:

9. Determine risks; and
10. Establish governance.

1. DESIGN YOUR BUSINESS MODEL

As an investment management operation, your first design element is your business model. Having clarity about the business model is essential to maximize business results. It is what helps you focus on the right value drivers and earn credibility with clients and what enables you to allocate resources appropriately. Use the following to clarify the business model:

a. **Manager's vision:** Describe the vision of your investment business. Typically, such vision will be developed by the manager and the investment advisory team.
b. **Manager's philosophy:** Provide the narrative and logic of your investment philosophy.
c. **Investment strategy and approach:** Clarify the investment strategy. If there are multiple products, clarify for each. Would the primary model be fundamentals based or quantitative? Would it be value based or growth?
d. **Structure:** Describe the structure for the offering. Clarify why that structure is best for the offering. Assess the pros and cons of alternative structures.
e. **Asset classes:** Identify the asset classes for the product.
f. **Investment vehicles:** Clarify the investment vehicles in scope.
g. **Products:** Using the above, define all products and services.
h. **Customers:** Identify customer segments for each product. Clarify the value attributes for each segment, i.e., what benefits customers receive and how each product creates value for clients.
i. **Positioning and differentiation:** Describe your positioning and competitive differentiation. Identify major competitors by products.
j. **Financial model (fee):** Clarify your fee structure for each product. Describe how you make money.

k. **Operating model:** Describe your plan to operate the firm. Do you expect the operation to be inhouse, outsourced, or hybrid?

l. **Go-to-market approach:** Define your go-to-market approach.

Based on the above, you can establish the core business model of the firm. However, an AI-centric business model takes the above information and translates it into an automated and intelligent model.

Plan big, execute in achievable steps: Companies do not have the resources and operating bandwidth to change everything. They must choose and prioritize. While I insist that when business models are changing, it is critical to improve all aspects of a firm, I also understand the constraints. This is akin to launching a new model of airplane in service. The differences between the airplanes from World War II, the Vietnam War, and modern planes are significant. The same goes for improvements in smart phones across generations of improvements. Similarly, architecting an asset management firm may require a complete overhaul—but one needs to start somewhere. The most important critical element in picking a strategic positioning is to understand the relative strength of the firm in accordance with: (1) internal capabilities, (2) competition, and (3) market needs.

In a world defined by the rise of competition from all angles, a firm needs to be cognizant of what makes it different. Is it the quality of its analysis? Is it a unique business model? Is it client service? Has the firm figured out a new way to create portfolio diversification? Is the firm able to extract new alpha signals? Has the firm figured out how to reduce cost to serve clients? Has the firm increased the ability of clients to feel more engaged in decision-making? Is the firm betting on its credibility to continue as a discretionary portfolio manager? Is it based on developing better insights about asset classes? Does the firm have a specific strategy to attract institutional investors? All of these are important questions.

These questions have become significantly more important as competition is knocking on your door. You can no longer count on preserving the integrity of the structural elements that constitute your business. Every single aspect of your business is getting redefined and is under attack from competitors. That is why I insist that asset management firms must rethink business models of who they are and what they do—since competition is constantly redefining them. The structural integrity of the business boundaries is no longer intact. Sometimes semantics keep us trapped in perceptual adherences to the past, and we stay stationary even when the underlying dynamics change. Our sensemaking tells us that we are in the investment management business, and that gives us a certain frame, or a mold, of what asset management is. It gives us a sense of comfort even though we know that the meaning is no longer applicable. Economic shocks, such as the coronavirus, will only accelerate our transformation.

Competition from fintech: When I use the term fintech, I refer to the start-ups and established firms that are exclusively focused on the finance sector. These firms are niche focused and they do have the ability to grab the attention of the masses. A large part of these masses are the generations who are benefiting from the generational transfer of wealth. Millennials, who are the recipients of the wealth transfer, are comfortable with technology. They are also used to getting and acting upon recommendations from machines. From selecting which movies to watch to understanding what clothes to wear, they rely upon machine advice. The coronavirus era has made the world even more reliant on technology and technology-centric relationship management. The concept of advice, therefore, has both machine- and human-centric components in a socially distanced world.

Techcroachment: Techcroachment happens when large and established tech firms decide to encroach into a new business segment. For instance, Amazon entered the groceries business, Apple entered the entertainment and financial sectors, Google entered health care, and Facebook is experimenting with digital currency. These firms have the data and insights to launch new business models in finance and provide automated services, as well as to acquire upcoming fintech firms and supercharge them with the data and financial backing necessary to alter the face of the industry.

Competition from legacy competitors: Competition also comes from traditional sources. Legacy competitors may take advantage of the weaknesses of a financial firm—such as the decline of Deutsche Bank due to regulatory compliance issues opening opportunities for other banks to fill the void. Legacy competitors may also strengthen their position from technological innovations. TD Ameritrade's move to acquire an AI firm shows the firm's willingness to build broad internal AI-centric capabilities.

As the second decade of the twenty-first century ended, Wells Fargo made an astonishing claim. In the next few years, the bank predicted, more than 200,000 human bankers will be replaced by robots (Kelly, 2019). While large banks have made several claims about trading human analysts with robots, a new and powerful economy is not built by automating back office jobs. To gain a true productivity edge, companies must approach automation as a phenomenon that fundamentally alters the way business is done today. While back office automation can be about automating deterministic processes, today's artificial intelligence technology offers us a way to truly transform business by creating a new type of investment and finance firm. This book shows you how. This book provides that systematic and comprehensive approach to reengineer the investment management business via machine learning.

Competition from foreign and emerging players: It is not so much about fintech anymore. China is embracing what can be termed as techfin, a *Financial Times* article claimed (Thornhill, 2020). In doing so, China is emerging as a global leader in finance. The approach taken by China is not just to automate the existing financial processes but instead to reengineer and re-envision how the new economy works. In this book we will show you how to develop and design a firm that can excel in the new financial economy by using artificial intelligence. The approach of this book is not academic. It is written for finance professionals, asset and wealth managers, investment firms, private equity, and corporate finance departments who manage internal funds. The vision developed in the book is contemporary and novel, but it maintains a pragmatic approach to business.

Based on the above competitive dynamics, a firm needs to architect the business model that will give it a sustainable competitive advantage and establish its goals for product and service designs.

 ## 2. SET GOALS FOR THE ENTIRE FIRM

Based on the discussion in the previous section, establish some concrete goals for your firm. These goals should be both long- and short-term, and each goal must reflect the strategic intent stated in terms of specific results and timing. The goals must address the following:

- AUM targets: What are the firm and strategy AUM targets? By when?
- Customer acquisition targets: How many and what size of clients are you seeking?
- Cost structure targets: What is an acceptable cost structure for business? Separately determine what capital is being allocated for business development.
- Capital: What is the target capital (partners and internal sources)?
- Customer retention goals: What is the acceptable customer churn?
- Human resources goals: What are your talent management goals?

3. SPECIFY OBJECTIVES FOR AUTOMATION AND INTELLIGENCE

A firm's objectives exist to support its goals. Translating goals into specific objectives for a firm, therefore, must be orchestrated in terms of AI technology. Specifically, the objectives can be articulated in terms of specific business processes. For example, the following can be the objectives to support a goal:

Goal: To streamline the quantitative strategy process by May 20, 20XX, such that we can identify at least five profitable strategies.

Objectives:

1. Restructure the organization by eliminating silos and creating specialist work areas;
2. Acquire and process new types of data;
3. Deploy data organization;
4. Develop models;
5. Begin search for viable strategies; and
6. Test and evaluate strategies.

4. DESIGN WORK TASK FRAMES BASED ON HUMAN-COMPUTER INTERACTION

Each objective can be segmented into work tasks. For example, *develop models* (objective 4 from the previous subsection) can be broken down into the following work outputs:

– preprocess the data;
– select a set of algorithms; and
– train models on data.

Work tasks tend to be cognitive, physical, or both. For example, preprocessing data, while a cognitive function (since typically a human may need to know how to organize data to make it ingestible in a machine), also requires some physical movement from a human (pushing keystrokes on a computer). Breaking down each task into physical vs. cognitive helps to understand the work segment better. When work links are connected, they form the work chain. While you can think of work tasks as processes, the terminology of processes tends to be more human-centric. To truly approach automation, we need to remove humans from the equation and only focus on the expected work output.

In general, the objectives refer to each of the goals and clarify how a business process supporting the goal is automated and made intelligent. Work streams are composed of interaction of what we automate and what we intellectualize.

5. PERFORM A DTC (DO, THINK, CREATE) ANALYSIS

The cognitive part of the tasks described above can be classified as follows:

1. **Doing:** Doing consists of those parts of your tasks that are relatively simple and deterministic. For example, when you order your phone to call a restaurant, it abides by that order. It is a simple command, and the phone has a clear process to dial the number you asked it to dial. For simple operations, you can implement rule-based systems.
2. **Thinking:** When a machine is expected to perform some level of thinking, even rudimentary, the space for possibilities becomes larger. For example, instead of just calling the restaurant, if you want your phone assistant to make a reservation for you, the task becomes more complex. This means you expect your assistant to be able to have at least some sustained conversation. Your phone assistant can perform that task with some level of training. However, it is likely that it will be able to respond to only a few types of speech patterns related to the task of making a reservation.
3. **Creating:** When a machine operates in high uncertainty, it has to deal with many options, and a large space of possibilities exist. For example, if the restaurant is busy and the scheduler says something like "How about if I bump you to the back and give you a seat near the band? Would that work?". Your virtual assistant may have trouble figuring out the contextual meaning and the complexities of language.

In design science, your job is to take each task and break it down into doing artifacts, thinking artifacts, and creating artifacts (Figure 3.1). One or more of these artifacts when deployed in a work configuration will create work outputs. They are all parts of the links that form the work chain.

DTC can be viewed as navigating through increases in uncertainty

		UNCERTAINTY	EXAMPLE	TECHNOLOGY
	Do	Absolute clarity on what needs to get done, little or no variability in task, high repeatability	Dialing a number. When you ask Siri to call a number.	Robotic process automation, machine learning, expert systems
	Think	Variability due to randomness or inability to process information, multiple possibilities and paths, less repeatability	Make a reservation in a restaurant, i.e., having somewhat of a sustained call with limited response options.	Machine learning
	Create	Unlimited set of possibilities, unlimited paths, no repeatability, novel and innovative	Ability to persuade when the restaurant says no tables available.	Machine learning (deep learning, deep reinforcement learning)

FIGURE 3.1   DTC Model

Doing Artifacts: These are simple command-action protocols. This will usually be accomplished by one or more of RPA, expert systems, and machine learning.

Thinking Artifacts: For these, a range of possibilities exist, which will require one or more machine learning models.

Creating Artifacts: For these, a very large number of possibilities exist, which will most likely require deep learning neural networks or deep reinforcement learning models.

For each work outcome, you will have one or more do, think, and create AI artifacts.

6. CREATE A SADAL FRAMEWORK

SADAL stands for Sense, Analyze, Decide, Act, and Learn. I developed the SADAL model, and it provides a quick way to translate your work automation into an intuitive and user-friendly way to take your business maps and turn them into AI projects.

Sense: Sense is composed of sensors that bring data into the artifact. You can think of it as the ears, nose, and eyes of a human. For a machine, digital data of various types is brought into the machine. Sensors capture the data of interest from the environment and bring it into the AI artifact.

Analyze: The AI artifact analyzes the data and tries to make sense about the environment. It creates a representation of the environment.

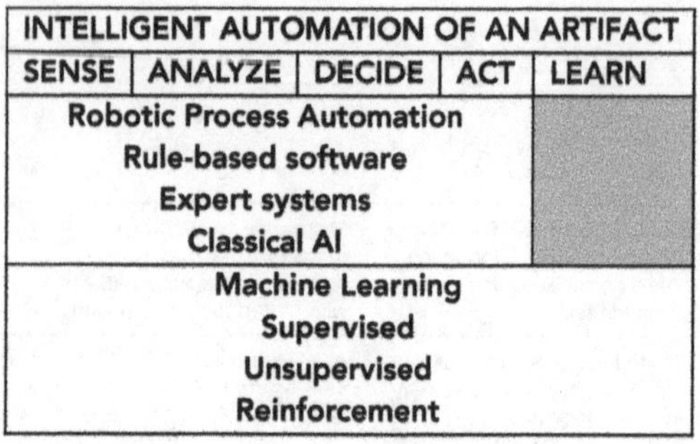

INTELLIGENT AUTOMATION OF AN ARTIFACT				
SENSE	ANALYZE	DECIDE	ACT	LEARN
Robotic Process Automation Rule-based software Expert systems Classical AI				
Machine Learning Supervised Unsupervised Reinforcement				

FIGURE 3.2 SADAL Model

TABLE 3.1 SADAL in a Work Task

Work task	SENSE	ANALYZE	DECIDE	ACT	LEARN
Artifact 1					
Artifact 2					
Artifact 3					
Artifact 4					

Decide: The AI artifact has some type of a guideline or a map that directs it to make some decisions about the data it has received. Those guidelines can be viewed as rules or trained algorithms.

Act: Based on its input data and the decision-making, the AI artifact then performs some actions. Its actions can be viewed as the outputs.

Learn: Not all AI artifacts have learning capabilities. As shown in Figure 3.2, many AI artifacts (RPA, Expert Systems) do not possess any advanced learning capability. Those artifacts can perform well with sensing, analyzing, deciding, and acting—but not with learning. Many of your "do" tasks will fit into that class. The artifacts that will require learning will apply supervised, unsupervised, or reinforcement learning (or a combination of these) to perform.

As you develop your requirements for each artifact, break it down into sense, analyze, decide, act, and learn components (Figure 3.3). Note that the best way to do that is to take the DTC artifacts for each work task and analyze them as shown in Table 3.1.

SADAL				
Sales forecasting using product reviews, sales data, media chat about firm, and products and service.				
SENSE	ANALYZE	DECIDE	ACT	LEARN
Product reviews (social media) Market share by markets Social media chat about firm Social media chat about product	Uses data from social media and internal sales data. Clean and preprocess data sets.	Forecast the sales.	Notify upon changes.	Learn to do it autonomously and constantly.

FIGURE 3.3   SADAL Analysis for a Sales Forecasting Artifact

7. DEPLOY A FEEDBACK SYSTEM AND DEFINE PERFORMANCE MEASURES

Once you have performed your SADAL analysis, your next task is to clarify the performance criteria for your system. Having a performance criterion means that you have some way of understanding and measuring the performance for your artifact. The performance measurement should be on both the business and the technical sides. The business performance measurement could be factors such as improved productivity, revenues, or profits. The performance measurement on the technical side usually is whether automation can beat human performance or not.

8. DETERMINE THE BUSINESS CASE OR VALUE

Your artifacts and automation plan must create value for your firm. Design science compels us to calculate and communicate the value proposition for automation. The typical value drivers include estimating the effect on:

- revenues;
- costs;
- risks;
- cost of capital;
- options (value of options, e.g., real options); and
- regulatory or compliance.

9. ANALYZE RISKS

Identify risks with the development and implementation of the AI artifacts. The risks might include factors such as:

- resource shortage;
- not having data;
- risk of overfitting; and
- risk of not being able to explain to auditors or regulators.

10. DEVELOP A GOVERNANCE PLAN

The AI artifacts are as good as the underlying data distributions of the problems they solve. When the data distribution changes, the model loses its ability to predict. It was designed for a different environment. AI models can also lose their utility. For example, if new features (if you are not familiar with features, think of them as additional dimensions of data about the problem—they are explained in the next chapter) are identified, your current model may be sub-optimized, as the presence of newly discovered features can improve the performance of your model. If that happens, your competitors will have an edge over you. AI models can become stale, irrelevant, or malfunctional. At all times you need to make sure that the models retain their relevance, performance, and functionality. In addition to the technical issues, AI models can create governance problems from an ethical and public policy point of view. These are covered in Chapter 19.

SOME ADDITIONAL IDEAS ABOUT DESIGNING INTELLECTUALIZATION

Intellectualize: Intelligence refers to the type of work where human cognition is used. Intellectualization can be applied in various ways. For example, we can think of various human work streams that require use of advanced cognitive abilities and that can be automated.

What is out there: In this work stream your machine is trying to discover the tasks it can undertake. This can be viewed as discovering a set of possibilities on what can be done—for instance, machine learning deployed to discover new molecules for drug development or identify novel patterns in the market that can help in identifying new investment opportunities.

What should we focus on: In this type of thinking tasks, machine thinking is deployed to identify the optimal tasks that should be undertaken by an entity. This can also be viewed as prioritizing tasks or goals. The input for this could be the output from the previous step of discovery. An example of this will be to select the most attractive investments from the patterns identified in the previous step.

How can we do something better: In this the learning machine implements a specific work task identified in goal setting. This is where most of the machine learning applications are. In this step more than one applications—both intelligence and action based—work together to form a nexus of capabilities to perform work.

How am I doing: This is a feedback system where goals are analyzed and compared. It is a step that helps ensure that tasks are achieving the corresponding goals.

SUMMARY OF THE DESIGN PROCESS

As shown in Figure 3.4, the design process begins with understanding the business model, clarifying goals, setting objectives, identifying activities and work tasks, and breaking them into DTC components and developing SADALs for them.

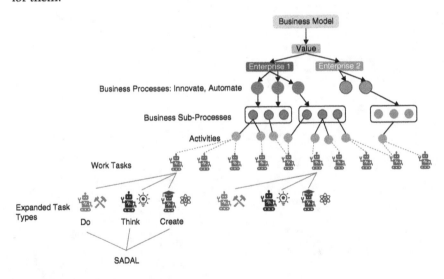

FIGURE 3.4 The Design Process

Ultimately what we are trying to approach is:

1. A state of awareness about AI and how AI is affecting the business.
2. A robust strategy that is designed to be successful.
3. A social fabric that understands, embraces, and achieves a shared sense of accomplishment.
4. A business model and architecture that is derived from the opportunities offered by the AI revolution and is consistent with the needs of our times.
5. A technology architecture that is consistent with the strategy.

 REFERENCES

Kelly, J. (2019) Wells Fargo Predicts That Robots Will Steal 200,000 Banking Jobs Within the Next 10 Years [online]. Available from: https://www.forbes .com/sites/jackkelly/2019/10/08/wells-fargo-predicts-that-robots-will-steal-200000-banking-jobs-within-the-next-10-years/#db949ad68d78.

Thornhill, J. (2020) "Three Technological Trends That Will Shape the Decade." *Financial Times.* January 6.

CHAPTER FOUR

Data

I N THE PREVIOUS CHAPTER WE BUILT the bridge between our business strategy and our AI strategy. In this chapter we will introduce the second transformational capability necessary for industrial-scale enterprise machine learning (ISEML): the data capability. We will cover how to build essential data capabilities for your artificial intelligence program. We will also differentiate between various data needs. Finally, we will also distinguish between data management and data management for AI.

Well-performing data management programs were critical even before the advent of the AI into mainstream. But solid data management programs have now become a must-have for companies to succeed. However, legacy data management does not necessarily encapsulate the specific requirements for data management for the AI era. It also does not easily relate to how to build a company around AI. We need to go beyond what the traditional or legacy data management entails. Traditional data management organizations would require restructuring to modern data organizations. We introduce one such model.

WHO IS RESPONSIBLE FOR THE DATA CAPABILITY?

The data capability is managed by the data organization. Many companies have established chief data officer (CDO) positions (Noh, 2016; Samuels, 2015). Many data executives are data management specialists. Many others come from different fields. Data science is often confused with data management. They are not the same. While data science deals with developing systems from data, data management organizations establish programs to organize, govern, and manage data.

To be fair to data management organizations, their job was never easy. They had to develop programs and educate executives when organizations did not really understand the value of data. Some still do not. Given that their starting point was so far behind, many CDO-led programs stayed focused on data governance, data management, and data quality. Creating data dictionaries, establishing data quality standards, identifying data stewards and owners, and exploring data lineage became their core focus areas. Some CDO organizations got dragged into creating enterprise data warehouse projects. Submerged under the heavy burden of tactical management of data, many CDO organizations were not able to function at a strategic level. As the AI revolution started, CDO organizations found themselves unprepared for such a powerful and strategic change. Political battles erupted between CIO and CDO organizations. Some made truce. Others attempted to get the other organization to report to them. Data management programs have acquired a credible and central position in the corporate world, but they are grossly unprepared to support the AI revolution.

In addition to the CDO organizations, in many companies, data science groups emerged. In many cases, these groups did not appear as a centralized organization and were scattered throughout the firms, often reporting to the departmental heads. Data science people were less concerned about organizing enterprise data as their focus remained on developing AI solutions and hence, they only paid attention to the data sets they needed for their artifacts.

All of the above developments have created massive confusion in the firms. The current setup is counterproductive and needs change. We are proposing to create a centralized data organization that is strategic, that performs all the functions of the CDO organization, and that is designed to support the AI transformation. That group can be led by the current CDO, but it is critical that CDOs in those positions develop a strategic data perspective. A strategic CDO organization:

1. manages data for the entire enterprise;
2. provides data for all the data science and AI efforts;
3. operationalizes data collection and sensing;
4. implements and supports data preprocessing for AI;
5. procures data and manages data supplier relationships;
6. understands the current and future needs for data; and
7. performs the traditional data management functions such as data governance, data quality, metadata management, and master data management.

DATA AND MACHINE LEARNING

Data is the lifeblood of machine learning. In fact, the rise of machine learning is very much related to data. The precipitous explosion of data generation happened when smart phones became our cameras, recording devices, and Internet access devices, which gave us easy access to social media. Billions of people all over the world began contributing to data in a variety of forms and formats. Machines were already creating significant data about their performance. With trillions of devices installed all over the world, data volumes became larger than our capacity to understand or make sense out of it. In an interconnected society composed of both humans and machines generating huge volumes of data, the times of algorithms had arrived. By some estimates, humans were generating more data within a span of days than the total data generated in the entire history of humankind. But increase in data was not the only major change. Boost in processing power due to GPUs, new algorithms, and the ability to handle large data sets was instrumental to launch the new era of machine learning. In this chapter we will cover the necessary capabilities that must be deployed by a firm to manage its data. However, managing data is one thing and managing data for AI another. Throughout this chapter we will build upon the existing data management theory and practice and add to it the specific requirements of data science–centric data management. We will start by explaining the two broad types of data. Then we will explain the various types of data used in investment analysis. Later we discuss the data management issues. After that we will cover the capability building for data preprocessing. Lastly, we will cover data sourcing and sensors.

 ## RAW DATA

Raw data is a representation of some aspects of reality. It is through data that we try to understand the reality relevant for our goals. Since we cannot absorb all aspects of reality, we need to focus on those aspects that help us develop a better understanding of it. For example, to know if something is a car, I do not need to know every little detail about that object. The reality of a car is far more complicated than what I can decipher. It is not necessary for me to know about every molecule, atom, and subatomic particle that exists in a car to know that it is a car. It may not be important for me to know what every part of the car is made up of to recognize that it is a car. But for a mechanic trying to fix the car, knowing about auto parts is valuable information. Thus, as we make observations about some real-world phenomenon, we call it data. These observations can come in various forms. We can have visual observations such as photographs and videos, or sound observations such as audio files, or metadata about the health and performance of a machine, and so on.

The raw data we acquire tells us something about some aspects of reality. When we thread together data, we discover more about the phenomenon, and reality takes shape. Our reality is generally composed of objects and their interactions and relationships. When data is pieced together, we can grasp the concepts of objects and their relationships and interactions. Each piece of data offers a little window into the phenomenon under study, and as we collect more data on more aspects or dimensions about the reality being studied, our understanding becomes more comprehensive.

This means that some basic questions such as the following are important considerations:

- What reality are we interested in?
- What observations can we make about that reality? What observations should we make?
- How much can we learn about that reality?
- How would learning about that reality help us?
- What pieces of data (windows into reality) do we need to make sense?
- How can we knit together various windows of reality observed to make more sense about the reality and to improve our understanding of the reality?
- How can our sensemaking evolve with more pieces of data?
- How can our sensemaking improve with more windows into various aspects of reality?
- Can we discover interesting patterns in data that we did not know exist?

STRUCTURED VS. UNSTRUCTURED DATA

The rise of information technology was accompanied by processing transactions and managing transactional data. Transaction data, for instance, data in accounting or supply chain systems, tends to be structured. It can be meticulously organized in tables with rows and columns, and it can be related to each other in a relational data model. Accessing data was easy. You needed to specify what you were searching for, and your database programs cranked to find exact matches for your search criteria. The advent of digital photography, digital videography, sound files, IoT, social media texts, global positioning satellite information, and many other types of information sharing led to the massive production of unstructured data. In the past such data did not lend itself to be easily analyzed. Unlike transactional data, this data lacks structure as it cannot be simply placed into row and columns. For example, suppose you visit a bank to conduct a transaction. As you walk into a bank, your video is recorded. As you talk to the teller, your conversation is recorded. Now, in addition to your banking transaction, the bank has your video and voice data. While the transactional data of your banking transaction is structured data, the video and audio files are unstructured data. Your bank can use that data to determine your satisfaction, mood, style, and preferences. Significant daily trading data generated by markets also comes in both structured and unstructured forms. The tasks related to managing unstructured data are to store it, organize it, index it, tag it, retrieve it, and use it. Managing, using, and making sense out of unstructured data is one of the biggest challenges of establishing an AI program.

DATA USED IN INVESTMENTS

Lately there has been a trend to break down data types into categories of fundamentals, market data, analytics or behavioral data, and alternative data. The reasons for such classification are obvious. First, this classification is specific to investment operations and does not represent the needs of other departments. Secondly, this classification represents the historical progression from mostly fundamentals and market data to, with the passage of time, adding other types of data (such as analyst reports) and alternative data (such as metadata). In the past, while fundamentals and market data were considered analyzable, analyst or constructed data and alternative data were not deemed analyzable by machines. That data was produced for human consumption or for recordkeeping's sake. With the rise of machine learning, it was more convenient to add two more data types and formalize them as separate from the core fundamentals and market data. The issues with such a classification scheme are as follows:

As shown in the previous chapters, in a modern investment operation, it is essential to understand the interdependence of all functions in a firm and not just the investment function. Furthermore, the AI capabilities are deployed across the firm, and therefore all data needs are considered equally important. This also means that at the level of strategic planning, we do not plan for just investment-centric data, we plan for data that is needed by marketing, by sales, by regulatory departments and others.

The second important consideration is that the term "alternative" data seems to imply non-standard data, and while this may have been true in the past, the use of the so-called alternative data is so pervasive that it has become a standard now. If we think about the usage of the alternative and analyst data, especially from an investment perspective, it is either used to understand and predict asset values and risks or to develop insights into markets for trading strategies. In other words, all such alternative data is used for one or both—fundamentals analysis and market analysis. For instance, analysts' reports and earnings call sentiment analysis help us develop better understanding of the stock we are analyzing. They help give us more clarity and a better assessment of the stock, its value, stability, economic well-being, and health. On their own, that data does not have much value for us. The extracted value comes from using the data for the purposes of position or valuation purposes. They become important when that data is placed in the context of fundamentals analysis. It comes from being able to evaluate portfolios, positions, and compatibility of various stocks (or other investments) in our portfolios.

DATA MANAGEMENT FUNCTION FOR THE AI ERA

To build a data function for the AI era, you need to work simultaneously on the twelve steps presented below. If you are a small firm, you may do these functions with a small team. If you are a large enterprise, I recommend each of the steps below be headed by a director or manager level position and organized as a separate team. All the directors report to the CDO. Although when these are separate teams, significant collaborations and coordination are necessary to create meaningful results.

- Step 1: Based upon the design exercise, determine the data needs;
- Step 2: Perform strategic data planning;
- Step 3: Know the sensors and sources;
- Step 4: Understand the supplier;
- Step 5: Understand the data type;
- Step 6: Organize data for usability;
- Step 7: Architect data;
- Step 8: Enhance data quality;

– Step 9: Implement data storage;
– Step 10: Excel in security and privacy;
– Step 11: Implement data for AI; and
– Step 12: Provide investment specialization.

STEP 1: DATA NEEDS ASSESSMENT (DNA)

The DNA group is responsible for connecting business and investment strategies with data. This function has the broad responsibility of understanding
what strategies will require what data.

The search or discovery for linking strategy is data relating business opportunities and problems to data. It answers the question: If we were to pursue a
certain business or investment strategy or solve a certain problem, what data
would we need?

The starting point for the DNA work is the SADAL model developed
in Chapter 3. Think of DNA analysis as a top-down approach, and use the
SADAL framework developed in the previous chapter to understand the data
requirements for each of the artifacts.

STEP 2: PERFORM STRATEGIC DATA PLANNING

This function is performed in a subunit of the CDO organization known as data
strategies unit (DSU). It has two functions and roles:

– DSU develops specialization to monitor the strategy of the entire company.
– DSU creates a bottom-up strategy. It addresses: assuming we had some data,
  what type of innovation, strategy, marketing strategy, business strategy, or
  problem solving could we pursue?

The first role answers questions such as:

– What are the various business strategies (market, position, differentiation,
  etc.) possible for the firm?
– Which are the most beneficial?
– What are the blind spots for the firm?

	Bad or No Data	Good Data
Good Strategy	high risk; results due to randomness	strategic science
Bad Strategy	extremely high risk	failure to convert data to strategy

FIGURE 4.1 Strategy vs. Data

Blind spots come from both not being able to convert data to information and knowledge and from not being able to have the data. As shown in Figure 4.1, a firm can have a good strategy supported by good data or bad data—and it can have a bad strategy supported by good data and bad data. A bad strategy supported by good data will intensify the bias or alternatively the firm will fail to convert good data to a meaningful strategy. A good strategy supported by bad data will mislead the firm into believing that the strategy was bad when in fact the data was bad. Hence both strategy and data need to be good to create meaningful value.

The second role emerges from exploring what data can enable which business or investment strategies. This is a discovery operation—even a thought experiment at early stages of exploration.

It relates data to a business problem and opportunities. A top-down strategy links strategy to data (previous section). A bottom-up strategy links data to strategy, and it is the reverse of the top-down strategy. This function keeps an eye on both new strategies and new types of data.

The bottom-up approach is a humble way of approaching strategy. In many cases we first design the strategic course and then seek data to test and support our strategic rationale. However, the bottom-up approach reminds us that data can generate ideas not only about novel strategies but can also guide us to think differently. It can show us patterns that we did not know exist. The idea here is to not only search for what we have determined as what we need as data but to also constantly identify new sources and types of data that can help us think differently.

Such analyses are constantly performed for each value chain segment and for the entire enterprise. As we explained before, both business and investment dynamics are constantly changing; this function is always on the watch for deciphering both business dynamics and data to determine the potential of new applications. Both bottom-up and top-down approaches to study strategy-to-data and data-to-strategy links are critical.

STEP 3: KNOW THE SENSORS AND SOURCES (IDENTIFY GAPS)

This function is performed by the data intelligence group (DIG). Knowing where data originates is essential for managing an effective data organization. This information can be obtained from data suppliers or developed internally. For example, data suppliers categorize data by data sources such as observed data, netnograph, crowd sourced, drone with camera installed, and so forth. Understanding the data sources is important not only for compliance reasons, but also so you can perform a build vs. buy analysis. It can also give you some ideas about how new data is being generated.

DIG is responsible for putting together an enterprise strategy for build vs. buy data. DIG collects and records metadata about the sources of data. DIG develops and indexes data by sensors and keeps track of sensor technologies being used to collect data. DIG must look at both upstream data needs and downstream data production that comes out of various machine learning algorithms. For example, if a machine learning classifier is classifying articles based on various fields (sports, business, health care, etc.), the upstream data is composed of all the articles—and the downstream data is the results of the classification that are added to the organizational knowledge base.

STEP 4: PROCURE AND UNDERSTAND THE SUPPLY BASE

The data procurement organization (DPO) is responsible for the procurement of the externally sourced data. It keeps track of all potential suppliers of data, conducts RFI and RFP, and obtain quotes of data. It is designed as a strategic sourcing organization. DPO establishes a data supply chain and maintains data supplier relationships.

The DPO function is managed by people trained in business, corporate strategy, procurement, finance, and data management. This function works with all other data groups to understand the type of data they will need as corporate groups transform to the AI era. Once they develop those requirements, they assess what data currently exists in the firm and what data needs to be generated or procured.

The DPO function is staffed by business and data management people. As data moves upstream, it enters the realm of machine learning. The DPO function must constantly evaluate the upstream data needs from the enterprise perspective and have a strategic plan to source the data from external sources and to make it available to the organization.

DPO also works with the compliance and data quality group to ensure that quality data is being procured from credible sources.

STEP 5: UNDERSTAND THE DATA TYPE (SIGNALS)

The data composition group (DCG) is responsible for understanding and architecting the composition of data. This organization studies data by its categories such as raw, signals, reports, sampled, social, aggregated, and others. The point, of course, is to assess the composition of data. This information is also part of the metadata necessary to make better decisions about data. Signal data are calculated metrics and may include analyst reports. In addition to understanding the data composition, this group also generates various usable forms of data from combining various data elements.

STEP 6: ORGANIZE DATA FOR USABILITY

This is led by the data use and governance group (DUG). All the metadata about the data is organized for easy retrieval. They collect and organize data by its usability, location of storage, ownership, statistical characteristics, and multidimensional classification. The core idea is to enable access for automation to the entire enterprise. This enables various organizations all over the firm to see and use data. Data terms, lineage, relationships, and all other aspects of data are recorded. Note that the traditional data governance usually applies to internal data that resides in company's internal systems. Since the field of finance requires significant external data sets, this group also organizes and manages metadata about all external data sets. To do that it needs to have extensive collaboration with other data organizations mentioned in this section.

Notice that some of the data that firms use for fundamental analysis can also be used to develop marketing and sales analysis. For example:

- Identify high-value clients;
- Determine the large investors in a target firm to understand the pattern of their investment; and
- Understand the unique needs of a target firm to assess products and services needs.

STEP 7: ARCHITECT DATA

The data architect organization (DAO) performs the functions of developing and maintaining enterprise data architecture, addressing integration and interoperability, content management, and reference and master data management. Many of these capabilities already exist in traditional data management organizations.

 ## STEP 8: ENSURE DATA QUALITY

The DQO, or data quality organization, ensures the quality of data. Data quality has many attributes such as timeliness, relevance, and comprehensiveness. In addition to the traditional data quality attributes, machine learning has added some other areas that should be considered by data quality. For example, a simple measure of ease of usability by algorithms is an attribute that can be added to the data quality toolset.

 ## STEP 9: DATA STORAGE AND WAREHOUSING

The data IT organization, or DITO, is the group that designs data storage and warehousing strategies, processes, and products, and develops plans. DITO evaluates cloud vs. internal vs. hybrid options, selects hardware and software, and deploys databases, repositories, marts, and data lakes for data storage. Some of these services are undertaken by traditional IT organizations. In our model, DITO should be part of the CDO organization.

 ## STEP 10: EXCEL IN DATA SECURITY AND PRIVACY

The data security and privacy, or DSP, group develops and implements data security and privacy. DSP focuses on data security and privacy, and this group can work in coordination with the centralized chief information security officer's organization.

STEP 11: IMPLEMENT DATA FOR AI

Data is the vital grub for algorithms. Learning can be viewed as training an algorithm to perform optimally. An algorithm gets trained on training data, and then when test data is presented to it, it demonstrates its learning performance. But feeding data into an algorithm is no easy task. Data needs to be organized in a certain structure to be fed into an algorithm. Besides preparing data into the structure that algorithms like, one needs to understand various aspects of data to make the algorithms run more efficiently. When it comes to algorithms, not all data contains equal levels of informative content. Certain elements of data are far more informative than others and hence contribute more to learning. Identifying those elements is a very productive exercise. In fact, in many cases some less informative content of data can be discarded since it does not help in learning and becomes an unnecessary burden on processing. More about that later in this chapter.

The AI-specific data management function is composed of three different stations. Each one of these functions requires separate and specialized skill sets. Ideally these functions can report to a central leadership structure. They must work together like a production chain to create best results. The functions are:

– data labeling;
– feature engineering, extraction, and selection; and
– preprocessing.

Data labeling: For supervised learning data needs to be labeled. While unsupervised learning methods work to identify clusters, in supervised learning, labeled data is critical. Labeling of data is a function by itself. In some cases, labels are part of the data. For example, predicting prices of assets using a set of features implies that the labels (prices) are contained in the data sets. In other cases, labels need to be attached, generated, or produced. Attached implies that the label data is in a separate data set and that needs to be integrated with the core data set. Generated means that an automated method is used to assign labels to data. Produced means that a human reviews the data and assigns values to it.

Data preprocessing: This is a specialized function composed of machine learning experts who also have a good understanding of financial data. The goals of the data preparation are to: (a) organize data in a form that machines can take that data in as input; (b) calibrate data in a context-specific setting to link it with use such as asset classes; (c) clean and index data for use upstream; (d) enhance data quality; and (e) preserve data informativeness. This is a specialization of its own, and it includes the following steps:

- Data curation, filling missing or incomplete records;
- Understanding the data statistics—outliers and anomalies;
- Managing non-standardized and categorical variables;
- Combining data sets from different sources to develop new features—feature enrichment;
- Normalizing or scaling data so variables do not represent values that are widely different (for example one variable has values that are less than 1, while the other has values that are all in billions); and
- Providing additional preprocessing to text data such as removing punctuation and common (stop) words, and stemming.

Feature Engineering: While this is also part of data preprocessing, I have listed feature-related adjustments because they constitute an important part of preparing your data. In feature engineering, you use domain knowledge to extract features (variables that are important in describing the reality) from your data sets. Once extracted, you can study which features are most informative and can select those features for your algorithm. In very large data sets, making these choices becomes immensely important since you cannot burden your algorithm with every possible variable in your data. If you are unclear what is stated in this section, do not worry. These things will become clearer in the next two chapters.

STEP 12: PROVIDE INVESTMENT SPECIALIZATION

While all of the above steps apply to any business, finance requires its own way to process data. This is particularly true for the quant side of the business. Some of the major global experts in this domain have offered clear guidance to make sure that data management and data science people understand that regular processes that apply in other fields do not necessarily apply in finance (De Prado, 2018). For example, from a data quality perspective you may want to make sure that the data is complete and accurate. But if you are evaluating your strategies and performing historical simulations, you want to re-create conditions that would have been prevalent at the time the simulation was running. If on a particular trading day at 3:45 p.m. you did not have certain data in real life, then you must not run strategy evaluation where data has been retroactively inserted or fixed. In other words, data that will be considered as bad quality data in traditional data quality will actually be good data quality since it represents the reality of the trading day.

Some other aspects of finance-specific feature selection include selecting the features that will generalize well in evaluation while ensuring that you are not overfitting. All of these will be explained later in the book. What is important, however, is that feature analysis is not something static. It is also not something that should be approached only after the SADAL analysis is finalized. Identifying information-rich features, cataloguing them, and facilitating their use is a necessary function for firms that pursue quantitative strategies.

In addition to working on features, this group also understands how to extract and sample data for use in quantitative models. For example, they know how to prepare and use the tick data. Other data includes fundamental data such as financial statements and quarterly reports (balance sheet, income statement, and cash flow statements). Other data may also include economic ratios, macro variables, and other economic data.

Most importantly, this group is staffed with people who understand finance and standards such as GIPS®, and who are knowledgeable about asset classes, investment vehicles, and data used in quantitative strategy development.

 ## ABOUT LEGACY DATA MANAGEMENT

The legacy data management departments mostly concentrate on data governance. These groups have a wide spectrum of responsibilities, but the primary responsibility is of governance and data quality. They may also interact with the IT function to understand where data resides in a firm, to understand data lineage, and to develop insights into data operations. While data management functions have done a reasonably good job in some firms to organize and govern data, in many firms the function has not kept up with the specific requirements of enabling enterprise-wide adoption of AI. This organization is mostly staffed with information or data management experts—and not investment professionals. Their understanding of finance function and specific requirements of finance is usually limited. They tend to focus on broad issues of data governance, such a data stewardship and ownership or data quality. Data management organizations—in our opinion—should be restructured in accordance with the process defined in this chapter.

REFERENCES

Noh, K. S. (2016) "A Study on the Position of CDO for Improving Competitive-ness Based Big Data in Cluster Computing Environment." *Cluster Computing.* [Online] 19 (3), 1659–1669.

De Prado, M. L. (2018). *Advances in financial machine learning.* John Wiley & Sons.

Samuels, M. (2015) "Chief Data and Digital Officers Rise to Threaten the CIO." ComputerWeekly.com. (February), 15–18. [online]. Available from: https://www.computerweekly.com/feature/Chief-Data-and-Digital-Officers-rise-to-threaten-the-CIO.

CHAPTER FIVE

Model Development

A T THE HEART OF BUILDING industrial-scale enterprise machine learning (ML) is model development. I use the term "modeling" to simplify and be consistent with single words in the process (data, evaluation, performance). This is where ML learning solutions are developed. ML helps machines to learn from data. ML methods are about extracting models from data such that we can extract patterns and make better predictions. In ML, we use methods to extract models. An alternative way to think about ML is to view it as fitting the model to the data.

Please note that in this chapter I will provide an introduction to ML. If you have some background in ML, you can skip this chapter. This chapter is meant for businesspeople who are trying to get a high-level introduction to ML. The main goal is to have businesspeople learn about the methods and tools that are used by this group. This can help facilitate communications between the data science and the business teams.

 ## WHO IS RESPONSIBLE?

In the previous chapter we focused on identifying data and features. Feature libraries helped us determine the most informative aspects of raw data. At that stage we did not know what model would fit best with what data. We did not know which model worked best for the data we have. Data function (Chapter 4) manages data but is not a model development group. Modeling group or station is where actual solutions are produced. This is where real strategies are developed and algorithms are tried and tested. This is the core research and development function. This is the heart of your firm's future.

This function is headed by a senior executive who reports to the CAIO/COO. Think about the upstream operation we discussed in the previous two chapters. In Chapter 3 we learned about design and in Chapter 4 we recognized how to manage data to support our design. Outputs of both chapters become the input for the third step in our upstream operation. This is the third step, and in this step we develop models for ML (or other methods depending upon the requirements). Developing a model implies three things. First, we need to understand the problem to assess what learning type or approach we will use. Second, within a selected learning type, we determine what learning architecture we will deploy (for example, neural network or support vector machines). Third, we select one or more algorithms to train.

 ## HIGH-LEVEL PROCESS

Let us take a quick inventory of the raw materials going into this group's operations:

- SADAL: The first is the SADAL documents. The SADAL documents are the foundation for our starting point. From SADAL we understand the project goals, business reasons, user expectations, value, timing, and so forth.
- DSU-brainstormed ideas about new strategies become important in our exploration for models. This is important for investment strategies where artifacts are being constantly innovated.
- Curated data: We have data that has been preprocessed and ready. If the modeling group needs data in different formats, it communicates that to the data group.
- Features: Features were identified, catalogued, and organized. Ideally, feature combinations and their informativeness were also explored and catalogued.

Using the above raw material, the modeling group trains investment and business/functional algorithms. We divide the AI artifacts into the following categories:

Enterprise Strategy: Enterprise strategy artifacts are corporate strategy–centric algorithms that attempt to predict, evaluate, and monitor the overall strategy of a firm. Whether approached as market-centric and competitive, resource-centric, or emergent, this function analyzes the core strengths and weaknesses as well as risks and opportunities of the strategic positioning of the firm. This area also includes a competitive intelligence function. The competitive intelligence and strategy-monitoring models cover various aspects of business including customer service, product launches, and competitor actions.

Enterprise Functions: Enterprise functions include all other functions except strategy and investment. It develops models for marketing, customer service, AUM expansion, relationship building, institutional client management, supply chain, and others.

Investment: The investment function develops artifacts and the theories behind investment. The theory is enabled by converting informative features into working algorithms. The link between data and algorithm is the catalyst for learning. The libraries of features provide clues to the configuration of the strategy. The strategy, obviously, needs to be clarified and defended based on solid economic and scientific principles. The strategy focuses on both asset classes and instruments, as well as on portfolios. In some cases, theory is reverse-engineered as the model (for example, in unsupervised learning) shows promise except we cannot explain the financial or economic theory behind it.

As we review the toolkit available for us to achieve the above, we should consider some guiding principles for this operation:

- The AI field is constantly developing, and every day new discoveries are made. We need to keep an open mind. As soon as we build something, it is possible that a better model has been created somewhere.
- The fit between data and model can be relative. Not all models respond to the data the same way. Some are far more efficient than others.
- Despite the hype surrounding certain technologies—for example, deep learning—one should match the problem domain with the methods. Simpler models may do the job better than more complex models.
- Build the modeling function with the spirit of research orientation, innovation, and constant experimentation. Give autonomy to data scientists to experiment.
- Develop strategy constantly. Strategies become stale. Conditions change. Competitors copy your strategies. And new data and new ideation can lead to new strategies. Always stay in the reinvention mode.

TABLE 5.1 Methods Used in Finance Applications (adopted from research by Andriosopoulos et al., 2019)

METHODS

Asset Screening and Selection
DEA, ANN, ANFIS, MCDA, Fuzzy GRA, GA, SVM, GP, Fuzzy MCDM, Copula models, SA

Capital Allocation (Mean Value Extensions)
Algorithmic approaches: solutions for complex optimization problems; modeling formulations: portfolio selection with multiple objectives and goals, stochastic approaches, multiperiod and continuous time models, fuzzy models, robust optimization, network models

Trading
Rule-based NFIS, RL, ANN, SOM, fuzzy logic, DST, GA, multi-agent system, ANFIS, boosting, GP, SA, online algorithm, SVM, GA, DP, TM, Markov models, ridge regression

Credit Risk Modeling
NN, kernel, classification trees, decision rules, fuzzy and neuro-fuzzy systems, Bayesian models, ensembles, hybrid systems; hazard model, ensembles, credibility theory, mixture model, LR and OLS, SVM, Bayesian, QR, DE, SURV, Probit and OLS, copula model, DL; stochastic and dynamic programming, computationally efficient simulation methods, Markov chain models, evolutionary approaches

Asset-Liability Management
GP, chance constrained programming, RO, SP, multi-objective stochastic programming

Sovereign and Corporate Debt Management
MSP, SP, LP

Venture Capital and IPO
Game theory, fuzzy goal programming, SVM, multicriteria analysis, ANFIS, GO, FS, Bayesian inference, Markov chain Monte Carlo

Operational and Liquidity Risk Modeling
Extreme value theory, Bayesian inference, Bayesian networks, copula modeling, adaptive fuzzy inference model, fuzzy cognitive maps

Derivatives and Volatility Modeling
Linear programming, neural networks, wavelets, DL, SVM

Financial Fraud Detection
Multicriteria analysis, integer programming, TM, stacked generalization, DT, Bayesian classifier, network analysis, graph-based models, random forests, nearest neighbors

With the above principles, we can take a quick look at the various applications being used in investment and finance. See Table 5.1. This is adopted from research performed by Andriosopoulos (Andriosopoulos et al., 2019):

Key for acronyms in the table:

ANFIS: adaptive neuro-fuzzy inference system
ANN: artificial neural network
DE: differential evolution
DEA: data envelopment analysis
DL: deep learning
DP: dynamic programming
DST: Dempster-Shafer theory
DT: decision trees
ETF: exchange-traded funds
FS: fuzzy systems
GA: genetic algorithm
GO: genetic optimization
GP: genetic programming
LP: linear programming
LR: logistic regression
MCDA: multicriteria decision analysis
MSP: multi-objective stochastic programming
OLS: ordinary least squares
QR: quantile regression
RL: reinforcement learning
SA: sentiment analysis
SOM: self-organizing map
SP: stochastic programming
SURV: survival analysis
SVM: support vector machines
TM: text mining

 ## MODELS

A model is a representation of reality that satisfies some goal. It enables us to represent a reality so we can understand it better. Think of language as a model that allows us to understand the physical reality around us. We cannot place a physical car or an airplane in our head, but we can represent those objects and their attributes and actions with words, and words can serve as symbols that we can understand. Language, therefore, can represent the reality and is a model. A map, for example, is a model of physical reality of roads, stores, buildings, and so forth. Financial statements are models of a business's performance. Transcripts are models of a student's performance.

A learning model uses some method (ML) to predict the unknown part of the reality that we are interested in. Let us give some relevant examples here:

- Predict the potential of fraud in a company (future)
- Predict a fraud that happened in the company (past)
- Predict a fraud that is taking place (present)

In general terminology, we tend to think about predicting as predicting some future event, but in the ML world, the word "predict" signifies the formula to estimate an unknown value.

Specifically, the prediction can be viewed as using the inputs (feature vectors) to estimate the value of the output (target variable). In other words, assuming there is some relationship between x and y, you ask the system, given x, what do you think y will be? These concepts are further explained below.

THE POWER OF PATTERNS

We recognize things by looking at patterns that form them.

Nature tends to achieve complexity from simplicity. It is through the simple interactions of simple agents that complexity is born. The human brain is a great example of how neural connections lead to the creation of complex ideas, thoughts, emotions, and feelings. Throughout our life, we progressively learn simple things and through the simplicity achieve complexity. We learn words and from words we form sentences and from sentences we form paragraphs and books. Our ability to identify even simple things is a powerful gift.

Imagine presenting a child a toy car and asking the child what it is. It is likely that a child will respond, "A car." The child knows that she cannot sit in this car, that her parents cannot put her car seat in the car and take her for a drive. But for her this is a car. She ignored the functional attributes of the car and observed a visual pattern in the toy. The toy looks like a car. We do that when we name an object from a picture. Our ability to extract the pattern is powerful. We generalize the concept of car and instead of narrowing our understanding of a car as a specific single object, we identify a pattern and apply it to create a broad concept of what a car's class membership looks like. This membership may include cars as different as sedans and sports cars, large and small cars, and cars in different shapes and colors. Thus, it seems like we develop a general idea of what is a car. Clearly, the functional aspects of what a car is—the mobility factor—is not something we take into account when considering what a car is. For example, we will not call a bus or a trailer or motorcycle cars, even though they all serve the function of mobility. However, if we consider a class of vehicles vs. trains, we will place trucks and buses in that category.

Just as we identify objects as patterns—visual or otherwise—we also understand the relationships between objects. Roads are meant for cars and not trains. Train tracks are meant for trains and not cars, and so on. Certain types of clouds and weather conditions mean rain. The idea is that patterns can be viewed as composed of indicators or pointers or markers. These markers give us clues to not only what objects are but also about relationships between objects. For example, windshield, four tires, doors, shape, and so forth, give us clues to what might be a car. These markers give us some information about some aspect of the reality (a car), and when we put them together, we develop a general pattern that gives us the confidence to recognize certain objects as cars.

This learning from patterns is a strategy that can be applied to machines. The attributes that give us clues can be viewed as features. The ability to generalize or define an abstraction—for instance being able to see different types of cars and still understand that it is a car—is achieved via algorithms. Non-AI machines do not have that capability. When you scan a barcode on a car, the machine takes in the barcode and finds an entry in the database and returns the name of the car. This is not an intelligent system. If there was no entry in the database, the machine would not have known that it is a car. It would have found no matching entry and returned a message like "did not find a match."

Another type of AI, known by some as first wave of AI (Launchbur, 2017), would require you to answer specific questions about the object and based on your answers could have told you if it is a car or not. Those are expert systems, and while their reasoning ability is strong, their ability to learn is low. Modern learning systems have come out of the ML branch of AI, and that area has made incredible progress.

TECHNIQUES OF LEARNING

What are the three types of learning?

If we are trying to learn from patterns, there are three ways to learn. I give the example of how children learn.

Watching others: Children learn from watching others. They try to emulate what their parents, friends, siblings, and others do. This means that the actions of others become examples for children of what to do or what not to do. This can be viewed as learning from example. In learning from examples, children are provided examples, and learning is generalized, not specific. If a parent shows a child that touching a cup of hot tea can burn the fingers, that learning is not specific for just tea. If tea is replaced by coffee, it is likely that the child will be able to extrapolate that the same thing can happen for coffee. Learning by examples is known as supervised learning. In supervised learning examples are linked with the labels of what they are. When many examples are provided, a pattern develops, and that pattern then helps to identify new examples. In other words, it learns to generalize. It knows that coffee can also be hot.

Discovering: Another way that children learn is by discovering or exploring. A child may enjoy walking around the backyard and discovering butterflies, flowers, insects, and plants. Imagine a curious child who records various patterns that she discovers in the backyard—a butterfly, a strange-looking bird, a flower. She then brings that back to her parents and asks them what they are, and they (based upon their own knowledge and research) inform her what those things are. In this case, the child did not start the learning process with an example. She just went out in the backyard and started discovering these patterns that she brought back to her parents, and they then assigned meaning to those patterns. Unsupervised learning is like that. It searches and explores for patterns in data and discovers interesting patterns. Humans can see those patterns and assign meaning to them.

Reward and punishment: Another way that children (as well as adults and animals) learn is by reward and punishment. When a certain behavior is rewarded, it becomes stronger. If punished, it becomes weaker and is avoided. This type of learning is known as reinforcement learning. In this case learning can be viewed as a guided process where feedback is provided to determine if the agent is moving away from the goal or coming closer to it. The reward and punishment become the feedback mechanism to guide the learning.

WHAT IS MACHINE LEARNING?

Here we provide some intuition about machine learning.

Learning can be viewed as predicting or finding the right answers based on some data. For example, if we are trying to predict whether the weather conditions will lead to rain or not, it is rain that we are trying to predict. We can call it the output variable (also known as the dependent variable, target variable, or simply, y value).

But we were trying to predict whether it will rain or not from some data. That data, hopefully, will be informative and relevant to helping us answer our question. For example, data such as clouds, cloud type, moisture, wind, and so forth, may give us information about the pattern that can predict rain. These data elements or properties or attributes are the **features** (Figure 5.1).

Features, Attributes, or Dimensions

x1	x2	x3	x4	x5	x6	x7	x8	x9	x10	y
687	0.613	420.912	257.89	0.240	61.995	14.90	0.619	9.826	5.71	1
868	0.738	640.163	472.13	0.422	199.290	84.12	0.443	37.243	16.49	1
745	0.141	105.164	14.84	0.724	10.745	7.78	0.800	6.224	4.98	0
83	0.929	77.107	71.63	0.022	1.544	0.03	0.887	0.030	0.03	1
381	0.052	19.816	1.03	0.370	0.381	0.14	0.806	0.114	0.09	1
570	0.291	165.814	48.24	0.899	43.349	38.96	0.027	1.049	0.03	0
326	0.546	178.044	97.24	0.813	79.078	64.31	0.914	58.770	53.71	1
48	0.958	45.987	44.06	0.066	2.904	0.19	0.443	0.085	0.04	0
568	0.434	246.282	106.79	0.554	59.123	32.73	0.791	25.879	20.46	0
88	0.689	60.650	41.80	0.255	10.647	2.71	0.361	1.034	0.39	0
150	0.259	38.864	10.07	0.471	4.739	2.23	0.393	0.877	0.35	1
689	0.728	501.604	365.18	0.728	265.867	193.56	0.690	133.501	92.08	0
671	0.494	331.356	163.63	0.713	116.700	83.23	0.865	71.962	62.22	0
162	0.260	42.102	10.94	0.829	9.070	7.52	0.513	3.858	1.98	0
128	0.982	125.657	123.36	0.379	46.731	17.70	0.561	9.936	5.58	0
252	0.361	90.971	32.84	0.060	1.972	0.12	0.158	0.019	0.00	1
484	0.985	476.585	469.28	0.047	22.036	1.03	0.052	0.053	0.00	1
169	0.143	24.138	3.45	0.262	0.905	0.24	0.402	0.095	0.04	1
842	0.320	269.073	85.99	0.687	59.106	40.63	0.964	39.162	37.7	1
33	0.630	20.784	13.09	0.216	2.830	0.61	0.414	0.253	0.10	0
220	0.796	175.090	139.35	0.870	121.294	105.58	0.207	21.824	4.5	1
493	0.805	397.086	319.83	0.753	240.976	181.56	0.884	160.455	141.8	1
620	0.295	182.662	53.82	0.388	20.888	8.11	0.244	1.975	0.4	1
466	0.639	297.859	190.39	0.722	137.386	99.14	0.241	23.926	5.7	0
686	0.751	514.874	386.44	0.436	168.606	73.56	0.272	20.005	5.4	1
403	0.695	280.264	194.91	0.155	30.265	4.70	0.279	1.313	0.3	1
434	0.842	365.488	307.79	0.041	12.482	0.51	0.671	0.340	0.2	0
110	0.736	80.987	59.63	0.494	29.477	14.57	0.001	0.008	0.0	0
359	0.474	170.335	80.82	0.545	44.035	23.99	0.936	22.452	21.0	1
226	0.603	136.202	82.08	0.890	73.018	64.95	0.427	27.762	11.5	1
704	0.245	172.658	42.34	0.983	41.613	40.89	0.829	33.904	28.1	1
948	0.987	916.701	886.43	0.043	38.009	1.63	0.064	0.104	0.0	1
501	0.676	338.921	229.28	0.228	52.170	11.87	0.075	0.895	0.0	1
70	0.698	48.834	34.07	0.805	27.428	22.08	0.459	10.133	4.6	0
73	0.832	60.735	50.53	0.383	19.345	7.41	0.479	3.548	1.7	0
599	0.862	516.546	445.44	0.523	233.176	122.06	0.693	84.542	58.5	1
577	0.418	241.042	100.70	0.150	15.151	2.28	0.593	1.351	0.8	0
960	0.790	758.844	599.84	0.074	44.241	3.26	0.979	3.194	3.1	0
568	0.231	131.169	30.29	0.314	9.520	2.99	0.735	2.199	1.6	1
768	0.251	192.781	48.39	0.014	0.671	0.01	0.828	0.008	0.0	1
961	0.226	221.895	50.19	0.766	38.437	29.44	0.860	25.302	21.7	0
785	0.322	252.556	81.25	0.807	65.555	52.89	0.315	16.674	5.2	0
387	0.836	323.676	270.71	0.749	202.832	151.97	0.189	28.775	5.4	0
799	0.110	87.717	9.63	0.181	1.744	0.32	0.165	0.052	0.0	0
236	0.740	174.688	129.30	0.678	87.671	59.44	0.126	7.501	0.9	1
835	0.598	499.009	298.22	0.606	180.784	109.59	0.429	47.040	20.1	1
976	0.871	850.444	741.04	0.857	634.856	543.89	0.906	492.751	446.4	1
156	0.069	10.781	0.75	0.176	0.131	0.02	0.168	0.004	0.0	1
917	0.501	459.829	230.58	0.843	194.386	163.87	0.418	68.421	28.5	1
843	0.496	418.048	207.31	0.561	116.367	65.32	0.547	35.712	19.53	0
658	0.607	399.155	242.13	0.164	39.787	6.54	0.804	5.256	4.23	0
761	0.296	225.210	66.05	0.387	23.805	8.50	0.973	8.273	8.05	1
623	0.649	404.062	262.06	0.614	160.971	98.88	0.018	1.808	0.03	1
819	0.544	445.886	242.53	0.892	216.360	193.01	0.986	190.329	187.69	1
790	0.895	707.128	632.95	0.609	385.659	234.98	0.423	99.514	42.14	1
259	0.457	118.486	54.20	0.813	44.063	35.82	0.599	21.453	12.85	0
356	0.652	232.172	151.42	0.950	143.851	136.66	0.010	1.421	0.01	0
356	0.811	288.818	234.31	0.558	130.757	72.97	0.716	52.236	37.39	0
297	0.323	95.807	30.91	0.045	1.383	0.06	0.637	0.039	0.03	0
134	0.920	123.266	113.39	0.802	90.916	72.89	0.289	21.045	6.06	1

$X = (x1, x2, x3, x4, ...xn)$
These are independent variables, input

Many general problems have binary values of "y", e.g., Spam = Yes or Spam = No
This is the dependent variable, target variable, or output

FIGURE 5.1 Data, Features, and Target

Features give us information about the output (rain) and constitute the input variables, independent variables, or simply, x values.

Each of the features represents some part of the reality that leads to predicting rain. These features have values. For example, temperature, cloud type, and so on, will be supported by data. This is the data that we will use to train the algorithms. It is known as the **training data**.

Imagine that data in the form of a table where each column represents a feature. Each row represents the values of features, and we call each row a **feature vector**.

Now we can study the relationship between features and the target variable. We want to understand the link between the variables that predict rain and the occurrence of rain. That is the pattern we want to uncover. We can express this relationship as a mathematical function. Let us call this a **function**. For example, see the following:

$$\text{Will it Rain }(Y, N) = w0 + w1 * \text{Variable } 1 + w2 * \text{Variable } 2 + w3 \\ * \text{Variable } 3 + \ldots$$

Or written differently:

$$y = f(x) = w0 + w1x1 + w2x2 + w3x3 + \ldots$$

Here w represents the weights assigned to each variable. Weights can be viewed as importance assigners. Variables with more importance in predicting the rain (output) get a higher weight. This means to predict whether it will rain or not, the variables (e.g., moisture) that have the highest predictive information will have a higher weight. In general, ML can be viewed as finding the function that links the features (input or independent variables) to the output variables.

Notice that this type of problem is opposite to what high school algebra trained us for. In algebra, we were provided equations (or functions) with the x values and we had to find the y value. We plugged in the x values, made some algebraic manipulations, and then calculated the y value as our answer.

In ML, we do not have the function. We find it. We discover it from the data. We are given the x values, and in many cases the y values, and our goal is to find the function that represents the data we are training it on. As shown in the figure, the x values can be viewed as the input data. Each x represents a feature. And y represents the output (0 means no rain, 1 means rain).

SCIENTIFIC PROCESS ON STEROIDS

A Machine as the new Scientist

Human knowledge is acquired through observation and experience. We developed science, which became the mechanism for identifying patterns and finding relationships between them. An apple falls to the ground and not toward the sky, so there must be gravity. This kind of observation linked to outcomes enabled us to establish relationships between different phenomena. Once the observation about the gravity was determined, Newton conceptualized the equations. That is what science does. It looks at data and tries to establish relationships between different factors. Machine learning is not too different.

In ML we work with the data to establish relationships. These relationships allow us to predict things—something we call learning. In machine learning, we understand what learning is and figure out how to embed the ability in machines to learn patterns efficiently and effectively.

THE LEARNING MACHINES

One way to think of learning is to be able to reason. For example, let us say we design a system that asks us a series of questions, and based upon the answer to each question asks the next question and then the next question. When we answer the last question, it gives us the answer to what we were looking for. This is one type of learning, but as you can tell, this learning is not very efficient. To design a system that asks questions, we would need to give it all the questions, and then it can ask those questions to provide answers. Think of it as a computer program with several layers of if-then statements. But even to do simple things, we would need to give the machine thousands, in some cases millions, of rules. Clearly, this is not the most efficient way to solve learning problems.

An efficient learning machine must be able to identify patterns and be able generalize that learning to situations that it has not seen before.

Let us say we are trying to develop a learning machine for predicting rain. This machine will learn how to predict rain. For that to happen, a learning machine needs the following:

1. An idea of what the properties are (i.e., preexisting simpler patterns) such as moisture, cloud type, and so forth. These are the variables that will be used to predict rain.

2. The values of those properties—numeric values.
3. Some type of a method that establishes the relationship among the variables so they can predict rain. For example, perhaps one variable, such as the type of cloud, could be the most informative to predict rain.
4. It helps to have a clear idea of what we want the machine to accomplish.
5. Some type of performance measure that shows how accurately the machine is performing.

In the ML world, there are names given to the above five:

- **Features:** The input variables are known as features. For example, predicting a stock price can have features as the fundamentals data about the firm whose stock price you are trying to predict.
- **Features vectors:** The numeric values that are associated with the features are the feature vectors. They can be viewed as the rows of data in a table where columns represent the features.
- **Method:** A method is the algorithm used in ML to learn. Unlike a program, the algorithm is not a set of coded instructions to a computer to do something. It is also not a set of rules. See the section below.
- **Goal:** Typically, we would like the machine to have a specific learning goal for us to develop our training strategy. For example, we want the machine to predict stock value or the performance of a portfolio.
- **Performance criteria:** The performance criterion assesses whether the machine is learning or not. It is a measure of your training success. This means that the trained algorithm has learned from the data that has been given to it during training but also that the algorithm performs when it is applied in new situations with data that it has never seen before.

 ## ALGORITHMS

What is an algorithm? Algorithms are the methods by which machines learn to think. Unlike coding programs where we give machines step-by-step instructions to do something, algorithms enable machines to find patterns to learn to do things on their own. They do not require specific instructions. They learn from data.

Imagine how many lines of if-then statements you would need to write a classification program whose job is to direct your legitimate emails to your inbox and spam to your spam box. You can write the names of the people who send you emails. You can identify the words that typically mean spam and write line by line instructions to warn your program:

1. If you see emails from such and such people, send them to my inbox;
2. If you see emails that contain such and such words, send them to spam.

Of course, you can recognize the problems:

1. You would need to write hundreds of names and emails;
2. You would need to write thousands or perhaps millions of lines of code to tell the machine the various combinations of words that would indicate spam.

That is why you use ML. If we can help machine to identify patterns, then we do not have to write millions of lines of code. We can just give them the data and have them learn from that data.

The methods that help machines identify patterns and make inferences are known as algorithms. Let us look at some interesting properties of data:

- **It discovers a mathematical link:** They can be viewed as the search to discover functions (as mathematical functions that express relationships between two or more variables). For example, a function can establish a relationship between the set of words (input features) and the output variable being spam or not spam.
- **It is goal oriented:** The goal of the ML artifact gets embedded in the function. The function to determine spam vs. not spam is trying to discriminate between spam and not spam. That algorithm will only be able to do that. It will not be able to tell you about the mood or intention or style of the email author who sent you the email. For that, you may need a different function. Similarly, the algorithm that tells you about the mood or sentiment will not be able to inform you about the writing style or educational background of the author of the emails. For that, you would need another function to represent that relationship, and so on.
- **There is a performance benchmark:** The algorithm is not just searching for a function; it is trying to discover the best one out there. An algorithm is not the function itself that solves your problem but instead it is a way of discovering the function that will solve your problem. Think of it this way: your algorithm is trying to discover a program from a large space of programs. Based upon the performance metric, your program discovers

the best one. In the spam classification example, there could be billions of functions that can try to establish a relationship between the input variables (text of the email) and output variable (spam or not spam) but many of them will not be good at it. Some may be successful 1% of the time, some 10%, some 30%. You want something far more reliable. Can you imagine a spam identification algorithm operating at 30%? Perhaps you want to aim for 95%.

- **It starts its journey randomly:** To find the function, the algorithm starts by finding a random solution. Then it finds a second solution. As the algorithm runs, it keeps trying to improve and uses feedback to evaluate whether it is moving in the right direction. It keeps adjusting the parameters till it comes to a point where it cannot improve any further. Hopefully at that point its performance is consistent with your expectations.

- **Computational efficiency matters:** In its journey to navigate through millions of possibilities, it is quite possible that the algorithm takes too long. Days can turn into weeks and weeks into months. Obviously, we want our algorithm to find a solution quickly. Hence, in addition to finding the solution, we expect our algorithms to run fast and scale efficiently.

Now let us move into more formal introductions to the learning types.

SUPERVISED LEARNING

Supervised learning is learning by examples, that is, where examples are provided (Figure 5.2). Examples can be seen as series of combinations of inputs and one or more outputs. For example, spam vs. non-spam email could be composed of words (text input) used in spam email and the output that shows spam email or not. In this scenario, the text becomes the input and the binary classification spam or not-spam is the output.

When we have thousands and thousands of examples of email text and spam vs. non-spam classification, we can give our algorithm many examples. We can designate the input as x-variables and the binary output as the y-variable. When x is given as input, the goal of the algorithm is to predict which value of y it belongs to.

We can convert all the data to numeric data. For example, the binary y-value of spam and no-spam can be 0 and 1. That is how we can now discover a function.

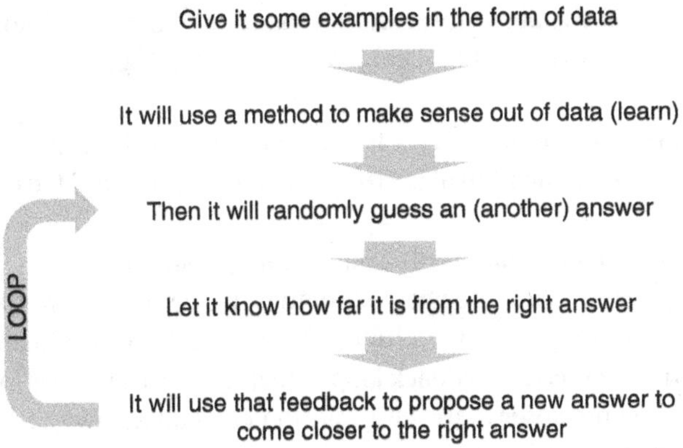

Give it some examples in the form of data

⬇

It will use a method to make sense out of data (learn)

⬇

Then it will randomly guess an (another) answer

⬇

LOOP

Let it know how far it is from the right answer

⬇

It will use that feedback to propose a new answer to
come closer to the right answer

FIGURE 5.2 The Process of Using Examples in Supervised Learning

The examples data is our data set. And there is a conceptual space where many functions link inputs with outputs. Somewhere in this space is the function we are looking for.

In the upcoming chapters we introduce many applications where documents are classified into different categories. For example, regulatory documents can be classified in different categories. Perhaps you already have documents that belong to those categories and you can use them as example for your algorithm to learn.

Just as documents and emails are classified, pictures and sound files can also be classified.

Let us now take a step back and review what is happening in supervised learning:

- We supply the examples. The examples are related to the task we want the machine to do, and the inputs are matched with the outputs. When inputs and outputs exist, we call it labeled data. The word "labeled" means that for each set of inputs the output is designated (spam vs. non-spam). The outputs are known as labels.
- Based upon the examples, the algorithm learns and finds the best function in the solution space.
- We aim for a preestablished performance measure—for example, 95%.
- Upon receiving the new input, our learning machine will correctly generate the spam vs. not-spam classification.

Recall that in the above discussion, I mentioned that we changed the text data into numerical data. This is known as preprocessing:

- The data is preprocessed to get it ready for machine ingestion.
- From many classification algorithms, an algorithm is selected to classify the data.
- The algorithm is initiated with some initial parameters.
- The algorithm uses specific techniques to discover the solution. For example, optimization or evolution. In optimization, for instance, a cost function serves as the feedback loop, which guides the algorithm to inform it if it is moving closer to the best solution or treading away. By doing that, the cost function helps it navigate toward the best solution.
- The data is separated in training and test data, where training data is used to train, and test data is used to check how the system will perform when used to classify unseen examples.
- The more data we have, the better. The algorithm can tune the function parameters better.

This was the general approach to supervised learning. Let us now see the two popular methods in supervised learning.

Supervised Learning Methods

Supervised learning includes two widely used methods: classification and regression.

Classification, just as we saw in the spam vs. non-spam example, uses the inputs to classify them into some classes of output.

We can have problems where inputs are classified in more than two classes. For example, classifying images of animals into dogs, cats, frogs, and horses. This is known as multiclass classification. In multiclass classification the input can only be classified as one of the given classes. For example, if an image is classified as cat, it is not classified as a dog, a frog, or a horse.

Another type of classification problem is a multilabel classification problem, or simply a multilabel problem. In multilabel classification, each set of inputs is classified into more than one label. For example, let us say we are scanning news and categorizing items by multiple topics (e.g., politics, religion, social, economics). In this case one document can be classified into multiple categories.

In classification the output is categorical. It means that the output could be 0 or 1 (binary) as in rain or no rain, or 1, 2, 3, 4, and 5 (each representing a class) as in various topics.

The other type of supervised learning problem is where the output is not categorical; it is continuous. It means that the output can take any number between a range of numbers. For example, temperatures, stock prices, and crop yields.

Regression is used to train an algorithm to predict a continuous-valued output. This can be viewed as estimating the expected value of a distribution on a continuous-valued variable. In simple words, when you are trying to predict something where the output can be over a range of values—such as prices of an asset from some data about the asset—we use regression. You can enter the earnings, sector P/E multiple, revenues, and so forth, of a firm to predict its stock value. To enable the algorithm to perform these and other time series–type analyses, you train the algorithm with the data of the inputs.

Let us review the classification methods used in practice.

SUPERVISED: CLASSIFICATION

In this section we will discuss several classification methods.

Classification: Decision Trees

A decision tree is a structure that looks like an upside-down tree, where the top is known as the root and the bottom nodes are known as leaf nodes. You start at the root node, ask a question about a feature, and, depending on the answer, you split the data set into branches. It is followed by another question about the next feature, and the data set is split again. These questions and answers continue till a point is reached where the data is segmented such that all members of the node carry the same label or no more features are left for classification. The beginning point of the decision tree is a labeled data set of features.

For example, if we are predicting whether citizens of a certain area will vote with party A or party B, and we are using features such as education, age, income, and so forth, we can start building a decision tree by asking questions about the data—for example, "College Educated? Age above 40? Makes above $100,000?" could be some of the questions—and based on the answers to a series of questions, we get to the bottom of the tree. The split at each question establishes a different path. At the bottom of the tree, we get information about how many people for each path voted for party A vs. party B. If at the leaf node we are left with a mix (impure), where some voted for party A and some for party B, we can calculate the probability.

Notice that each path gives us some rule paths also—for example:

IF (Education = College, Age = 40+, Income = 100,000+) THEN Class
= Party A

Notice that sometimes full paths may not exist. If the answer to our second question was that all college educated and age above 40 voted for party A, then there is no need to further explore that path. The path has become pure.

Which questions get asked first is important. Sequence matters. Some questions may carry more prediction-worthy information (i.e., information that contributes most to the prediction)—they are more informative. Different features will provide different prediction-worthy information. Some features are more informative. Can we find out which ones? There are processes that are employed (e.g., entropy) that can help us identify the most prediction-worthy participant features in the data set. Thus, a better way to build decision trees is by segmenting the data in a manner that increases the accuracy of the prediction, and that means to identify the features that carry the most information and then structuring the order of questions in accordance with that knowledge.

CLASSIFICATION: RANDOM FOREST

Decision trees sometimes overfit the data. That means that they do not generalize to new situations. They can fit the examples well but lack the ability to predict new examples. It happens because they pick up both noise (due to outliers and randomness) of the data and the signal (the insights obtained from the sample data).

A random forest is an ensemble method that takes the average or weighted average of more than one decision tree where each tree represents a subsample of features. At training time, the random forest creates multiple decision trees and then calculates the mode for classification or the median for regression. The averaging of multiple trees increases the quality of the result and addresses the overfitting problem by generalizing the model so that the model can recognize new situations.

CLASSIFICATION: USING MATHEMATICAL FUNCTIONS

In the decision trees, we discovered models that predict the target output based on other descriptive attributes (inputs). The trees enabled that by subdividing the set of all instances into series of successive, more informative subsets (purer), which enabled our ability to predict. They contained more information (a better, cleaner, stronger relationship) between the output and the inputs. The decision tree gave us the structure and the parameters of the model. The structure was the specific tree model, and the parameters were the probability estimates that we discovered once we got to the bottom of the tree at the leaf nodes.

Another way to develop a predictive model is to specify a mathematical function (Figure 5.3) such that the structure of the model and the parameters represent the data set. The model is set up by choosing the parameters. The initial model is developed with the modeler knowing something about the data set from domain expertise or by using some mathematical concepts (such as entropy) to develop some insights into the data. Then the parameters are tuned for learning. This process, known as parameter learning, searches for the best parameters from the space of all parameters that describe the data set.

The general idea of the classification via mathematical functions is to split the data in a manner that it can predict the output better. In a two-dimensional system, this can be viewed as a partitioning straight line that can separate the data into two classes (e.g., voting for party A or party B). This is known as a linear classifier. It is explained in the next section.

Many problems require us to think in terms of binary answers. For example, is there a fraud or not; should a person get the credit or not; should an

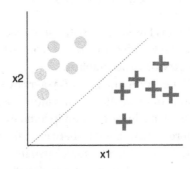

FIGURE 5.3 Function Based Split

investment be made or not. We can have more than 2 dimensions—implying we have more than 2 features (dozens, hundreds, or more)—and that can be viewed as a plane (for three dimensions) and a hyperplane (four or more dimensions) that splits the data into different classes.

CLASSIFICATION: SIMPLE LINEAR CLASSIFIER

Let us return to our previously used example of classifying (predicting) citizens as voting for party A or party B based on two variables of education and income. A linear classifier can be viewed as a line that attempts to split the data into two parts. The reason I used the words "attempts to" is because in many cases it is not possible to get the data cleanly split between sets. Some values can appear on the wrong side of the divider line.

Like any line in the two-dimensional system, the best divider line has a certain slope and a y-intercept. This means we can represent this line as an equation. Let us say we discover that the equation is as follows:

$$\text{Income} = (-1.75) \times \text{Education} + 50$$

Here −1.75 represents the slope and 50 represents the y-intercept—linear discriminant. In fact, we can move the income to the other side of the equation and set a simple rule that says if the value of the function is above zero, this means the point resides above the line, and if it is below zero (or equal to it), then it is below the line:

$$\text{Class}(x) = \text{Party A if} -1 \times \text{Income} - 1.75 \times \text{Education} + 50 > 0$$
$$\text{Party B if} -1 \times \text{Income} - 1.75 \times \text{Education} + 50 <= 0$$

Note: the assignment is based on how the line separated the data. Recall our target variables (output variables) are party A or party B. Let's review what the above equations are trying to accomplish.

Our goal is to predict party A and party B voters by studying two features of income and education. To make numerical values, we have converted education from 0 to 20 (years of education) and income from zero to $200,000. Our plotted data therefore gives us points where each point is a mixture of education and income, or $(x1, x2)$. Based on our known information, each of those combinations produced a party A or a party B classification. By dividing the data set into two regions, hopefully our data can be nicely split between party B

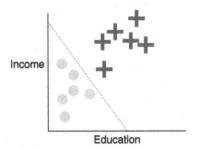

FIGURE 5.4 Predicting Voting

and party A (Figure 5.4). To split the data, we calculated the weighted sum of the values of the two attributes and based on that determined a line that split the data into two regions (party A and party B). In Figure 5.4, they are shown as plus signs and circles.

The line was represented by an equation, and the equation when viewed as a function helped us split our data by calculating the value of the function and figuring out whether the value is above zero. A general function is:

$$f(x) = w0 + w1x1 + w2x2 + w3x3 \ldots$$

Here the weights of the function are the parameters, and the classification is based on negative or positive values of the function. The higher the discovered weight, we can generally assume that attribute (input) is better for predicting the output. We now have both the structure and the estimates embedded in a mathematical function. We have successfully fit our model to the data by representing it mathematically. This is what we call our parametrized model.

The function $w0 + w1x1 + w2x2 + w3x3 \ldots$ shows that in addition to income and education we can use other attributes such as age and number of times previously voted for classification.

Also, the data we used (income and education) in the example was numerical. What about other types of data? If the data is text or image, it is changed to numerical values. As part of getting the data ready for ingestion, we also normalize the data. This is done to make the parameter values closer to each other. The parameter values can turn out to be widely different if there is wide difference between the numeric values of the variables. For example, in the above example, while the education scale runs between 0 and 20, the income scale runs between 0 and $200,000. To eliminate that problem, we can normalize the data before using it in the classification algorithm.

Classification: Picking the Right Line

Picking the right linear classifier is not trivial. Notice the space in between the two types of features. Many lines appear to qualify as the partitioning line (Figure 5.5). Which line then represents the best line that partitions the data sets better than any other line? Of all the lines that can part our data into regions, which line is the best line?

One way to think about it is that based on the features, we are hoping that the data will split into some natural partitions. As shown in Figure 5.3, we hope that based on the feature vector provided (i.e., X1, X2), the data points will clearly occupy separate areas in the two-dimensional space. Hence, the problem of classification can be defined as finding the line (2-dimensional), plane (3-dimensional), or hyperplane (more than three-dimensional) that can separate the data into segments of the output variable (target). The word hyperplane is generally used for the separation plane. A hyperplane in a two-dimensional system is a line. A hyperplane in a three-dimensional system is a plane.

Notice that in the above function, while we considered several inputs, we were only doing binary classification (i.e., two outputs—party A or party B). A more advanced system (multi-classifier) will be able to classify among several classes (e.g., party B, party A, party C, independents). Those problems are known as multi-class classification problems. In a multi-class classification problem, feature vectors are classified in three or more classes.

As previously mentioned, there is another type of problem in classification, and it is known as multi-label classification. Notice that in both binary and multi-class classification, each feature vector was classified as only one class. If a feature vector belonged to party A, it did not belong to party B. In multi-labeled you can classify in two or more classes.

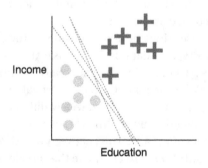

FIGURE 5.5   Solution Space, Many Lines Possible

While simple classifiers can address some trivial problems, some more complex problems can be solved with more advanced and powerful methods explained below. These methods display different levels of effectiveness for different types of problems.

SUPERVISED: SUPPORT VECTOR MACHINE

In our example, when provided the input values for education and income, the classifier classified as party A voter or party B voter. How can we make this classification more reliable?

One way to increase the reliability is to consider a band or a bar between the data, instead of a line. This band will have two boundaries, one on one side and the other on the other side. Each can be viewed as the best boundary drawn closest to the data. Now we can draw a line that runs right in between the two boundaries and that becomes our separation line. The distance between the two boundaries of the corridor (stripe, band) is known as the margin. See Figure 5.6.

A support vector machine (SVM) is a classifier that separates data into classes by establishing a boundary space between the data (Boser et al., 2010). The boundary space looks like a street with a line in the center (Figure 5.6). The street is laid out in the middle of the data such that the distance between the closest points and the central line of the street is maximized. Maximizing that achieves the goal of finding the optimal hyperplane that separates data.

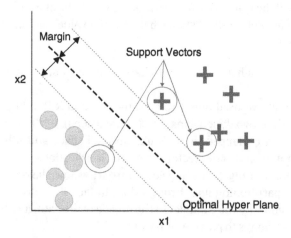

FIGURE 5.6 Support Vector Machine

Margin is the perpendicular distance between the hyperplane (i.e., the middle line) and the lines on the side. The lines of the side are defined by the class that contains support vectors. Support vectors are the vectors (points) that are closest to the hyperplane on all sides of the plane.

If we drop a test vector and it falls on either side of the plane, away from the middle, we can be reasonably confident that it belongs in those categories. What if the test vector falls extremely close to the middle line or on it? That can go either way. Assuming you have a reasonable divider line in between the data, the further away a point is from the margin, the more likely the point belongs to that class.

What about cases in which points end up on the wrong side of the line? For example, we may have a party A voter whose attribute values indicate that she should be a party B. She is on the wrong side of the partition (misclassified). Her misclassification raises an important issue: how to handle misclassifications? A related question is: do misclassifications decrease the predictive ability of our function? To measure that, we can define something known as the loss function. The loss function is measured by calculating the distance between the misclassified values and the margin. In fact, we can have simple rules that can alleviate our problem:

- There will be no loss if the values fall where they belong (party A or party B), that is, the predictor gets it right;
- If the values fall inside the boundary but have not crossed the margin, we will not penalize it;
- However, if the values end up on the other side of the margin, we can penalize it by calculating the distance between the values and the boundary of the margin.

Now we are in a better position to handle those values that end up on the wrong side.

Even though we used only two features (X1 and X2), real problems will involve more than two dimensions (i.e., N dimensions). In those problems, the feature vectors are mapped to an N-dimensional space and a hyperplane is discovered that separates the vectors into two classifications.

What if our training data is hopelessly mixed as shown below in Figure 5.7? Try putting a partitioning line through that. In fact, if we drop a test feature vector (represented by the triangle) in the middle of the data, it will be tough to determine if it belongs to party A or party B.

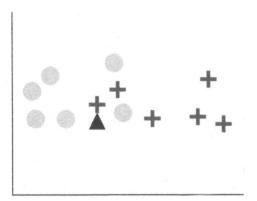

FIGURE 5.7 Non-Separable

You cannot get a line (hyperplane) to divide the data precisely into two camps (Figure 5.7). They are known as non-separable (linear) cases since the data is not easily separable with a straight line. The triangle is the test vector, and clearly it is difficult to determine whether it belongs with the circles or the plus signs. In that case advanced versions of SVM give us some creative ways to handle those situations. One simple solution is to simply tolerate a few misassignments. The dissenters or rebels are tolerated as a necessary evil. The misclassified element can be in the margin area, even if they are on the wrong side of the decision boundary or they are deep inside the wrong territory. The algorithm attempts to make sure that it is optimizing the trade-off between maximizing the margin and minimizing misclassification.

Another way to achieve better classification for tough cases is to transform the existing features by using mathematical transformations. For example, you can square, multiply, or create a mathematical transformation that alters the state of features in a manner where they become more separable.

Figure 5.8 shows that it seems impossible to separate the data since it is right in the middle surrounded in a manner where you cannot easily separate party A voters from party B voters. A mathematical transformation can help split the data as shown in Figure 5.9. A new dimension (Z) can be introduced by squaring x and y and adding them to form a new feature. When plotted, the transformation makes the data clearly separable, so we can now easily part the data into two segments.

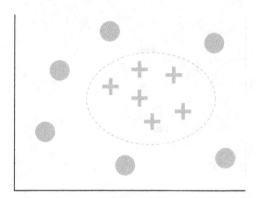

FIGURE 5.8 Inseparable

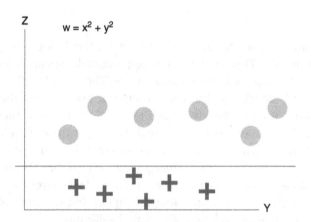

FIGURE 5.9 Inseparable Separated via Transformation

CLASSIFICATION: NAIVE BAYES

The Naive Bayes algorithm classifies by calculating the probability of different classes or outcomes. The probabilities are measured based on previously known examples presented in the training data. This algorithm is based on the Bayesian theorem, and it assumes that each feature is independent of the other features. The core strategy of the algorithm is to assume that the features are independent and then estimate the probability (think of it as the relative participation) of the feature in a class. The probabilities are then multiplied to determine the influence of features in a class.

CLASSIFICATION: BAYESIAN BELIEF NETWORKS

Bayesian belief networks (BBN) are also based on the Bayesian theorem, except unlike naive Bayes model, which assumes that features are independent of each other, BBN considers the probabilities and dependencies among features.

CLASSIFICATION: k-NEAREST NEIGHBOR

Just as the name states, this algorithm looks at the nearest neighbors of the instances being classified and classifies based on that. For example, let us say you are trying to classify a family by its income. One way you can estimate the income is to find out the income of the, say, ten neighbors and based on that you can estimate a family's income. Here we assumed that the family lives in a neighborhood and it is likely that their income will be not too different than its neighbors' (the surrounding points in the decision space).

Had we picked only one neighbor to estimate the family income, we may have gotten it wrong. But just by looking at the ten nearest neighbors, we are more likely to get a more reasonable estimate. The k in the k-nearest allows us to specify how many nearest data points we want the algorithm to look at.

In Figure 5.10, we can represent our test data as a triangle. We are trying to see whether the triangle belongs in the plus class or in the circle class. When we use k = 4 (the inner circle), it picks up the 4 nearest neighbors and determines that there are more plus signs (i.e., 3 out of 4) than circles (1 out of 4) and therefore classifies the triangle as a plus. However, if we increase the size of k

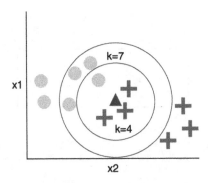

FIGURE 5.10 k-Nearest Neighbor

to 7, the 7 nearest neighbors of the triangle give a different output: 4 out of 7 are circles, and 3 out of 7 are plus signs, so we classify the triangle as a circle.

This concludes our coverage of classification algorithms in supervised learning. Let us move to regression.

SUPERVISED: REGRESSION

Supervised learning is applied in methods such as classification and regression. Classification is when the output is composed of discrete values such as spam or no spam, cancer or no cancer, type of car, or identifying a person in an image. Regression is when the output has continuous variables such as prices, temperatures, or stock prices. Unlike classification where you have specific classes, in regression you have range of possible values.

For example, see Figure 5.11 where we are trying to predict the GPA of students (y-values) based on their SAT scores (x-values). Hypothetical data is provided on both sides, and the middle is kept as empty space for the function we are trying to discover.

To find the function, we can start by plotting the data (Figure 5.12).

Looking at the plotted data, we can see that it would help if we can find a best-fit line that passes through the plotted data. That line could become the predictor to which we can feed the SAT values (input), and the output will come out to be close to the projected GPA. The best-fit line through the plotted points is the one for which the average squared distance between the points and the line will be minimized.

PREDICT GPA BASED ON SAT

SAT		GPA
850		2.8
900		2.9
950		2.9
1000		3.0
1050		3.1
1100		3.4
1150		3.5
1200		3.5
.		.
.		.
.		.

FIGURE 5.11   Finding the Function

We start by randomly placing a line and then calculating the average distance (squared, to eliminate the negative and positive values from being above or below the line) between all the points and the line (Figure 5.13). Our first attempt at it is not very informative. We need a few more lines to figure out whether we have minimized the average squared distance.

As we place a few more lines (Figure 5.14) and calculate the average distance, we can then determine whether the average squared distance of our first

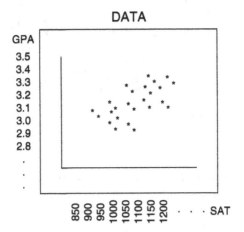

FIGURE 5.12 Plot

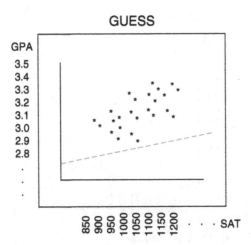

FIGURE 5.13 Random Placement of a Line

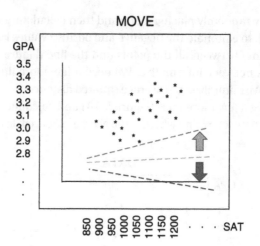

FIGURE 5.14　Adding Lines

line and the average squared distance of our second line increased or decreased. We can just keep changing the parameters (slope and y-intercept) and iterate closer and closer to finding that ideal line where the average squared distance is minimized (Figure 5.15).

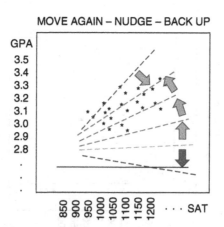

FIGURE 5.15　Finding the Best-Fit Line

If we pass that ideal line, we will know, as the average squared distance will start increasing again, which is something we do not want. When we reach that point where the average squared distance is the lowest, that is the line we are seeking. We have found out the optimal line.

Since this is a linear model, this equation is of the form: $y = a + bx$

We are saying:

$$GPA = a + b \times SAT,$$

where

a = the y-intercept
b = the slope.

In this, we tried to find a and b. Finding that best-fit line happens when we minimize the "cost function," where the cost function is the mean squared error, which we measured by calculating the average squared distance. More formally, we can define it as the squared distance between an observation's actual and predicted value. We use the gradient descent method to minimize the cost function. It simply means exactly what you saw in the figures above. We started with a random line—which translates into some random values for the coefficients (a and b)—and then based on that we calculate the gradient by plugging those numbers and repeatedly iterating till we minimize the mean squared error.

Every time we plugged in a combination of a and b, we got a new line. Our goal is to reduce the error—or in other words, minimize the cost function.

 ## SUPERVISED: MULTIDIMENSIONAL REGRESSION

What we saw above was one x-variable (SAT scores) to predict the y-value GPA. Most real problems will have many features (x-values). For example, to improve our chances of predicting the GPA values, we can add variables such as how many hours a student spends on social media daily, gender, hours spent on extracurricular activities, and whether the student plays active sports. That will give us many x-input values. The overall concept, however, of minimizing the cost function, will remain the same.

The above discussion concludes our coverage of supervised learning models. Now we proceed with unsupervised learning.

UNSUPERVISED LEARNING

Unsupervised learning is learning by finding patterns; it is when machines find patterns from the data given to them as input, but they are not given any examples. There is no expert or supervisor telling you how to label the data. There is no y-data—it is all x-data (features or input). In unsupervised learning, we have the inputs but no outputs. Since our supervised learning algorithms are unable to learn without examples, we must do things differently in unsupervised learning. The underlying assumption here is that class membership is defined by commonly shared feature input patterns. Even without any external guidance, the patterns should just stand out and point us to some classes.

Unsupervised learning is an answer to many business problems in which we have lots of data, and we expect to discover new patterns in the data that can create new knowledge for us. For example, customer segmentation. Since we do not know what those segments are when we start the inquiry, all we have is the data on our customers. We want our algorithm to identify those segments for us— even though we do not know what the algorithm will find. Notice that we are not giving the learning machine the answers or output—and therefore our data sets are not labeled. Another example will be trying to group documents but not knowing which groups we may end up discovering. Detecting fraud by discovering anomalies also uses unsupervised learning.

Some of the methods used in unsupervised learning are known as association rules, clustering, and self-organizing maps.

One way to get intuition about unsupervised learning is to think about data convergence due to proximity (how close) of features. For example, if we were teaching a machine to learn to classify fruits and we were using supervised learning, we would train it by giving it examples of oranges, apples, bananas, and grapes from features shape and size. In unsupervised learning, we will only have input data and no labels (outputs). Think for a second, if all we have is the size and shape data about the four fruits, it is highly likely that you will be able to tell the distinction between bananas, grapes, oranges, and apples. I only gave you the size and shape information, and you were able to tell what the fruits are. If the same problem was given to the machine, the unsupervised learning methods will aggregate the data into groups or clusters that are close to each other. Thus, apples will cluster around apples, oranges around oranges, bananas around bananas, and grapes around grapes. Here we did not tell the algorithm the right answers but simply based on the features, the algorithm found the clusters. If our unsupervised algorithm placed oranges and apples close to each other, perhaps by adding color as a feature, we would be able to get better clusters.

Unsupervised: Clustering

In unsupervised learning you sometimes find what you did not know you were looking for. You allow data to form natural groupings. It is as if data accumulates around other data with which it has some type of affinity. Once the data groups together, you can then start looking at the groups and determine if you found something interesting.

One of the clustering algorithms, known as k-mean clustering (MacQueen, 1967; Lloyd, 1982), works by randomly placing a certain number (k) of data points (known as centroids) in the middle of the feature (inputs) data points and then calculating the distance between feature data points and the centroids. Each feature vector is considered a data point, and the centroids are dropped at random locations between the data points. You then calculate the (Euclidean) squared distance from the points to the centroids, and those points that are closer to each of the centroids are grouped together. Then the process is iteratively repeated till the position of the centroids is optimized.

Let us say we have two features, X1 and X2, about customers, and we want to find out how to group customers based on those features. We start by dropping two centroids (the dark triangles) at random locations, as shown in Figure 5.16. Based on Euclidean squared distance, we start by identifying points closest to them and then establishing two groups (Figure 5.17).

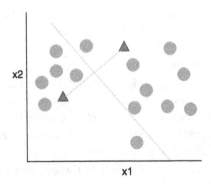

FIGURE 5.16 Step 1 of Clustering k-Means

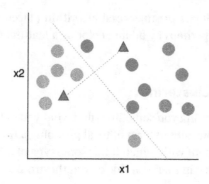

FIGURE 5.17 k-Means Clustering Step 2

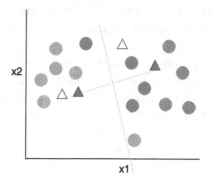

FIGURE 5.18 Step 3 k-Mean Clustering

Now we have split our data into two groups—notice the line parting the two groups. But we must not stop there. Let us calculate the average of the data points in each group and force our centroids to again move to those new average positions.

You can see in Figure 5.18 that the new positions (darker triangles) are now identified for the centroids. They left their original positions (white triangles) and moved to the center of their respective clusters. But their moving does something unexpected. The Euclidian distance between the original points and the centroids has now changed. This means we can now re-divide the clusters—shifting members based on the new division.

As shown in Figure 5.19, we now have them re-divided into new clusters. We can calculate the new average for the points and once again force our centroids to move. We keep on iterating till our average position of the center of the

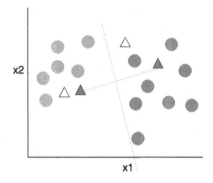

FIGURE 5.19 Step 4 k-Mean Clustering

cluster does not result in changing the memberships of the data. This means that we now have our final clusters—we have achieved success (at least in terms of splitting). We can no longer split the data into any more clusters.

Now we can look into these clusters and see whether our clusters represent meaningful information. Perhaps we can start naming them.

In real life, you will have many features. Take the example of fraudulent transactions. Let us say we have accumulated data on fraudsters and fraudulent transactions. We can cluster the population with the goal of discovering some unique patterns of the fraudsters that we did not know before. For example, we may realize that the group of younger fraudsters committed fraud in high-frequency, low-size transaction vs. older ones, who did low-frequency, large-sized transaction frauds.

 NEURAL NETWORKS

Unlike the methods that I have explained up until now, neural networks are a different way of approaching the problems. They emulate how a human brain functions.

It can be viewed as a specific configuration of neurons where neurons are divided into layers. There is an input layer where data comes in. There is an output layer where the output comes out. And there are hidden layers in between. This forms the network of neurons.

It will look similar to Figure 5.20. All we did was replace seeking a function with seeking a neural structure. Let us first understand how it works.

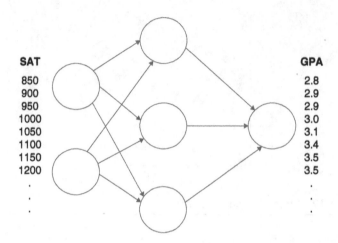

SAT		GPA
850		2.8
900		2.9
950		2.9
1000		3.0
1050		3.1
1100		3.4
1150		3.5
1200		3.5

FIGURE 5.20 Using a Neural Network to Predict

When the training starts, each neuron (also known as node) is a blank slate. Passing the feature vector data to the input layer activates neurons. They quickly pass the data to the next layer. But before passing the data to the next layer, they tune themselves in relation to the data they just received. This tuning is done randomly. At this stage, all they can do is arbitrarily pick some numbers for themselves and then hope for the best (I will explain later what "best" means). As the next layer receives the data and just like the previous layer, this layer too tunes itself and then sends the data to the next layer. This goes on till the data goes to the output layer and then gets sent out of the network in the form of a predicted value. The predicted output (say in classification) is compared to the actual target value (the y-value, the dependent variable). The difference between the two is seen as the feedback that must be provided to the neurons so they can improve their tuning.

Let us repeat the above process in a slightly different form. When the network starts, all neurons are ignorant. As the data comes in, each neuron in the first layer takes the data and assigns a weight to it such that its value becomes:

$$\text{Input} \times \text{weight} = \text{guess}$$

The weight is assigned randomly. Each neuron in the first layer will calculate the guess. And the sum of guesses from the first layer will be passed on to the neurons in the next layer—which becomes the input for the next neuron. Once there, we determine whether this neuron should be activated or not.

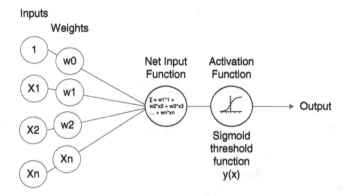

FIGURE 5.21 How a Neuron Passes the Output to the Next Layer

Just like the human brain, certain neural pathways are better to solve a specific problem. To make that determination, we taper our "guess" by multiplying it with something known as an activation function. The activation can be viewed as something that can turn the guess from a number of any size to a number between 0 and 1 (think probability) and then serve as a gateway that determines whether the number should be passed to the next neuron or not. Passing values from one neuron to another neuron in the subsequent layer is known as firing the neuron. If it passes on the next node (neuron), the node becomes activated and repeats the process. It takes in the input, assigns a weight, and then tapers it with the activation function to take it to the next layer, and the next layer, and the next layer, till it reaches the output.

What you see in Figure 5.21 is repeated for each neuron. As the output layer is reached, a final answer is spitted out of the network.

This output represents the output of the entire network. Thus, the output is compared to the actual or the correct answer such that:

$$\text{Correct (actual) answer} - \text{guess} = \text{error}$$

The error is now fed back into the network and used to adjust the weights such that on the next iteration the network learns to close the error gap.

$$\text{Error} \times \text{weight's contribution to error} = \text{fine-tuning}$$

This back-feeding into the network to fine-tune the weights is known as back propagation. Based on the fine-tuned weights, the network iterates

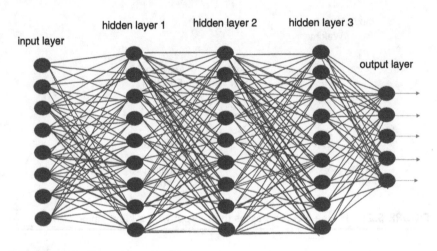

FIGURE 5.22 Deep Learning

through the forward propagation process (i.e., nodes from each layer passing the fine-tuned calculations to the next layer) to make another attempt at guessing the answer and based on the error generated once again back propagates. This back and forth continues till the error is minimized. Once minimized, we can declare that our neural network is now trained. In other words, the structure of the network has become such that it has learned the data on which it was trained. If we give this network the input test data, hopefully, it now has the capability to give the right answers.

Deep Learning

Unlike an ordinary neural network, deep learning is a neural network that has many hidden layers (Figure 5.22).

This technology is so extremely powerful that it is being used to teach machines how to perform sophisticated tasks such as analyzing pictures, videos, and voice for patterns. Deep learning networks develop the ability to understand which features are more relevant for predicting the output.

REINFORCEMENT LEARNING

Reinforcement learning—learning by reward and punishment—has recently shown miraculous success in various areas. It is a powerful form of learning that can be used in sustained strategy-making areas. Reinforcement learning works on the basis of rewards and punishment where the algorithm learns through success and failure. Thus, agents in the reinforcement learning try to maximize their cumulative reward. It is based on exploration and exploitation where it explores the unknown territory and exploits the current knowledge while maximizing its reward.

 ## REFERENCES

Andriosopoulos, D., et al. (2019) "Computational Approaches and Data Analytics in Financial Services: A Literature Review." *Journal of the Operational Research Society*. [Online]. 70 (10), 1581–1599. Available from: https://doi.org/10.1080/01605682.2019.1595193.

Boser, B. E., et al. (2010) "A training algorithm for optimal margin classifiers." [Online]. Available from: http://findit.dtu.dk/en/catalog?utf8=✓&locale=en&search_field=all_fields&q=training+algorithm+for+optimal+margin.

Launchbur, J. (2017) "A DARPA Perspective on Artificial Intelligence." [Online]. Available from: https://www.youtube.com/watch?v=-O01G3tSYpU (Accessed March 11, 2019).

Lloyd, S. P. (1982) "Least Squares Quantization in PCM." *IEEE Transactions on Information Theory*. [Online]. 28 (2), 129–137.

MacQueen, J. (1967) "Some Methods for Classification and Analysis of Multivariate Observations." *Proceedings of the Fifth Berkeley Symposium on Mathematical Statistics and Probability*, University of California Press, Berkeley, Calif. 1281–297. [Online]. Available from: https://projecteuclid.org/euclid.bsmsp/1200512992.

CHAPTER SIX

Evaluation

G ETTING THE MODEL RUNNING IS ONE THING; ensuring that it works, another. The term "works" implies two things:

The model works: This means the algorithm is efficient, generalizes well, and is accurate. Efficiency implies it does not take forever to run. Generalizes well means that it performs when introduced to data beyond the data on which it has been trained. Accurate means that it performs with high accuracy.

The solution works: This is specific to investment solutions. This includes backtesting, which implies that the strategy for which the model was developed is tested for performance.

In this chapter, we will introduce the organization, work process, and some best practices in evaluation. The discussion in this chapter mostly relates to classification methods where labeled data is used to train an algorithm.

WHO PERFORMS THE EVALUATION?

The evaluation function is headed by an executive with strong background in machine learning and finance. The organization reporting to the executive is composed of two different teams: (1) the investment strategy evaluation team, which has specialists who understand investment, asset classes, and instruments; and (2) the business/function team that works for enterprise and function-specific systems (Figure 6.1). The investment strategy team performs

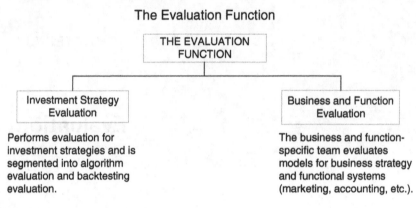

FIGURE 6.1 Roles in the Evaluation Function

evaluation for investment strategies and is segmented into algorithm evaluation and backtesting evaluation. The business and function-specific team evaluates models for business strategy and functional systems (marketing, accounting, etc.).

Both business/function and investment strategy teams support the modeling team. In many cases the modeling teams will perform initial evaluation as they test and deploy their algorithms. However, the formal evaluation group provides specialized services to support those efforts. In addition to being the service providers, this team also serves as the quality control and audit team that makes sure that the product being designed and pushed is a quality product that will perform in accordance with its goals, be stable, and be the best solution given the technological choices available at the time. These teams also understand the life cycle of the products. They work with the design group to develop and recommend the life cycle of strategies. They also study technological innovation to recognize if the existing solution in a firm has become outdated or has lost its competitive advantage.

Thus, evaluation is product specific, but it goes beyond simply testing the product for performance: it keeps track of the utility of the product as well. It is this goal of the utility of the product that ensures that backtesting is performed in an unbiased manner.

In smaller firms, the evaluation function may be composed of fewer people than in a large company, but depending on the work, the same team can perform both investment and strategy/business function evaluations.

Regardless of whether it is an investment team or a business/function evaluation team, all members of the team must have a strong background in machine learning.

PROBLEMS

Developing machine learning applications includes solving many problems. Recall that in machine learning we create systems from data. There are many issues that arise:

- The model works for the data you have but does not generalize well when new data is introduced.
- Various algorithms are explored for the one that performs better than others.
- The features selected were suboptimal. New features need to be added.
- The underlying distributions based on which the solution was developed may have changed. This means that the solution will no longer work.
- The model works well in the research setting, but when it is backtested on actual market data, problems appear.
- The backtesting of financial strategies was performed with conditions that fail to emulate actual market conditions.
- The training data does not represent the actual distribution where the algorithm must perform.
- Performance in terms of efficiency, computational power, and other factors that can affect the quality of the product.

We will first start with explaining how to make the models work. This is applicable to both investment and business/function operations. Then we will focus on backtesting, the second part of evaluation, which is applicable to investment strategies and automation.

MAKING THE MODEL WORK

As AI experts develop solutions, they typically pursue the following broad objectives:

1. **Ensure the problem-data-algorithm affinity:** Problems for which solutions are sought require the presence of certain types, quantity, and quality of data. This obviously varies by the nature of the problem being solved. Thus, there is a link between how much data you have and the

types of problems you can solve. The second part is the relationship between the algorithms and the data. Not all algorithms can do the same job well. This relationship can be viewed as affinity between algorithms and data. This three-tier relationship between *problem → data → algorithm* is usually not fully clear in advance. In other words, in many cases this relationship is determined through experimentation and testing. One starts with a few simple models and then gradually improves their complexity. Through iterations you discover that some models work better than others. The sooner one can figure out this relationship, the better.

2. **Accuracy:** A model that is not accurate is not helpful. Improving the model's accuracy is critical for a viable product. Accuracy can be improved by adding more data for training, using diverse data sets, training for longer duration and more iterations, and in neural networks tweaking the network for better accuracy.

3. **Computational efficiency:** An algorithm that scales well, trains faster, and uses less computational power can be advantageous over those that do not.

4. **Performance on new data:** Algorithms should perform beyond the data set on which they have been trained. An algorithm that only performs well on the training data but fails to perform with test data or in actual deployment when exposed to production situations is not very helpful.

To pursue the above broad goals, evaluation for *making the model work* includes techniques that can rapidly and effectively be deployed to maximize the efficiency and effectiveness of the overall product development. This is true for both business/function teams and the investment team.

Making the model work includes the following steps:

1. Evaluate and assist in evaluation of the best algorithm for the problem at hand. Different algorithms can be used to solve the same problem, but their performance may vary. Some algorithms perform better than others. Some scale better than others.

2. Keep track of learning from previous projects to hypothesize which algorithms will perform best.

3. Study the new research to track and catalog more effective solutions and examples of how to improve performance.

4. Maintain a set of best practices for *problem → data → algorithm* affinity.

5. Develop best practices for possible interventions to improve performance and for picking the right algorithms. Formalize and develop best practices for changing the neural network layers, architecture, tuning parameters, selecting features, and other interventions to improve performance.
6. Ensuring that the best algorithm will perform beyond training.

OVERFITTING AND UNDERFITTING

As discussed in Chapter 5, generalization is a major benefit of machine learning. Generalization implies that unlike rule-based systems (for example, expert systems), learning is non-specific. The machine develops a sort of intuition about things and can perform when exposed to new situations.

In supervised learning, the goal is to discover a target function that maps input variables to an output variable. As you can tell, the data used to train the algorithm is the sample data we obtained from the real world. That data has noise, and it represents some subset of the total population. This means that it is possible that the data used for training purposes may not represent the actual problem domain distribution well.

It is possible that we find an algorithm that works great for our training data and shows high accuracy. But when we test our algorithm on test data, it fails to show good results. This is overfitting. Overfitting is when the algorithm trains well with the training data but fails to perform in test or actual situations. This could be because the data used for training purposes did not capture the properties of the data for which the solution would be used.

Underfitting is when the algorithm fails to achieve acceptable learning performance. This means that the algorithm fails on both training and test/actual performance tasks.

SCALE AND MACHINE LEARNING

One way to overcome overfitting is to feed more data to the algorithm. However, older algorithms do not scale well with more data. Their performance plateaus as additional data is added. This means more data does not mean more learning in older algorithms. Neural networks tend to perform well on large data sets and can achieve computational scale. Adding layers in neural networks can lead to better results. Adding more data, when combined with adding layers, can result in better training performance.

NEW METHODS

In the past, the approach followed was to divide the data into two groups of training data and test data. The data was randomly selected—generally 70% for training and 30% for test. In many cases, algorithms worked well on both training and test sets but failed when deployed in live or actual situations. The reason was that the live distribution was different than both test and training situations. When algorithms did not perform as expected in testing, data scientists used that information to tweak the algorithms in attempting to improve the performance—and that led to overfitting in both training and test data. In other words, the test data is no longer test data when it is used to improve the performance of the algorithm, as the algorithm will absorb the properties of that data and hence it defeats the purpose of the test data.

The solution to that problem was to divide the data into three groups instead of two (Figure 6.2). The three groups are as follows:

- Training data: Training data is used to train the algorithm.
- Development data or cross-validation (CV) data: This set is used as an intermediate step to improve the performance of the model by selecting better features, tuning parameters, and applying other interventions to improve the performance prior to testing.
- Test set: This is used strictly for testing and not for making improvements to the algorithm. This set provides unbiased assessment and evaluation of the algorithm's performance.

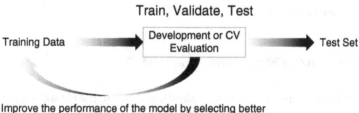

Train, Validate, Test

Training Data → Development or CV Evaluation → Test Set

Improve the performance of the model by selecting better features, tuning parameters, and applying other interventions to improve the performance prior to testing

FIGURE 6.2   Train, Validate, Test

In practice, the evaluation teams will help perform the following activities:

1. Apply methods to randomly select the training, development, and test data sets.
2. Understand and apply the right quantities of data in each set.
3. Ensure that the CV and test data sets are drawn from the same distributions. If the CV and test data sets are chosen from different populations, assuming training works well, we may end up overfitting to the CV set.
4. Understand the reasons behind performance failure and recommend actions to mitigate. Despite applying the above methodology of three-way split of data, the algorithm may still not perform in accordance with the expectations. It may overfit the CV data set or the distributions of CV and test data could be different. The team evaluates such issues.
5. Develop metrics such as accuracy, precision, recall, and F1 score. Clarify satisficing metric (good enough) vs. optimizing metric. Study algorithm performance against those metrics.
6. Study variance and bias (explained in the next section).
7. Perform error detection and correction. For example, identify mislabeled data.
8. Help select the algorithms that perform best.

 ## BIAS AND VARIANCE

The following discussion is based on Andrew Ng's book *Machine Learning Yearning* (Ng, 2018). Bias and variance are two measures that help identify where the problems are originating. Training error is a measure of the performance of the algorithm with the training data. If the algorithm is correctly classifying 90% of the data, then its training error is 10%. If it is classifying 99% accurately, then its training error is 1%.

CV or dev error: This is the error from the CV or dev data. When the algorithm is run on the CV data, if it performs correctly with 95% of data, the dev error rate is 5%.

Bias measures the training error. If the training error is 1%, then bias is 1%.

Variance measures the difference between dev error and bias. If dev error is 10% and training error is 1%, then the variance is 9%.

High variance means that the data is overfitting. The intuition behind that is that while the algorithm is performing well on training data, it is failing to generalize on dev data. Since it produces significantly greater errors on dev data, it is not generalizing on data on which it was not trained. In general, high variance means overfitting.

If variance is low but bias is high, that means data is underfitting. For example, if bias is 12% and dev error is 13%, then bias is 12% and variance is only 1%. If the algorithm was expected to do better, this implies that it is doing poorly on both fronts of training and dev data.

If both bias and variance are high, this could mean that the algorithm is performing poorly on the training data and worse on the dev data.

Ng (Ng, 2018) noted that bias can be both avoidable and unavoidable. Unavoidable bias, he clarifies, is the level at which humans perform. That bias may be unavoidable since the labeled data used to train algorithms is coming from humans. If we can get machines to perform at the level of a human, we have done well. The goal can be then to concentrate on avoidable bias. Ng recommends that if there is high avoidable bias, then it helps to increase the size of model by adding layers and nodes. If there is high variance, he suggests adding data to the training set.

 BACKTESTING

In the finance field, evaluation is far more complex than determining whether the algorithm performs for training, validation, and test data. Just because the artifact works on the data used for training, validation, and testing does not mean that it will perform when placed in a real active production environment. The reason is that unlike applications in other fields where machine learning artifacts automate established business processes, investment strategy is a constantly evolving phenomenon. For example, if you design a recommendation engine for marketing, the recommendation engine will continue to perform based on customer actions, attributes, and previous choices. The utility of the recommendation will not run out since patterns of customer choices, attributes, and actions may stay relatively stable. This means that the life cycle of the artifact will be long and its utility stable. In the investment field, the utility of a strategy will likely erode due to changes in market conditions and competitors identifying (via discovery or copying) your strategy. This means that your strategy will require constant innovation, and hence, you will be constantly developing artifacts that find new and emerging patterns.

Thus, investment-related machine learning applications not only represent specific strategies, they may also exhibit declining utility with time. This also means that each of your artifacts represents a specific strategy—which leads to the second problem. Strategy reflects a promising pattern that takes shape under specific market conditions. In other words, strategy takes shape, manifests, and materializes in conditions that represent the existing reality at a given time. It enables us to find patterns of profitmaking in the daily disarray of markets. The real challenge is that we need to discover those patterns that are easily transportable to market situations that may be different from where the strategy was discovered and architected. This interplay between strategy and market conditions is represented in the underlying data. Hence failure to backtest properly implies that our strategies may turn out to be useless in real situations. This means what we call a strategy is not much of a strategy to begin with.

Backtesting is when you test your strategies in different market conditions than those where the data was used to architect your strategies. You are trying to determine whether your strategies will work outside of your innovation lab. You apply backtesting by performing historical simulation of the investment strategy developed via algorithms. You try to measure the performance of a strategy over a time period and try to determine what profits or losses the strategy would have produced during that time period. We can then assess if that strategy is viable or not.

What makes backtesting critical is the distinction between in-sample (IS) testing and out-of-sample (OOS) testing. In-sample testing happens when you test your strategy with the data that was used to develop the strategy. Out-of-sample testing happens when you test your strategy on data that was not used to develop the strategy.

One would think that this should be a relatively trivial task to accomplish. All you have to do is draw sample data from a different time period than the one used to develop your strategy and then run your strategy on that data to determine how well it performs. As De Prado has cautioned in many of his writings, this is an extremely slippery slope (De Prado, 2018; Bailey et al., 2014; López De Prado and Bailey, 2001). He argues that years of experience is needed to do this right. And others have agreed with him about the issues in backtesting (Arnott et al., 2019).

Limited data: Other than the tick data, other data in finance is extremely limited. For example, 55-year monthly and quarterly data for a stock will give you only a few hundred observations. The limited data on fundamentals, as well as on economic indicators, severely constrains the ability to both develop and test strategies.

Economic foundations: While machine learning can discover profitable strategies through brute force or randomness, in many cases such strategies lack economic logic or explanation behind them. In other words, you can show that the strategy works, but you cannot explain the economic rationale behind it.

Force-fit economic explanations: In some cases, when researchers discover strategies that show promise but lack economic explanation, they develop economic justification. Such rationalization of economic logic is dangerous since it cannot be easily tested.

Failure to remember humans in the mix: In some cases, financial modelers are detached from the on-the-ground realities and forget that their models represent actual real-world events. These events and transactions represent human emotions such as fear and greed, herding behavior, and the underlying asset values. Such factors imply there is significant noise in the signal.

Overfitting: As explained in the previous section in this chapter, overfitting happens when a model works during training (in some cases even testing) but fails to perform in actual situations. One of the reasons is that a winning strategy can emerge simply due to randomness. For example, if your strategy would work in 1 out to 20 chances, and you conduct the backtest where the first test turns out to show promise, you cannot assume that you have a successful strategy. If you had run the strategy 19 more times, you would have recognized the futility of your strategy by observing 19 out of 20 failures.

Intellectual integrity: De Prado has identified the issue related to abusing the facts by researchers disclosing only the winning tests without disclosing the number of times the tests failed. As in the previous example, in some cases researchers will only show results about the model that worked but fail to mention tens, hundreds, thousands, and in some cases millions that did not work.

Good models fail, bad models thrive: In some cases, good models could be forgotten or ignored due to peculiarities of data—a false negative. In other cases, we can accept bad models on the basis of false narratives or play around with models till they start appearing as profitable models but in real situations they will fail to perform—a false positive. In investment, both false positives and false negatives are dangerous. False negatives lead to our failure to bring forward good models for our investors, and that can give competitive advantage to our competitors. False positives create situations where we will compromise and endanger the interests of our investors by losing money for them.

Forcing bad models to work: As explained in the previous section, in machine learning we often try to make models work by playing around with features and parameters (hyperparameters). When that happens, our models can perform better, and that means we achieved success. Unfortunately, in finance such an approach may not work. When we make models work, we may tweak the model to a point where they conform to our hypothesis but fail to work in actual conditions. Making models work is not only achieved by traditional machine learning–centric interventions, but in finance it can also be achieved by selectively ignoring certain asset classes, time periods (for example, recession or depression), transaction costs, turnover, and corporate events. When that happens, we are no longer creating a strategy for our real environment; we are modifying both—the strategy and the environment—to coerce them to function together. For obvious reasons, the actual market conditions will likely diverge from the fantasy conditions we created to make our model work.

Data issues: De Prado has pointed out that in many cases researchers (especially academics) ignore the realities of data when sampling. They fail to consider that market data is not necessarily available at the close of the day or that fundamentals or economic data is not retrospectively adjusted. In other words, had they used the actual unadjusted data, their strategies may not have worked. Prado has also pointed out that in addition to having credible suppliers of data, the modelers should be familiar with various standards such as GIPS® of the CFA Institute.

BACKTESTING PROTOCOL

The above points show that to make models work, we tend to aggressively tinker with them and create fantasy environments in which they seem to work. These fantasy environments tend to be widely different than actual conditions and hence lead to large-scale failures in investment. For that reason, the main function of the backtesting team should be to validate strategies based on the following protocols addressed by Arnott et al. (Arnott et al., 2019):

Provide economic logic: In the world of modern deep neural networks, in many cases we find patterns that seem to work but that lack economic explanation or logic. These weird relationships require explanations. We can show the results but cannot answer the "why it works" question. One can either provide an ex ante explanation or an ex post explanation. Ex ante explanation implies that we have a clear understanding of the underlying economic theory and we try to explain the results in accordance with that. Ex post is the reverse process where we observe the results and then try to develop or identify a theory. Researchers and practitioners insist that an ex post explanation is critical to develop a good strategy. From that perspective, your machine learning model is consistent with the finance theory and therefore the model's finding can be explained in accordance with the economic logic. The propensity to justify results by creating an economic narrative is deemed dangerous. While in general I agree with the approach, I believe that finance theory is limited, and as we discover patterns that include human behavior (behavioral finance), we can expand the theory. Therefore, results that withstand vigorous testing but are hard to explain using the current financial theory may require ex post analysis to augment the theory. However, I do agree with the practitioners that deploying such findings in actual investment scenarios would be irresponsible.

Multiple strategies: It is important to track and record randomly selected strategies. Correlation between strategies needs to be understood. Researchers should also keep track of the variables used. Arnott et al. explain that as new variables are used or created (for example, from the interaction of existing variables), such interactions produce a significantly large number of strategies.

Sample choice and data: Arnott et al. recommend that the training sample should be justified in advance and held consistent after that. This ex ante selection of sample implies that the data should not be massaged only to make the model work. Data quality should be understood and maintained. Having accurate data is one thing; having strategy-compliant data means that the conditions of the testing environment should be re-created as they existed in the time frame when the strategy is being tested. In other words, data quality in this case may not mean correct data; it means that if the data at the simulation time was incorrect, then the incorrect data becomes more relevant since that is how the real world was at that time. This is a hard-to-understand concept for data management professionals who tend to prefer correct data over incorrect data.

Cross-validation sampling: Since researchers have the hindsight and complete information about the prevailing conditions from which the cross-validation data is being selected, it is important to recognize that bias does not enter the models. Selecting cross-validation samples from data with the knowledge of specific market conditions can lead to biased samples. The authors warn that if your model works in-sample but fails out-of-sample and you use that information to tweak in-sample such that now the model works in both, then the model is overfitting for both. Lastly, including transaction costs and fees is important. Strategies that do not take that into account may fail in real situations even if they pass all tests.

Model dynamics: Ensuring that structural changes in the economy and human behaviors are represented and not excluded is important. Authors give the analogy of the Heisenberg uncertainty principle from physics where a particle's position and momentum cannot be ascertained simultaneously with certainty, and state that a similar dynamic exists in finance where historical cross-validation may not apply to the present or future as the underlying conditions may have changed. They remind again that tweaking the model to make it work may be the right approach in other fields, but in finance it leads to overfitting.

Dimensionality: Adding more variables means models require more data. As more explanatory variables are added, some variables may have very limited data. Moving to higher dimensions leads to sparsity of data. Furthermore, more complex models may be harder to explain. Being able to develop interpretable machine learning models is valuable in finance.

Research culture: Finally, creating a research culture where research orientation and search for truth are valued and rewarded is important. Pushing people to come up with strategies may force people to cut corners and ignore good science.

REFERENCES

Arnott, R., et al. (2019) "A Backtesting Protocol in the Era of Machine Learning." *Journal of Financial Data Science* (Winter), 64–74.

Bailey, D. H., et al. (2014) "Pseudo-Mathematics and Financial Charlatanism: The Effects of Backtest Overfitting on Out-of-Sample Performance." *Notices of the American Mathematical Society.* [Online]. 61 (5), 458.

López De Prado, M., and Bailey, D. H. (2001) "Quantitative Meta-Strategies." [Online]. Available from: http://ssrn.com/abstract=2547325.

Ng, A. (2018) *Machine Learning Yearning, Technical Strategy for AI Engineers in the Era of Deep Learning.* Draft version. deeplearning.ai.

De Prado, M. L. (2018) *Advances in Financial Machine Learning.* John Wiley & Sons.

CHAPTER SEVEN

Deployment

T HE DEPLOYMENT PART PLAYS A CRITICAL role in an AI-centric transformation and includes two distinct groups. The deployment department is headed by an executive who is responsible for the technical deployment of all the artifacts developed in the previous stages (Noh, 2016). While the role can be viewed as the traditional CIO role, the best person to lead the deployment unit is one who has a broad understanding of systems, infrastructure, and information technology. Note that the emphasis is on technical deployment of artifacts and not the strategy deployment in the investment process. The investment strategy deployment—which covers how to test strategies in the production environment, determine the strategy life cycle, allocate capital and other such details—will be discussed in the next chapter. This chapter only covers the technical deployment.

AI artifacts are a new addition to the corporate technological assets and artifacts. In the last several decades, we have collected multiple layers of IT assets: the ancient legacy systems (mainframes), the more modern ERP and CRM type business software, analytics and reporting layers, data storage (for example, databases, data marts, and large data warehouses), data centers, data lakes, cloud, networking infrastructure, security, Extract Transform Load (ETL) technologies, and several other components of corporate IT infrastructure. On top of the base architecture we have deployed applications, processes, and analytical software.

The introduction of AI requires a fundamental rethinking of the IT infrastructure. Specifically, we can identify some critical needs:

1. **Enterprise AI platform:** You need an enterprise-level ML system. Using such an AI platform you can build your AI applications. There are many systems these days—all with different strengths and weaknesses. Some of those systems are IBM Watson, AWS, DataRobot, and CogntiveScale.

2. **High computing capacity:** You need CPUs and GPUs for powerful processing capacity. In Prado's recent book, he discusses the importance of upcoming quantum technology (De Prado 2018). In many cases processing power and response times are critical sources of competitive intelligence in finance (for instance in high-frequency trading), and hence computing capacity is necessary for artifacts to do their jobs.

3. **Preprocessing:** Preprocessing of data has been covered in the data chapter. This is a necessary step for machine learning. Preprocessing performed for machine learning is different than anything done in the legacy IT artifacts. Traditional artifacts (for example, reporting software, analysis software, or applications) did not require the intense and model-centric preprocessing that is needed for machine learning. This means that firms that want to implement industrial-scale enterprise-wide machine learning must deploy efficient processes for preprocessing of data. As stated in the previous chapter, preprocessing also requires additional steps in the finance field. For example, preprocessing data to train an algorithm may require preparing data in a numerical format to feed to an algorithm or to scale features or to add the missing data and so on. However, in finance, you may need to restore the data in its original form that would reflect the state of the data set as it would have been, say, near the end of the trading day or on the date of the release of the financial statements. This could imply that you may have incomplete or even incorrect data; however, to test a strategy, you need to re-create the conditions that would have existed in the period being simulated.

4. **Data infrastructure:** The data infrastructure needs to be designed not only for big data–centric storage and processing of both structured and unstructured data but also for figuring out how to tag data and to be able to efficiently retrieve it on demand. One should keep in mind that data will come in multiple formats, for various uses, and from a wide spectrum of sources. In addition to the data that comes into the firm from external sources, internally generated data—such as preprocessing data, features and feature catalogs, research ideas, investment strategy ideas, feature

notes, libraries, machine learning code, preexisting functions, and other machine learning–specific data— will need to be addressed and may require building new capabilities that do not currently exist.

5. **SDI and ADI:** *CIO* magazine covered an article to show the distinction between software-defined infrastructure (for example, for data centers and cloud) was once important for managing knowledge assets and scripts to run the infrastructure. Now, in the age of artificial intelligence, AI-defined infrastructure, the article claims, is the modern approach to manage infrastructure. ADI is composed of machine learning–based intelligence algorithms that can learn, adapt, and self-adjust to various challenges and problems that arise in infrastructure management.

    The article clarifies that AI-defined IT infrastructure environments can help with:

    – Responsive resource deployment that adjusts with the workload requirements.
    – Developing awareness for itself to function and adapt to the constantly changing behavior and state of other infrastructure components.
    – Autonomous actions to eliminate errors and problems that generally arise in infrastructure (Buest, 2017).

6. **Automation library:** Automation library tracks all the automation artifacts that are being developed, their function, data of commissioning, life cycle, integrations, governance issues, quality issues, and all other metadata that is necessary to manage the life cycle of the artifacts. Just as humans carry identity cards and have health records, this can be viewed as the identity card and health record of an AI artifact.

7. **Data and process discovery:** Since data is usually spread across companies, spreadsheets, and applications, data discovery and lineage become important considerations. Exploring data relationships across the firm is necessary to understand what data the firm has and how it can be used to define various features. In many cases companies come together through mergers and acquisitions, and it becomes even more challenging to identify such associations. In that case, data discovery tools help to identify data. Process discovery refers to understanding processes in a firm. Data provides clues to how processes manifest in a firm. Process discovery tools analyze transactional data and metadata to suggest potential processes. From an automation strategy perspective, data and process discovery become essential tools.

8. **RPA and chatbots:** Robotic process automation (RPA) technology is used to automate repeatable processes. RPA can be used to automate

simple functions such as invoice processing, building small rule-based applications, and screen scraping and data entry. Chatbots can help with customer service.

9. **Function as a service and microservices:** As firms realized that large-scale ERP systems are inflexible and expensive to change, concepts such as microservices and function-as-a-service have gained popularity. Microservices are built to replicate the functionality that was once considered as encapsulated within an ERP-type system—however, such a functionality in a microservice environment is flexible, cheaper to maintain, and can be changed as the business model changes.

10. **Cloud:** Since many firms now keep data in the cloud, the presence of private, public, and hybrid cloud has become a critical element of modern-day businesses. Deploying AI capabilities such that they are closest to the data is important. Moving data up and down from the cloud could be challenging, and hence deploying models to run in an efficient environment requires good planning and execution.

11. **Integration and network:** AI is introducing new needs for integration and essential plumbing in the IT infrastructures. For example, data transfer based on service requests for preprocessed data will require channeling data to the algorithms. Additionally, a high-performance network is critical for AI success. This means it should be a high-bandwidth and low-latency network.

12. **Security and privacy:** While security and privacy have been at the forefront of legacy IT for decades, the arrival of AI will place greater requirements on security and privacy.

13. **Governance:** AI governance is an entirely different area and any industrial-scale enterprise AI deployment will necessarily involve AI governance.

14. **Development for the production environment:** Once testing is complete for both business/function and investment systems, the final development (coding) for the production environment is undertaken for speed optimization, environment consistency, and overall compatibility with corporate standards.

In addition to the above, having a research orientation implies that all new academic research (published in journals) in various fields is analyzed by a dedicated team. The infrastructure needed to catalog, classify, and analyze that research in accordance with the capabilities of the firm will require building new capabilities in legacy investment firms. I have covered that in the design chapter.

REFERENCE ARCHITECTURE

The reference architecture for the industrial-scale enterprise AI development can be viewed as shown in Figure 7.1.

Let us understand various components of this architecture.

Data interface: The interface to data includes being able to bring various types of data into the firm. This could include textual, numerical, videos, GPS, or any other form of data.

Data governance: The data governance layer ensures that the data is being tagged and that quality is being ascertained, governed, and managed. It includes managing metadata and master data, and categorizing data not only by type but also by utility and use. The use shows how the data can be used to create value.

Financial data management: Quantitative finance-specific data management is a specialized unit that concentrates on building a financial data capacity.

Data lake and private, public, or hybrid cloud: Data lake and cloud are where data is stored. The cloud can be private, public, or hybrid.

Applications: Applications include all the ERP, CRM, and other systems. It also includes the AI artifacts that are deployed in production.

Preprocessing: Preprocessing requires significant manual work; however, advances in technology are now enabling us to automate several aspects of preprocessing. The preprocessing area of the reference architecture includes request interpreter and queuing of data (input), temporary storage (holding area), and preprocessing processes that are applied on the data.

Services: The service layer is designed to sequence and feed data back for ingestion into the enterprise brain.

Enterprise brain: The brain is composed of your AI artifacts. These intelligent applications function in a communal manner, often relying on each other, functioning individually but also collectively to achieve goals. They are composed of the following:

- **Deep learning neural networks:** Advanced modern neural networks.
- **Traditional machine learning:** Statistical learning and traditional machine learning.
- **Expert systems and RPA:** Rule-based systems are valuable for many applications. Generally, their reasoning ability is higher than machine learning–based systems.
- **Knowledge engineer:** The knowledge engineer contains ontologies and data dictionaries.

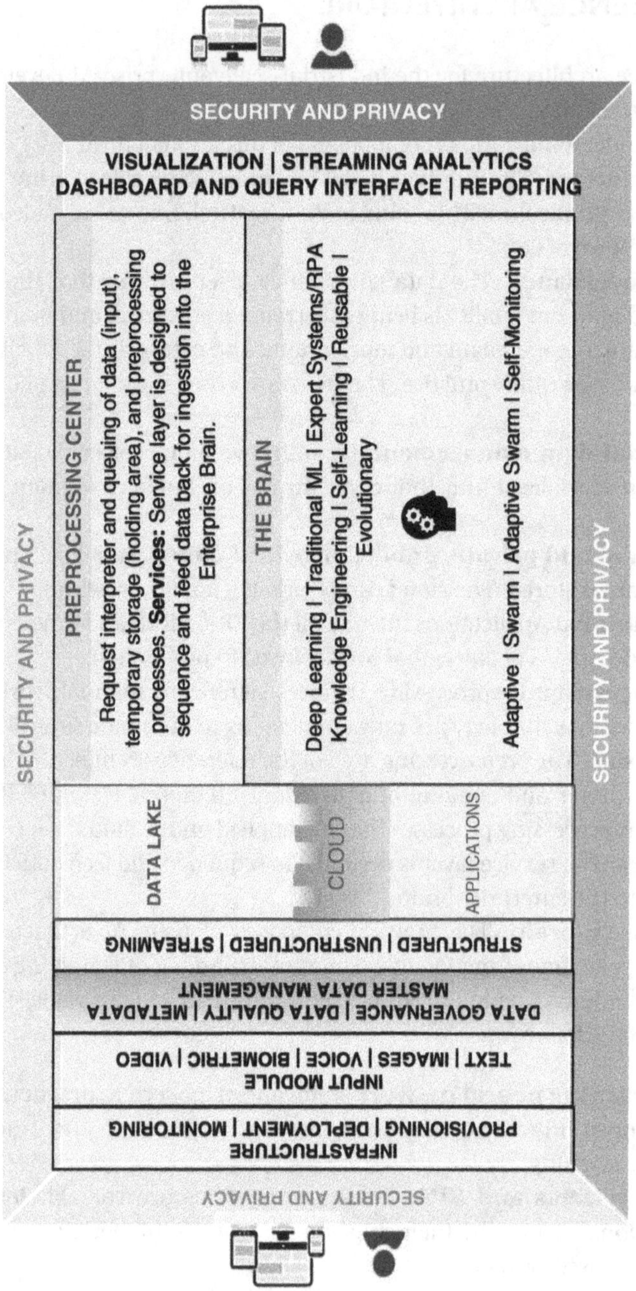

FIGURE 7.1 Reference Architecture

– **Self-learning:** Self-learning is that part of the brain that serves as a critic to individual artifacts and learns via methods such as reinforcement learning. This is accomplished by establishing a meta-learning layer enabled by a meta-feedback loop. Self-awareness happens when algorithms are abstracted for the purposes of analyzing the system's own behavior, and based on that, enabling the system to improve learning, improve their processing or absorption of sensor data, and adjust their actions. Self-regulating is a powerful way to improve the overall performance of the artifact and for its governance.

– **Evolutionary learning:** Evolutionary learning uses evolutionary algorithms to solve problems and find optimized solutions. While this can be classified as traditional machine learning, this area is constantly advancing with new research.

– **Reusable learning:** Developing profiles of solutions by problem areas and having metadata on them enables you to understand how to reuse solutions developed for one problem for another similar problem domain.

Meta cognition: Meta cognition includes those elements of the system that are designed to study, learn, and adapt to the collective dynamics of the entire system. They deal with the functionality and intelligence as it manifests through the collective action of various intelligent artifacts. This includes five types of systems:

Swarm intelligence: Individual AI artifacts can be combined to work together by forming AI swarm intelligence (Aydin and Fellows, 2017, 2018). These artifacts display intelligence that is greater as a whole than the intelligence manifested in each of the parts. They are smart systems that adjust to the changes in the environment and respond to the feedback from various systems. Not that different than birds in a flock, these artifacts adjust their behavior dynamically. Based on the desired functionality, the system can dynamically commission, decommission, change, or rearrange component artifacts.

Adaptive AI: As you have recognized by now, machine learning involves training and testing data on the distributions that represent some form of reality that you are trying to model. The data distribution and its quality and quantity are important factors to select learning algorithms. But what if after deployment at some point in the life cycle of the algorithm the data distribution of the underlying reality changes or new features are recognized or made available due to tracking additional data. This means your algorithm is no longer effective. It also means that your competitors will be able to develop a solution that has greater competitive advantage over your system. How do you fix this situation? Since algorithms depend upon the quality, quantity, and distribution of data, you cannot be sure that your existing algorithm can be updated. The best way is for machine learning to determine when your algorithm has become sub-optimized in relation to the reality by assessing the state of the reality and, based upon that information, automatically change and select a new algorithm or update the existing. This adaptive AI is at the center of adjusting to new realities. Machine learning and adaptive systems is an emerging area of research (Farhi et al., 2014; Quin et al., 2019; Jamshidi et al., 2019).

Adaptive swarm intelligence: Making algorithms function collaboratively and developing a sense of coordinated intelligence involves bringing diverse and uncoordinated swarm behavior to a focused and directed behavior. This means enabling self-assembling swarms that function well collectively and also individually.

Security and privacy: The security and privacy layer ensures the privacy and security for all—intelligent and non-intelligent systems and data. Intelligent security and privacy layers include AI-based security and privacy systems.

External layer: The external layer provides visualization, streaming analytics, analytics, and other requests from external systems.

 ## THE REFERENCE ARCHITECTURE AND HARDWARE

The reference architecture shown above is designed for an industrial-scale enterprise AI firm. As mentioned before, every asset management firm must strive to become that. For trading-centric firms, one of the most important assets is their hardware. To build an industrial-scale enterprise machine learning operation, hardware is a critical consideration. It improves computational performance (Duarte et al., 2020). In addition to advances in the classical CPU server technology, there are recent developments in GPU technology—and now quantum computing is on the horizon. The performance of quantum algorithms leads to substantial improvements (speed-ups) relative to classical algorithms (Orús et al., 2019). Regardless of the size, a firm must constantly evaluate its hardware options.

 REFERENCES

Aydin, M. E., and Fellows, R. (2017) "A Reinforcement Learning Algorithm for Building Collaboration in Multi-Agent Systems." [Online]. Available from: http://arxiv.org/abs/1711.10574.

Aydin, M. E., and Fellows, R. (2018) "Building Collaboration in Multi-Agent Systems Using Reinforcement Learning." *Lecture Notes in Computer Science (including subseries Lecture Notes in Artificial Intelligence and Lecture Notes in Bioinformatics)*. [Online]. 11056 LNAI201–212.

Buest, R. (2017) "Introducing the AI-Defined Infrastructure." *CIO.* September 27. [Online]. Available from: https://www.cio.com/article/3227608/introducing-the-ai-defined-infrastructure.html.

De Prado, M. L. (2018). (2018) *Advances in Financial Machine Learning.* John Wiley & Sons.

Duarte, V., et al. (2020) "Benchmarking Machine-Learning Software and Hardware for Quantitative Economics." *Journal of Economic Dynamics and Control.* [Online]. 111103796. Available from: https://doi.org/10.1016/j.jedc.2019.103796.

Farhi, E., et al. (2014) "A Quantum Approximate Optimization Algorithm," 1–16. [Online]. Available from: http://arxiv.org/abs/1411.4028.

Jamshidi, P., et al. (2019) "Machine Learning Meets Quantitative Planning: Enabling Self-Adaptation in Autonomous Robots." *ICSE Workshop on Software Engineering for Adaptive and Self-Managing Systems.* [Online]. May 2019, 39–50.

Noh, K. S. (2016) "A Study on the Position of CDO for Improving Competitiveness Based Big Data in Cluster Computing Environment." *Cluster Computing* [Online]. 19 (3), 1659–1669.

Orús, R., et al. (2019) "Quantum Computing for Finance: Overview and Prospects." *Reviews in Physics.* [Online]. 4 (September 2018).

Quin, F., et al. (2019) "Efficient Analysis of Large Adaptation Spaces in Self-Adaptive Systems Using Machine Learning." *ICSE Workshop on Software Engineering for Adaptive and Self-Managing Systems.* [Online]. May 2019, 1–12.

CHAPTER EIGHT

Performance

THE CONVERGENCE OF BUSINESS AND technology strategies in other industries (for example, Walmart, Amazon, Tesla) is also transpiring in asset management. This convergence implies that the business strategies and technology strategies are not developed separately but instead are viewed as integrated, interdependent, and identical. That is why the performance of AI business strategy is measured by looking at the two components: (1) Was our overall strategy influential and are we achieving results? and (2) Were we successful in deploying and operationalizing our strategy via AI project implementation and building industrial-scale enterprise machine learning? The first one is a measure of business results and denotes our ability to formulate good strategies. The second one is a measure of our execution and operationalization of the stated strategies.

We have come a long way. Our journey began with strategy and design—which linked our business strategy with our AI strategy. Our design and data practices enhanced our AI capabilities symbiotically. When we manage data effectively, we can build more AI artifacts faster, and our artifacts perform better. When we come up with good designs, we can create value through automation and insights. Once we had data under control, we entered the modeling stage. In modeling we recognized that we are dealing with a large set of potential learning models and approaches. We learned about the three primary approaches for teaching machines. After we developed our models, we wanted to check whether our models will perform in the real world. We recognized that in the investment world, having a model is one thing, making it work in real situations, another. Once we crossed that bridge, we entered the deployment phase. We were comfortable that the solution worked, and it was ready for prime time. At that point we recognized the vulnerability of our models. Our models were only as good as the underlying data, and our models—regardless of their performance—are subject to performance deterioration and even termination at the end of their life cycle. Since the concept of AI-centric automation is based on achieving business results, we need a performance system that measures performance as both a business and technical phenomenon. At the highest level, we can view performance as a construct of two factors:

- The business is achieving its goals through a strong strategy; and
- The AI artifacts are achieving their goals through a strong development and implementation program.

Please note that the term "performance" used in this chapter is in the context of measuring performance of our stated strategies (as captured in Chapter 2) and of the data-centric process (operationalization, Chapters 3 to 8). Performance reporting for portfolios is addressed in Chapter 15 as part of GIPS.

WHO IS RESPONSIBLE FOR PERFORMANCE?

The performance office (in the context that we are presenting) does not exist in legacy organizations. The performance function is headed by a person who reports directly to the CEO. This person also has a dotted-line reporting relationship to the board. The performance management team is a diversified team that comes from business, investment, and data science backgrounds.

The performance head from the CEO office takes an integrated strategy outlook and evaluates the collective (whole vs. the parts) of the firm while vetting and integrating the functional strategic components.

WHAT ARE THE WORK PROCESSES OF PERFORMANCE?

On the business side, the goal of measuring performance is to make sure that the business is achieving business targets and the return on investment from the various automation projects is being realized. The work processes of business functions are as follows:

- Vets and integrates the strategies and designs developed in the design function. Note: if firms sense that there is a conflict of interest in the performance department being responsible for integrated (whole) strategy vetting and then measuring its performance, the initial vetting function can be performed by a special team in the design function.
- Works with the CFO office to evaluate the performance of various business functions (marketing, sales, etc.). This includes CSR performance.
- Evaluates the performance of investment strategies in the long run.
- Helps build investment rollout allocation path for quantitative strategies.
- Establishes various performance measures.
- Keeps track of return on investment calculations for all the projects deployed.

On the AI front, the performance office measures and reports on five things:

- **Productivity:** How quickly can the machine learning organization create new AI artifacts? This can be viewed as how many SADALs get implemented. It can also show what percentage of the total automation goals are accomplished in a given time frame (year, quarter). This will be measured by the number of total projects completed vs. total projects identified by SADALs.
- **Effectiveness:** Do the artifacts created meet the stated goals? This measures the performance of the artifact. It uses measures such as bias, variance, and overfitting to further test the evaluation and determines if the business objectives were achieved. There are two aspects of measuring the effectiveness: (1) the artifact performs; and (2) the artifact's performance achieves business goals.
- **Collaboration:** The performance group also evaluates whether the solution footprint is achieving collaborative work automation. In other words, instead of treating AI artifacts only as individual work units, the performance group also measures how these machines perform work in a work chain. This includes looking at machine-to-machine and human-to-machine interaction to complete work processes.
- **Adaptability:** The performance function measures how adaptable the solutions and systems are to changed environment (data distributions).

- **Self-awareness:** The performance function also measures the metacognition of the network of systems that function together to perform work. Typically, these measures include being able to induce change in work chains by shutting down or diminishing the role of a set of systems while invoking and commissioning others based on the stimulus.

The performance function also:

- Vets the investment strategy performance. It helps evaluate the rollout sequence of the investment strategy. In that regard, this function works with the evaluation and deployment teams to set standards for how to introduce evaluated strategies. Under the supervision of the portfolio managers or investment leaders, they collectively determine the stages of testing. It can be tested with paper money, followed by small allocations of capital, and if successful, it can lead to additional capital allocation.
- Establishes processes, best practices, work documents, and protocols for handover of work from design to the data function, from data to model development, and from model development to evaluation.
- Measure performance of governance and CSR standards.
- Measure performance of AI governance.
- Reports the total performance to the board and the CEO.

Recall from a previous discussion that our goal is to create powerful business results from automation and insights (intellectualization) via an industrial-scale assembly line for enterprise machine learning.

 ## BUSINESS PERFORMANCE

Remember from the design chapter that the business strategy was linked with business goals. Each goal was segmented into objectives, and each objective was analyzed for automation of work and intellectualization of work. Automation was about improving productivity of work and intellectualization was about making us smarter.

Clearly, the performance measurement for the business side is very much related to measuring whether the business is meeting the goals that we had set. Performance monitoring is implemented in every area of the value chain as well as for the entire firm. Performance monitoring implies having a state of awareness that you are moving in the right direction and achieving your strategy. Since we have outlined in this book that our business and industry are experiencing powerful transformational forces, the measures stress and accentuate *transformation*.

For this discussion we segment performance management into six areas: business strategy performance, investment performance, functional/business performance, corporate social responsibility, governance performance, and return on investment on technology. For an AI-centered investment management firm, we use a comprehensive measurement system that tracks different areas of capabilities. The six primary capability areas are as follows:

1. **Strategy performance:** For strategy we measure factors related to the competitive advantage of a firm. The measured factors inform us about the competitive dynamics in the industry at the time of measurements, organizational readiness to embrace change, business model performance, and strategic direction. These measures give us an understanding of whether our business model is helping to create a competitive advantage for the firm. As shown in Chapter 3 ("Design"), the business model clarifies how we deploy our resources and how those resources create value. Conventional measures such as AUM, number of clients (retail, institutional, others), niche client markets, and brand power all belong in this section. In addition, we can also deploy a machine learning–based automated strategy analyzer.

2. **Functional/business performance:** We measure the performance of each department and function (except investment management). This includes measuring the performance against the established goals of these departments. For instance, we measure the performance of the regulatory department, marketing and sales, procurement, or the compliance department.

3. **Investment performance:** The industry provides a mechanism for measuring the investment performance (GIPS). As you implement your AI technology, your expectation should be to improve investment performance.

4. **CSR:** In this area we measure the performance of CSR. Our goal is to develop metrics that show us the progress and effect of our social responsibility programs.

5. **Governance/regulatory:** The fifth performance measurement is about a firm's improvements in corporate governance and regulatory compliance.

6. **Value/ROI:** An overall assessment of the return on investment on the AI technology is measured. The logic behind this evaluation is that investment in AI should provide a decent return on investment. The ROI is measured at the project level but also its integrated effect at the firm level. Like everything else, performance measurement is also automated by RPA and machine learning.

 ## TECHNOLOGICAL PERFORMANCE

Technical performance measures factors related to technological transformation to the new economy. It emphasizes the application of the science and AI in every area of the asset management business.

Automation: The automation measures the following performance:

- *Number of work processes designed for automation:* Divide the work processes by do, think, create, automation, i.e., DTC system, as introduced in Chapter 3. If the create part is too complex, put it on the back burner for automation, but since you have examined it and included it in the DTC analysis, your performance score for design will be higher. Compare that to a business process or function that has not been analyzed for automation, which will bring down the performance score. Measures such as percentage of each work task automated and percentage of total work automated belong here.
- *Data availability for all prioritized SADALs* This measures performance of the data organization to assess factors such as whether the data was available for developing the SADAL. Was it quality data? And did the data serve the purpose for which it was sought?
- *Number of AI artifacts developed:* Modeling is the development measure, and it shows the performance of the efficiency of the model-building department.
- *Number of AI artifacts evaluated:* The performance of the evaluation function can be measured in output; however, this could be a wrong incentive for investment strategy where churning out half-baked strategies could be counterproductive and backfire.
- *Number of AI artifacts deployed:* the speed, quality, efficiency, and state of IT infrastructure, deployment, and support. This area also covers cybersecurity, security, and privacy.

Insights: How developed are our strategic insights? Strategic insights can be viewed as the generation of predictive (in some cases descriptive and prescriptive) information to improve our decision-making, actions, and business results. For example, a recommendation engine that helps with sales by predicting what customers will likely bundle-buy uses prediction to create business results. Presumably, it also helps customers to make better decisions.

	Automation	Insights
Strategy	What parts of the strategy development work process are automated?	What insights are being provided from AI?
Business functions	For each business function, what processes are automated?	For each business function, what incremental insights are being provided by AI?
Investment	What parts of the investment process are automated?	How is AI enabling better investment strategy?
Operations	What parts of operations are automated?	How is AI providing greater understanding of operations?
CSR, governance, and regulatory	What parts of CSR, governance, and regulatory can be automated?	What insights can make us improve our CSR, governance, and regulatory functions?

Recall what a SADAL looked like. It is a business document that lays out the plan for a single artifact. This artifact can be a "do, think, or create" artifact. It may or may not have learning features. Each SADAL is assigned its own project. Each SADAL relates to work task automation.

SADAL				
SADAL# 6-1812 Sales forecasting using product reviews, sales data, media chat about firm and products and service.				
SENSE	ANALYZE	DECIDE	ACT	LEARN
Product review (social media) Market share by markets. Social media chat about firm. Social media chat about product.	Analyze how the data relates to sales. Does it have predictive power to forecast sales?	What are the most important predictors of future performance?	Notify the results. Monitor and inform when predictions and forecasts change.	Learn to perform the function autonomously and constantly.
LEARN				
WHAT DATA YOU SUGGEST FOR USE?		HOW WILL THE ARTIFACT CREATE VALUE? HOW WILL YOU MEASURE IT?		
Social media CRM Client interaction		■ Achieve better sales forecasting (value comes from ability to plan better). ■ Reduce the need for sales forecasting staff (value comes from cost reduction).		

- **Productivity:** Productivity measures the ability of the industrial-scale enterprise machine learning team to take a SADAL design as an input and convert it into a working product. The typical measures will be as follows:
  - Number of SADALs implemented;
  - Number of SADALs completed but not implemented (designed, modeled, and successfully evaluated); and
  - Ratio of number of SADALs completed vs. total number of SADALs assigned.
- **Effectiveness:** Effectiveness measures whether the artifacts achieved their stated goals. There are two aspects of measuring the effectiveness: (1) The artifact performs in accordance with its goals; and (2) The artifact's performance is optimum. The first measure is a technical measure that calculates whether the artifact performs as expected from the SADAL. The second measure is bit more complicated. It measures whether the artifact's performance is optimum in the domain it was established. There are four things that can alter the effectiveness: (1) the underlying distributions of the problem domain have changed; (2) new elements (features) of data have been identified that can solve the problem better; (3) a better algorithm match is now possible (due to new research); and (4) a better processing unit (hardware or infrastructure) is now available. For a dynamic and rapidly evolving discipline, performance cannot be static and stale. Also, when you are seeking competitive advantage, performance measures are not about measuring your performance against yourself. You measure your performance against competitors and also against what is technologically achievable.
- **Collaboration:** The performance group also evaluates whether the solution footprint is achieving collaborative work automation. The performance group measures the performance of machines in a work chain. The work chains are composed of humans and machines working together to form chains that create value. These chains evolve dynamically. Remember that AI is not only giving us automation, it is also enabling us with intellectualization. That means it is constantly evolving us to become smarter, to have more insights. With intellectualization comes the constant innovation and reinvention of work chains. Our work chain today may be different than the work chain two years from now. The performance group keeps track of that.
- **Adaptability:** The performance function measures how adaptable the solutions and systems are to a changed environment (data distributions). While effectiveness measures the ongoing relevance and utility of an

artifact in terms of the change in the underlying distributions, new features, algorithms, and hardware, adaptability measures the ability of a solution set to dynamically transition to a better path when a change event happens. See Jamshidi et al. (2019) for self-adaptation in quantitative planning where robots self-adjust at runtime. For instance, if we implemented a regulatory monitoring system by classifying data using algorithm A, but the system observes that algorithm B can achieve better results and can switch dynamically, we can have an adaptable system.

- **Self-awareness:** Being able to work together also requires metacognition. For example, when a human makes coffee, we understand the combinations of various functions to get the task completed. Walking to the coffee station (legs), holding the coffee pot (e.g., right hand), holding the cup (left hand), and so on. We know when one part finishes the task and it passes on the work to another part. Once we have finished making the coffee, the hands pass the work to the legs so we can return to our desk. The ability to switch by shutting down, starting up, or diminishing the role of certain systems while invoking and commissioning others based on work tasks is self-awareness or metacognition. As we design our intelligent artifacts, being able to have that metacognition will become increasingly important. For example, the perception of risk in trading can be used to adapt to the market forces and hence leads to adaptive behavior (Dempster and Leemans, 2006; see also Deng et al., 2017).

The combination of business and AI performance measurement gives the firm a holistic picture of its progress. These performance measures are reported to the board and the CEO on a regular basis and are used as a yardstick to measure the future performance potential of the company.

 ## REFERENCES

Dempster, M. A. H., and Leemans, V. (2006) "An Automated FX Trading System Using Adaptive Reinforcement Learning." *Expert Systems with Applications.* [Online]. 30 (3), 543–552.

Deng, Y., et al. (2017) "Deep Direct Reinforcement Learning for Financial Signal Representation and Trading." *IEEE Transactions on Neural Networks and Learning Systems.* [Online]. 28 (3), 653–664.

Jamshidi, P., et al. (2019) "Machine Learning Meets quantitative Planning: Enabling self-adaptation in autonomous robots." *ICSE Workshop on Software Engineering for Adaptive and Self-Managing Systems.* [Online]. May 2019, 39–50.

CHAPTER NINE

A New Beginning

N PART 1, WE LEARNED HOW TO think in terms of building our firm with AI. We learned that strategic transformation of our business happens when we organize our firms with the AI mindset. The AI mindset is both a strategic and operational paradigm change. It orients leaders to think differently about business. From a strategy perspective, you achieve by enhancing strategic performance potential, flexibility, innovation, market share, and profitability of your firm. You reduce costs through better coordination of work across the firm. You innovate and launch new products. You market and sell more effectively. You manage change in a profound way. You increase collective awareness about the firm. You hire the right talent and manage the talent more effectively. You avoid mistakes and regulatory problems. Your ability to predict improves. As various functions across the firm work in a coordinated intelligent manner, the overall performance increases.

To garner the power of those benefits, you need an operational transformation. Operational transformation comes from the steps of: design, data, model, evaluate, deploy, and performance. Building an AI-centric firm means that you develop the capabilities to implement industrial-scale enterprise machine learning. We learned those in Chapter 3 to Chapter 8.

In Part 2, we shift attention back to the value chain and strategic transformation. In this chapter we will develop a high-level functional model of an investment management firm.

BUILDING AN INVESTMENT MANAGEMENT FIRM AROUND ARTIFICIAL INTELLIGENCE?

What is your flywheel?

Amazon calls it "flywheel," and it has done wonders for Amazon. The concept is simple to understand. In my assessment, it has five parts.

- First, decide that you are an AI-centered company and reorganize your firm around machine learning and AI capabilities.
- Second, embed the AI capabilities both in your products and the operations platform required to develop and deliver the products.
- Third, deploy the AI capabilities across the entire value chain and do it in a systematic way.
- Fourth, share and reuse innovations developed by one team across the firm and even make it available for customers as a service.
- Fifth, hire the right AI talent.

What is so special about flywheel? More importantly, why do so many firms—in all sectors—struggle to embrace the concept of flywheel? Why are so many executives and managers trying, but failing, to get it right?

The difference, in a nutshell, is that firms are not thinking competitive advantage. In a fast-paced world where competition can strike from any side, investment management firms have not figured out how to blend their artificial intelligence pursuits with their firm's overall strategy. They approach them as two different areas. This creates a void, and that void is being filled by siloed projects.

Siloed innovation is not modernization. It is a burden. Sooner or later, it will lead to value loss. Machine learning, when approached in a siloed piecemeal manner, will create more problems than solve them. In fact, companies are finding out that 75 to 85% of their AI projects are failing or failing to impress executives (Nimdzi 2019). The real problem is not that AI projects are failing. I firmly believe that the real problem is that firms are approaching AI as projects. AI is not "projects." AI is a way of life. It is a transformational change. It is a strategy. It is the new way to operate your business.

What you must do is modernize your asset management firm and do it systematically and with a plan. You do that by moving your firm to a science-oriented firm. Becoming a science-oriented firm is key to acquiring the competitive advantage your asset management business needs, and these days the only way to become a science-oriented firm is by building your firm around artificial intelligence.

The question is how to build a flywheel for an asset management firm. What would that plan be? What will an investment science firm look like when it is transformed?

Part 2 will show you how to build your firm around AI. It will challenge you to think differently. It will link business outcomes with an artificial intelligence–centric transformation.

In a world dominated by hard-core technology researchers and mathematicians on one side and soft-skilled graduates of management schools on the other side, we will erect a bridge where the two sides can meet. The innovation spark happens when the two come together.

The line of thinking is built upon approaching strategy from a flexible perspective where innovation and change in markets are constantly tracked and considered. The execution layer is designed to be responsive and adjustable to the changing plans.

However, before we introduce the model, it is helpful to first address two questions:

- What about all the cognitive and digital automation projects that IT teams are currently engaged in in your firm—isn't that building your firm around AI?
- Why should you shape your firm around AI?

Both are fair questions, and here are the answers.

THE FALLACY OF GOING DIGITAL

I recognize that you have been led to believe that your firm is on its way to become digital and cognitive. Well, you are not alone in that. Many firms have fallen prey to that false narrative.

The reality is that only a handful truly understand what the cognitive change entails. I provided the example of Amazon.

When the Internet came, many firms found themselves in a similar self-deceptive fallacy.

Let us reflect on what happened in the department store retail sector when e-commerce matured. Nearly all large retailers (Kmart, Sears, Macy's,

Nordstrom, Toys R Us, etc.) launched major digital transformation programs. All were advised by leading consulting firms. All believed that they were on their way to become a major online sensation. The consultants assured them of that.

But despite building significant digital presence, nearly all retailers lost ground and could not withstand the powerful force unleashed by Amazon. For decades they slowly simmered and festered as Amazon took market share away from them. These stores did not recover.

Well, to be fair, all except one. Walmart was not only able to thwart Amazon's competitive advances, it emerged as a formidable force.

As we learn from the past, the first lesson is that just having a digital program is not enough. Just because you joined the automation club does not mean you get a seat at the table. There are ranks within the club and only the ones at the top matter. Others simply survive, pulling one stunt after another, until there is no act left.

Sears, GE, Toys R Us were American icons. They all thought they were technologically advanced. They all had powerful technology programs. But disconnected silos of innovation are not transformational. You need a coordinated strategy.

A second and perhaps more interesting lesson is that it is indeed possible to transform a legacy firm to keep it at the forefront of technology. Walmart's example gives us hope.

Take the example of the wealth management market. On one hand you have firms such as Wealthify, who have declared their intent to partner with traditional advisory firms, and on the other hand you have companies such as Nutmeg and Betterment, who are adding human advisors to their robo-advisors.

These are very interesting developments. Firms such as Wealthify can partner with a few firms. Their partnership can last only to the point when they can figure out how to scale without the help of legacy firms. And even if they open their platform to all advisors in a partnership model, does this mean there is no competitive advantage for the partners? If all the asset management firms will have access to the same platform, where is the competitive advantage?

Conversely, if only a handful will have that access, then what if you are not one of those handful of firms? This means you will be left behind. This is one side of the dilemma.

What if these robo-advisory firms get acquired, and the acquiring entity shuts the door on previous partners or worse, the acquirer now has access to your customers. Does that make you feel uncomfortable? Wait till you hear the other side.

Firms such as Nutmeg that are now adding human advisors can challenge your traditional business and relationships. They will become like you—except a better you. They will even poach people from your firm. They will blend advanced analysis with human relationships and try to move up the ladder, from younger generation and smaller clients to eventually mid-market and larger clients. Why not? Who says technology is only good for younger people? It can do wonders for all age groups.

As the artificial intelligence economy matures, you will need to do what Walmart and Amazon do. You will have to lead the transformation of your firm by building your firm around AI. You will need to develop your own capabilities. An AI-centric transformation cannot be outsourced. It cannot be deployed by off-the-shelf software.

An unknown author once said that there are three phases in life: you believe in Santa Claus, you don't believe in Santa Claus, and you are Santa Claus. It appears we have experienced a similar path in fintech.

Just a few years back fintech was both fascinating and enchanted. The charming IPOs and massive funding rounds of start-ups with "behavioral algorithms" and peer-to-peer lending created an aura of mystery and wonder. The future of traditional business was over, many projected. Then came the realities of business and peak-to-trough declines of 80 to 90% in share prices (e.g., OnDeck, Lending Club) of fintech firms took the air out of the balloon. Suddenly, we stopped believing in magic.

With the crash came the truce—an unsustainable armistice—as both the traditional firms and the tech firms withdrew to their comfort zones. Legacy firms recognized that they lack the innovation culture, the technology, and the innovative spirit to create a powerful future. And the tech firms realized that they do not have the deep pockets, the staying power, or the customer base to challenge the established firms. Fintech took a breather after a long battle—but the game has only begun. FinTech is only recharging and preparing for the next and the major combat.

The stage is set for the decisive battle to begin.

In the third phase the tech firms will break through the barriers of scale. Most importantly the tech giants learning and waiting on the sidelines will finally decide to enter the market with models that will create new value for customers—while breaking the bank (no pun intended). Legacy firms are not ready for that.

Now let's return to the question of why do it.

WHY BUILD YOUR FIRM AROUND AI?

There are several compelling reasons to adopt AI. I am sure you can think of a dozen reasons yourself.

Pick any magazine or newspaper these days, and you will see articles and references to artificial intelligence. Recently, Arizona became the first state to offer sandbox flexibility to fintech. This means firms can get a license to trade (limited and small scale) and experiment to drive innovation.

Think about your clients. They now expect their phones to follow orders and their cars to park themselves—they sure would want their asset managers to equip them with a fully loaded investment management performance platform.

Customer preferences are changing. Let us first start with the younger generation and then move up. Wealth is moving toward the younger, more technology savvy generation. Generational wealth transfer is expected to be somewhere around $30 trillion.

Besides being technology literate, younger clients (millennials and gen-Z) have also experienced the Great Recession firsthand. Even if they were in school when it happened, it is likely that they heard their parents and grand-parents talk about the anguish of losing life savings or reading about Wall Street greed.

These are also efficiency- and cost-conscious generations that prefer solutions that minimize waste and utilize available capacity to the max (e.g., Airbnb, Uber, Lyft).

In some ways the definition of "expertise" for these generations has shifted. They can access vast amounts of information quickly. They can educate them-selves with thousands of DIY courses and videos for free. It is natural for these generations to feel they can learn and do anything themselves. Why pay an external party if meaningful and usable expertise develops from your own research and from the wisdom of the masses in a network?

The above factors have contributed to these younger generations seeking greater control over the outcomes that they believe they can influence. Not trusting the specialists and instead relying upon their own research skills and the opinion of their network comes naturally for them. Whether that confidence is warranted or not is a different issue.

But it does not stop at younger generations. Older high-net-worth (HNW) and ultrahigh-net-worth (UHNW) individuals also want greater control, more flexibility, and higher transparency. They want to be understood and respected.

They too want excellence in customer service. Same goes for the institutional investors. We cover institutional investors in detail in Chapter 12.

Covid-19 has affected our society in a substantial way. Many believe that we will never go back to the pre-Covid-19 business style. The online adaptation is here to stay and could become a permanent work model. This could mean traditional physical meetings–centric relationship management may change to more online-centric businesses.

But regardless of how your meetings materialize, traditional relationship management with both high-net-worth individuals and institutional clients can only go so far. Sooner or later firms would need to demonstrate how their strategy and the ability to understand client needs are different from or better than any competitor's.

One small miss, and clients will be inundated with alternative options claiming to possess the magic bullet. Clearly, to gain the respect and attention of younger generations and to maintain and sustain the existing relationships, firms need to do something different. They must innovate.

This means that from a positioning perspective a firm needs to be able to demonstrate that it knows more, it knows better, and what it knows cannot be easily picked up from reading a few articles or taking some courses.

This means that firms need an edge that comes from proprietary insights not widely available to anyone. Additionally, firms will have to be a low-cost operator, provide excellent service, build trust, and show exceptional command on the regulatory and compliance parts of the business.

YOU MUST RELY ON YOUR OWN CAPABILITIES

In investment management, where does your competitive advantage comes from? Is it from your relationships? Is it from your strategy? Is it from your investment research? Is it from your ability to understand your clients and their goals?

I think you would agree that all these factors affect your competitive advantage. Your advantage comes from your ability to accomplish the above better and faster.

In today's world where automation is the key to strategic transformation, "intelligence" is becoming the new source of competitive advantage. But sustaining competitive advantage is not easy when technology firms are automating what you do. I call this "techcroachment"—i.e., encroachment by technology firms in various sectors.

In a business environment characterized by techcroachment and fast innovation, it is not possible to build your competitive advantage by installing packaged software or configuring some solution or even by depending on a partner. The reason is simple—your machine learning automation is a function of your data, data processes, and your algorithms. Your data and algorithms are your proprietary knowledge, and it is likely that you will not share that with your competitors. Third-party configurable software and point solutions do not provide this type of assurance. If an implementation partner installs that at your firm, they repeat the process at another firm and so on. The world of algorithms is proprietary, and confidentiality is key to developing competitive strength.

Hence, AI development is something you must do yourself. It is plain and simple: Your competitive advantage comes from your data and your algorithms. It depends on your own creativity.

 ## WHAT IS ASSET SCIENCE?

To lead your firm to the modern times you do need to start thinking like a research scientist. The AI revolution is being shaped by research scientists, and even if you are not trained as a scientist, learning about the scientific method is not rocket science.

The key point is that you are moving from a soft management paradigm to a scientific management paradigm. The soft management paradigm was shaped by our instincts, emotions, and rationality. It artfully concealed our biases and delicately fused them with our decisions.

The scientific method is not just about rationality. It does not aim to make us purely rational. Its job is to create a higher state of awareness. It recognizes our instincts, emotions, and rationality. It understands our biases and their sources. It gives us the ability to rediscover ourselves and our clients.

Asset science is the application of the scientific method to help create investment success for clients.

It is neither dogmatic nor constrained by the theoretical battles (mean-variance vs. behavioral) that rage in the finance field. It does not push theory top-down but instead enables bottom-up dynamic theory generation based on client needs and market changes.

It does not limit the application of science just to the investment management part but instead applies it in all areas of the firm including sales and business development. It is not based on deploying tactical tools but instead is powered by a strategic framework of building interlinked and interdependent capabilities across the value chain.

It has been talked about for a while, but it has not been adopted due to the mismatch between theory and execution. In 2014 Statman provided three lessons in his book *What Investors Really Want* (if you haven't read the book, I strongly recommend you do) and summarized them in a presentation (Statman, 2014, 2015). He writes:

- *First Lesson:* Know yourself. Know your clients. Know their wants. Know their goals. Know their cognitive errors. Know their emotions.
- *Second Lesson:* Know science. Teach science to your clients. Teach the science of financial markets. Teach the science of human behavior.
- *Third Lesson:* Be your clients' financial physician. Good financial professionals are like good physicians. Good financial professionals promote both wealth and well-being. Good financial professionals ask, listen, empathize, educate, prescribe, and treat.

Statman then provides the basis for why he recommends science. He argues that only through science we can be aware of our cognitive errors and misleading emotions and that science gives us the tools to correct such errors and empowers us with logic and empirical evidence. He goes as far as claiming that knowledge of science is what makes investment professionals different from individual investors.

Despite the stern warnings issued by the leading voices in finance that asset managers are really asset scientists and that they need to act as empathetic advisors, little progress has been made toward the transformation.

One reason why it is hard to make any progress is that unlike natural sciences, social sciences are not governed by natural laws. Social systems are dynamic, constantly evolving, and subject to constant change. Approaching such systems with the scientific rigor of positivist science may only provide half the picture. The other half is trapped in the philosophical wisdom that reality can be socially constructed and that knowledge is conditional and relative to time and space (Burrell and Morgan, 1979; Morgan, 1980; Kuhn, 1970).

The second reason is that we need tools to help asset managers become asset scientists. These tools need the ability to capture both—the purely rational and empirical part of science and the socially constructed part.

Let us look at the first lesson from Statman. He expects us to know ourselves, our clients, their wants, their goals, their cognitive errors, and their emotions. How in the world can you get all that knowledge? Even if you can somehow get that knowledge, how accurate would that knowledge be? Self-knowledge is neither effortlessly acquired nor quietly accepted. So what makes Statman recommend what is so complex to achieve in practice?

The answer is that Statman knows that today we do have the power to decipher that knowledge about ourselves and others. We are all digital natives, and we are leaving a digital footprint about ourselves every microsecond. Nothing about us is a mystery. We carry ourselves on our digital sleeves. It is only a matter of who wants to know and has the capability to know, and we can be read like an open book.

Statman insists on science because gone are the days when you needed to burden yourself with understanding personalities and behaviors by horoscopes and four-color classifications. Science provides a medium that you can trust. It gives you evidence. It establishes trust in your decisions.

Approaching asset management from a scientific viewpoint does not mean that the person becomes dehumanized, a zombie, or a machine. It simply means that we bring rigor and discipline in our strategic thinking about what our business model needs to be.

I believe the goal of artificial intelligence is to improve our behavior and the behavior of our clients so we can help clients achieve maximum success in an emo-rational world.

This is exactly your goal too. You want what is best for your clients.

Artificial intelligence enables two types of capabilities—first, it automates processes, and by doing that, it reduces errors and increases efficiency. This capability, known as *task automation*, lowers costs and risk. The second capability is known as *skill augmentation* or intellectualization and comes from the ability to know more, better, and faster. In skill augmentation, a firm not only automates, it increases its skill level to perform all its functions better and faster. Skill augmentation increases revenues and lowers risk and cost of operations. When combined, the above two capabilities lead to a powerful return on investment:

$$AI = task\ automation + skill\ automation$$

There are three steps to transform into an asset science firm. First, we need to understand the broad structure of the value chain of asset management. Second, we need to recognize the major activity areas within the value chain. Lastly, we need to develop a framework for automation to improve those activities.

The high-level structure of value chain of asset management can also be viewed as a cycle composed of two loops. Chains have ends, but cycles continue, and hence I like to think of value creation as a perpetual and ongoing process. Also, since our firms continue to be run as twentieth-century departmental and functional bureaucracies, we lose sight of why we do things. You will notice below that when we think in terms of loops and cycles, we are focusing on main processes and not departments. The asset management value cycle is composed of two interconnected loops covered with a protective shield and with a command center in between.

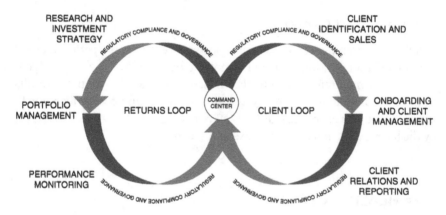

FIGURE 9.1   Value Creation Loops

The Client Loop

The client loop forms when firms direct their activities to identify, establish, and manage client relationships. This is the process of bringing clients to the firm and then keeping them and deepening relationship with them. This can be viewed as a process that results from coordinated activities across various functions and initiatives such as marketing, sales, customer service, customer lifetime value, customer experience, and channel management.

The Returns Loop

The returns loop forms when clients achieve investment success from investment and portfolio management activities. It is composed of three broad areas:

- The first is your research capacity. It focuses on building your firm's investment strategy and research.
- The second part is about asset allocation, portfolio management, rebalancing, account management, and transactions.
- The third part is about performance management.

Artificial intelligence plays a key role in all three by doing both task and skill automation.

The Protective Shield

As shown in the figure, the protective shield runs around the two loops, layering and covering them as thermoset insulation covers a copper cable. It is composed of four layers: (1) compliance; (2) governance; (3) corporate social responsibility; and (4) cybersecurity. This protective shield secures the two loops and builds trust.

The Command Center

Finally, the command center exists to constantly evaluate the performance of both loops by integrating them and managing their health. The command center's role is to maintain the health of both loops. It is a new function that results from the combination of strategy, investor relations, and competitive intelligence. It is supported by various back-office and support functions and it is led by the board, CEO, and the C-level executive team.

 ## A HEALTHY CYCLE

Let us look at the two loops. Why view our firms from that perspective? Think about it: you can have a great investment advisory side, but if clients don't know about it or fail to use or access it or are disappointed by other elements of service or you fail to communicate your value proposition to institutional investors, your firm will not be successful.

Conversely, if you are a marketing magnet and can do a great job in bringing clients and capital to your firm, but the advisory and investment management side keeps disappointing customers, you will lose clients faster than the sellout when markets hiccup.

When both loops perform and stay intact, the cycle stays healthy. When one or both loops fail to perform, the cycle and the firm collapses. One can observe that at least four breaches are possible:

- **The returns loop collapses:** Advisors and managers are unable to deliver acceptable returns. Performance declines, and the loop begins to degenerate. It then affects the client loop, and the firm starts losing customers to competitors.
- **The client loop collapses:** The client loop collapses when the asset management firm ignores customers, fails in customer experience and service,

fails to meet customer expectations, or is unable to provide the value proposition provided by competitors.

- **The protective shield ruptures:** The compliance and governance shields breach when the firm fails to uphold excellent standards in compliance and governance. When that happens, it loses customer and regulator trust and runs into major, often extremely expensive to fix, problems. We have seen numerous examples where unethical practices, fraud, and governance issues destroyed asset management firms.
- **The control room disappoints:** The control room disappoints when executives fail to notice that the business environment around them has changed and that change demands a corresponding change in the strategy.

THE TOOL SET

Asset science is enabled by taking an enterprise perspective to identify a value creation processes. Processes are composed of various jobs. The jobs are performed by humans and machines. The jobs are composed of basic tasks and skilled tasks, which display larger variability, require decision-making and cognitive thinking, and may include complex physical movements (as in robots).

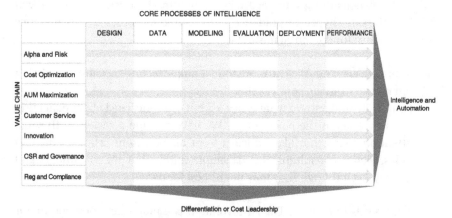

FIGURE 9.2 The Core AIAI Model

This takes us back to Chapter 1 in the book in which we introduced the value chain–centric investment management transformation system. The vertical capability building is the strategic excellence, which comes from each part optimizing its pursuits, accomplishing the goals of the enterprise.

The horizontal capability building is about implementing industrial-scale enterprise machine learning and transforming your firm to a science- and research-centric firm.

This leads to the making of a powerful firm that can deploy functional areas that not only pursue automation but by their very nature perform as a science-centric organization. Sales, marketing, human resources, customer experience, operations—all become sales science, marketing science, HR science, CX science, ops science organizations. That will be the focus of Part 2. This is the only formula for the long-term survival of the investment management firm.

 ## THIS IS NOT JUST AUTOMATION

As I mentioned in the previous section and what is also one of the most important messages and central themes of this book, you are transitioning to a science organization. Just as the introduction of science challenged many false beliefs, this change will also require us to break free from the old molds.

The way the AI revolution is being sold to you is very shallow and superficial. Call any consulting firm, regardless of their merit or orientation, and you will hear the same hyped-up guidance: automate your processes. This guidance is based on two fundamental mistakes:

- Many are viewing AI as no more than a simple technology and are missing out on the strategic power of this change.
- Some fully understand what is needed but are concerned about educating executives about the power of AI. We have become a society with small attention spans that likes to learn from memes, mini articles, and TED Talks. Hence consultants sell us simple things that we can understand quickly, even though they may not be best for us.

That needs to change. The AI revolution is a major development, and it will change how the entire economy operates. We need to pay attention to this change and be ready to embrace more complex learning.

Consulting firms offer significant experience from their past projects in digital automation and business process reengineering. They have gone through the waves of automation, gained deep experience, and established strong practice areas. The problem is that previous automation experience of the digital (classic computing) revolution is not applicable in the AI revolution.

Automating business processes is not what intelligent automation is about. In typical business processes, we ignored the component that required human thinking, decision-making, and cognitive powers. We only considered those simple automatable tasks that did not require much thinking. However, the real business dynamics were shaped by human rationality and emotionality. That combination of human rationality and emotionality is what is being automated now. And for that, we do not have a game plan or a manual. This book is the first such comprehensive manual.

The key point is that business process reengineering cheat sheets from the 1990s will not help in this revolution. Trying to automate using consulting approaches from the 1990s BPR is like trying to use the toolbox used to repair horse buggies to fix modern cars. AI is neither a trivial change nor can it be modeled using the standard business process reengineering templates.

 REFERENCES

Burrell, G., and Morgan, G. (1979) *Sociological Paradigms and Organisational Analysis: Elements of the Sociology of Corporate Life.* New York, NY: Routledge.

Kuhn, T. S. (1970) *The Structure of Scientific Revolutions.* Chicago, University of Chicago Press.

Morgan, G. (1980) "Paradigms, Metaphors, and Puzzle Solving in Organizational Theory." *Administrative Science Quarterly* 25 (4), 605–622.

Nimdzi Insights Pactera EDGE. (2019) *Artificial Intelligence: Localization Winners, Losers, Heroes, Spectators, and You. Technical Report.* [Online]. Available from: https://www.nimdzi.com/wp-content/uploads/2019/06/Nimdzi-AI-whitepaper.pdf.

Statman, M. (2015) "What Investors Really Want: Lessons from Behavioral Finance (Presentation on the book)." [Online]. Available from: http://www.cfasociety.org/poland/Documents/Meir_Statman_presentation.pdf.

Statman, M. (2014) *What Investors Really Want: Lessons from Behavioral Finance,* 1–28.

CHAPTER TEN

Customer Experience Science

T HERE WAS A TIME WHEN GENERATING returns was considered sufficient in investment management. Today, firms have recognized that to build a strong and sustainable business, many other areas are equally important. One of those areas is managing customer experience. Customer experience is one of the major drivers of a firm's success and is critical for existing client retention, new client acquisition, increasing growth, and enhancing a firm's reputation. In this chapter we will discuss the role of AI in favorable customer experience optimization.

CUSTOMER EXPERIENCE

At the highest level, one can view customer experience (CX) as what existing or potential customers experience when they interact with the firm. One way to accomplish that is to study all the touch points of those interactions and try to optimize experience in each one of them. For example, if you meet clients physically, your office location, interior decoration, style, reception area, restaurant selection, and other similar things may constitute the physical aspects of the meeting. In addition, how you scheduled the appointment, follow-up, professionalism, and many other such intangible factors are also involved in experience optimization. From a digital perspective, an example of customer experience can be your website or online software. However, while exploring touch points and responding to them is one way to approach customer experience optimization, strategic customer experience optimization involves process-specific actions.

Colin Shaw, CEO of Beyond Philosophy, identifies what he calls "Seven Imperatives" for customer experience (Shaw, 2015):

1. Recognize that customers decide emotionally and justify rationally;
2. Embrace the all-encompassing nature of customers' irrationality;
3. Understand that customers' minds can be in conflict with themselves;
4. Commit yourself to understanding and predicting customer habits and behaviors;
5. Uncover the hidden causes and unintended consequences of why customers want things to be easy;
6. Accept that apparently irrelevant aspects of your customer experience are sometimes the most important aspects; and
7. Realize the only way to build customer loyalty is through customer memories.

While the above points may apply to retail customers, in investment management we deal with institutional customers, and those customers can be extremely analytical, rational, information and data dependent, and experienced buyers of services. They are cautious in dealing with new firms and expect transparency from the firms they deal with. To establish a framework that can maximize customer experience, we need to consider various ways in which CX manifests.

 ## VALUE, STRENGTH, AND DURATION OF RELATIONSHIP

Forming strong, lasting, and value-creating relationships can be viewed as a goal and a measure of CX success. However, being able to do that consistently is important. Since it can be expected that at times your clients will have to be patient with your strategy and understanding of your performance, it is relationships that carry firms during turbulent times. Relationships matter.

To identify, cultivate, enhance, deepen, and strengthen relationships, a firm needs to develop an empathetic approach. This applies to both retail and institutional customers. There are no exceptions. While the approaches may vary, the underlying theme of understanding the human side, developing empathy, and recognizing the humanness of clients is important.

While AI has often been presented as cold, rational, emotionless, robotic, and unhuman technology, the truth is that AI can be deployed to create extreme empathy. In fact, customer experience can only be optimized by maximizing empathy, and empathy can only be maximized by using AI. The previous comment may feel like a hyperbole or exaggeration, but as you will observe in this chapter, it is not. With AI we can observe, sense, and feel aspects of other people that we cannot detect with our senses. This is what makes AI the perfect solution for CX.

Specifically, AI is applied to determine CX and influence clients as follows:

1. Deploy machine learning to learn about customers. This requires an empathetic and deeper level of awareness about customers.
2. Use machine learning to find the best way to influence customers so they can learn about your offerings, discover your brand, and understand how you can help them.
3. Implement machine learning to enhance customer experience at all touch points.

UNDERSTANDING CUSTOMERS: EMPATHY FOR CX

In 2014 I developed a five-level program for AI CX. I called it empathy-based marketing and taught the model to students from my MBA strategy class. In that model, there are five levels of developing a deeper understanding of customers. Deeper understanding of customers means you understand their emotional needs, physical needs, spiritual needs, fears, concerns, values, ambitions, aspirations, experiences, pains, expectations, and other such things that make us uniquely human. The five levels are as following:

Level 1: You understand customers based on basic information such as demographics—including name, ethnicity, physical features (image), social and financial status, profession, nationality, contact information, and other such factors.

Level 2: You use your own understanding of who people are and what they need. Your understanding stems from your experience and knowledge. You project your own understanding of feelings, needs, concerns, aspiration, and so forth, of other people.

Level 3: You develop a basic understanding of people's needs, feelings, emotional states, concerns, aspirations, and so forth.

Level 4: You develop a deep understanding of people's needs, feelings, concerns, emotions, and so forth.

Level 5: You acquire mastery of understanding people to the point where you understand them better than they understand themselves. At this state you can project what people may want but not based on your own projections of what people want. Instead, you have developed a true and deep understanding of your customers.

STEPS TO BECOME AN EMPATHETIC ASSET MANAGEMENT FIRM

There are three steps to acquire excellence in becoming an empathetic AM firm:

- Know your "empmeter";
- Expand empathy awareness and understanding; and
- Incorporate into products and services.

KNOW YOUR EMPMETER

Knowing your empmeter is not learning about your customers; it is learning about yourself. Do you have companywide recognition, awareness, executive support, and organizational readiness to develop CX programs? Have you deployed formal programs for CX? Have you taken initiatives to develop a deeper level of understanding of your customers? If yes, your empmeter is high. If no, you need to work on that. You cannot achieve what you do not desire. If there is no awareness in your firm about the value of developing deeper understanding of customers, then there is a huge gap. You should test your firm for CX programs, assess organizational awareness and customer-centric culture, and evaluate what technology has been applied to maximize your empathy.

EXPAND EMPATHY AWARENESS AND UNDERSTANDING

Once you have recognized the need for CX and assessed the gaps, the next step is to figure out how to close the gap. Your CX strategy will have the three components: what you can learn about your customers, why it is important, and how to do it.

How much you can learn about your customers will depend on how much data you have or how much data you can have. It will also highlight areas for which you need the data, but either the data does not exist or you have not identified the right provider. Secondly, it will depend on the speed of your industrial-scale machine learning adoption. Think of it as putting a puzzle together. As the pieces of the puzzle come together, you will have a better picture of your customers. In the CX literature it is known as the single view of a customer.

As the picture emerges, connect it with how you can help your customers. Evaluate the benefits of that helping strategy. Synthesizing that information can help you configure solutions and offerings that meet customers' goals. It also helps you to segment customers, develop new products and services, and personalize customer experience.

INCORPORATE INTO PRODUCTS AND SERVICES

With the in-depth knowledge of customers acquired (explained in the previous subsection), you can now position, propose, develop, design, and explore products and services that meet the needs of the customer. Remember that there could be instances where you know the customer better than the customer knows him- or herself. Your ability to match customer needs with products and services will be a powerful mechanism for retention and new client acquisition.

WHAT IS AUTOMATED EMPATHY AND COMPASSION (AEC)?

Empathy can be broadly conceptualized as being able to take the customer's perspective or reacting to an observed experience of the customer.

Automated empathy refers to the ability of machines to develop cognitive and affective responses to a customer's situation. The depth, structure, and capacity of empathy is a function of technology design, use, and state of the technology development.

There are two types of empathy. Cognitive empathy helps you to identify a customer's situation from his or her perspective. Emotional empathy places you in the customer's situation such that you feel the same emotions as the customer does.

Studies show that empathy alone can be a source of significant bias. For example, in consumer marketing, in many cases managers tend to impose their own biases on consumer preferences (Hattula et al., 2015). This happens due to self-referential tendencies whereby managers impose their own private consumer identity and reduce their reliance on actual research or empirical evidence.

That happens because when you feel another person's emotions, you risk assuming the same outlook that the person has but also bringing in your own emotional bias. However, being able to use an emotional state of a client as a data point can be an important consideration. We do not want to impose our feelings but also do not want to be completely detached and hence unable to recognize our customer's feelings.

Also, creativity and empathy have a delicate relationship (Form and Kaernbach, 2018). Too much empathy can hamper creativity. Too little can impede customer insights. A balance is necessary.

So our first task is to separate cognitive empathy from emotional empathy. Our second task is to use both as inputs to understand our customers better without contaminating them with our biases.

Our third and most important task is combining empathy with compassion to develop a comprehensive picture of the customer and his or her problems and goals.

To remain competitive and to be able to respond to the customer's needs, asset management firms need an automated AEC capability. This ability augments the sales team to be able to understand thousands of customers, develop individualized compassion, and help prepare a response.

There is another benefit of AEC-centric marketing and relationship management. While good salespeople tend to have empathy, it is also a source of stress for professionals. Automation helps put things in perspective and in many cases hides the unimportant details from the asset manager.

INCORPORATING AEC MARKETING

Building your automated empathy and compassion marketing engine requires looking at both structured and unstructured data. Prior research shows that there are four dimensions of customer relationship management: (1) customer identification; (2) customer attraction; (3) customer retention; and (4) customer development (Swift, 2001). Keeping those action dimensions in mind, I will identify 12 areas for you to work on. When you think about your solution, you need to approach it in an integrated way. Here they are:

i. **Customer segmentation:** Ability to segment customers not only in terms of standard metrics but also in terms of advanced behavioral and psychological traits. Remember that you are segmenting customers and potential customers to serve them better. You are also doing it to reduce your noise-to-signal ratio. Finally, segmentation of customers can be a powerful source of innovation. But discovering behavioral or values segments is one thing; knowing which ones are most important for individuals and then forming a customer group based upon that priority is the key. Different types of neural networks are being used in practice for various kinds of segmentation purposes (Ayoubi, 2016; Thakur and Workman, 2016).

ii. **Client enablement:** Supplying real-time news, updates, analysis, market intelligence, and value-added services is critical because today's investors need your help to understand and develop an investment perspective. However, what clients need is actionable and usable information for their specific situation. This also means that information should be packaged for easy consumption, noise free (as much as possible), reliable, and relevant. Inundating clients with a million links to articles is not client enablement. Natural language processing (NLP) is being used to identify relevant articles, and to understand meaning and context, sentiment, and events (Chaturvedi et al., 2016; Junqué De Fortuny et al., 2014).

iii. **Customer with god traits:** Are you still stuck in the 360-degree customer view? That perspective is rudimentary and mostly transactional. Most importantly, it is outwardly focused and not internally guided. It tells us little about the values, thoughts, goals, aspirations, fears, and biases of customers. Treat those 360 degrees as nice to have, but the world has moved far beyond that. What you need is introspection-enabled 360. Discovering, managing, and enhancing ways to develop client relationships is central to building the asset management business (Ngai et al., 2009). Studies have shown that performance alone is like flying a plane on one wing—magic happens when performance is combined with trust (Gennaioli et al., 2012). Artificial intelligence provides a way to systematically measure and manage customer satisfaction and loyalty (Aktepe et al., 2015).

iv. **Customer-led innovation:** Customer-led innovation comes in many forms (Judge, 2018). Perhaps a customer has designed a portfolio that is performing well. You should probably know why. Perhaps a unique customer need (driven by some customer behaviors) has identified an opportunity to readjust and realign the portfolio. Perhaps a customer insight has guided you to discover the idiosyncrasies that can help design new products or services. These innovations can come in many forms, and artificial intelligence technology can be deployed to facilitate the development and sharing of such information. It can also be a vehicle for determining incentives.

v. **Anticipation:** When you turn 50, AARP sends you an invitation to become a member. When your teenager reaches the driving age, you get a call from your insurance agent. When you reach Medicare age, some local hospitals help you transition. But when daily changes happen in your client's world, asset managers don't have a mechanism to find out what happened. You don't know if a family member passed away, if your client was diagnosed with a disease, when your client's daughter got admitted to an Ivy League school, or your client fell in love with London and she wants to retire there. You have no idea about these things because you are not linked to the customer's world. Your customer is a digital native, and you need to anticipate customer problems and opportunities before they happen. Humans are inherently predictable—or else you wouldn't be able to drive to work. Asset managers never claimed that their clients don't have goals, aspirations, or personal situations. It was just that they had a crude way of both understanding those situations and incorporating them in helping clients build portfolios in accordance with their goals. Turn that crude model into "anticipation-based" and "goal-directed" and you can do wonders for your clients. For example, customer churn is a major issue in banks, and it can cost up to 5 times more to acquire a customer than to keep one. With artificial intelligence you can predict when and why a customer might leave (Tsai and Lu, 2009). Some banks have used similar platforms to predict employee churns also.

vi. **Real-time selling:** Real-time selling is not about manipulating clients. It is about being able to understand their needs better and to dynamically develop a value proposition and solution for them. One of the goals of cross-channel marketing needs to be giving firms the ability to develop real-time customer needs fulfillment capability. Recommendation algorithms can use explicit (e.g., ratings) or behavioral (e.g., data on your usage of a system and your profile) to make recommendations. Recommendations can be tied to your goals, personality, and needs.

vii. **Innovate and surprise—give them the power and control:** Never give customers a reason to leave your firm. Innovate for them. Don't chase innovation made by others. Pioneer it. Stay ahead of the curve. Return on innovation is high. People who are innovating didn't come from Mars. They are scientists and researchers who need a good work environment, and they will make your customers happy beyond imagination. Intelligent automation is about passing control to machines in a responsible way. One of the most dangerous things you do daily is driving. If machines are becoming reliable enough that we can pass the control of driving to autonomous cars, the time is coming when your customers will be giving control of their portfolios to trustworthy machines. Are we ready for that world?

viii. **Customer care system:** Every firm needs an elaborate and comprehensive care system that focuses on discovering and managing all aspects of customer care and experience. Optimize the channel by allocating proper resources across multiple channels, managing them, optimizing them, making them work as an integrated whole (Ngai et al., 2009). Customers should have a flawless multichannel access to their accounts and analysis. This means they should be able to switch between digital devices and humans easily and find the best possible service from the combination of the two.

ix. **Rewards and incentives:** Can you figure out ways to learn from customers such that their insights and experience can be leveraged, and they can be rewarded for being a partner? We often ignore that even wealth and asset management is a two-way process where we learn from customers as much as they depend on us. I vividly recall that once I was on the customer side and was able to share my insights with the asset management firm that readjusted my (and many other clients') portfolio based on my insights. Customers are a great source of information.

x. **Education and coaching:** Wealth management is more than just about wealth. It is about the well-being of your client. Including the well-being coaching and investment education are important considerations for empathy-compassion-based marketing. Are your machines capable of educating and coaching your customers?

xi. **Community:** Humans are social creatures. Giving customers the ability to form groups and become part of the communities is a powerful incentive for customers to stay in the world you create for them. In this world, customers can interact with other humans or machines. They can play games, relax, explore, and make sense of their environments. Can you provide them an environment where they can do all of the above?

xii. **Partners in governance, CSR, and compliance:** Customers can be a big source of governance, CSR, and compliance. Being able to tap into customers is a major source of ensuring that the protective shield stays intact. Having the ability to quickly observe and learn from customers about their positions and views on challenges such as climate change, poverty, corruption, and so forth, are important data points for architecting CSR programs.

CX gives us more than just the 360-degree customer view and enables us to leverage the full power of customer data. Companies today compete on the basis of CX. With those foundational concepts, we move to the next chapter to focus on marketing.

 REFERENCES

Aktepe, A., et al. (2015) "Customer Satisfaction and Loyalty Analysis with Classification Algorithms and Structural Equation Modeling." *Computers and Industrial Engineering.* [Online]. 8695–106. Available from: http://dx.doi .org/10.1016/j.cie.2014.09.031.

Ayoubi, M. (2016) "Customer Segmentation Based on CLV Model and Neural Network." *International Journal of Computer Science Issues.* [Online]. 13 (2), 31–37. Available from: http://ijcsi.org/contents.php?volume=13&&issue=2.

Chaturvedi, I., et al. (2016) "Learning Word Dependencies in Text by Means of a Deep Recurrent Belief Network." *Knowledge-Based Systems.* [Online]. 108144–154.

Form, S., and Kaernbach, C. (2018) "More Is Not Always Better: The Differentiated Influence of Empathy on Different Magnitudes of Creativity." *Europe's Journal of Psychology.* [Online]. 14 (1), 54–65.

Gennaioli, N., et al. (2012) "Money Doctors." Chicago Booth Research Paper No. 12–39, June 11, 2012, 1–40.

Hattula, J. D., et al. (2015) "Managerial Empathy Facilitates Egocentric Predictions of Consumer Preferences." *Journal of Marketing Research.* [Online]. 52 (2), 235–252. Available from: http://journals.ama.org/doi/10.1509/jmr.13.0296.

Judge, K. (2018) "Investor-Driven Financial Innovation." *Harvard Business Law Review.* [Online]. 8291.

Junqué De Fortuny, E., et al. (2014) "Evaluating and Understanding Text-Based Stock Price Prediction Models." *Information Processing and Management* [Online]. 50 (2), 426–441.

Ngai, E. W. T., et al. (2009) "Application of Data Mining Techniques in Customer Relationship Management: A Literature Review and Classification." *Expert Systems with Applications.* [Online]. 36 (2 PART 2), 2592–2602. Available from: http://dx.doi.org/10.1016/j.eswa.2008.02.021.

Shaw, C. (2015) "Unlocking the Hidden Customer Experience." [online]. Available from: https://engagecxmarketing.com/wp-content/uploads/2015/12/11.40-Colin-Shaw-Beyond-Philosophy.pdf. [online]. Available from: https://engagecxmarketing.com/wp-content/uploads/2015/12/11.40-Colin-Shaw-Beyond-Philosophy.pdf.

Swift, R. S. (2001) *Accelerating Customer Relationships: Using CRM and Relationship Technologies.* Upper Saddle River. N.J.: Prentice Hall.

Thakur, R., and Workman, L. (2016) "Customer Portfolio Management (CPM) for Improved Customer Relationship Management (CRM): Are Your Customers Platinum, Gold, Silver, or Bronze?" *Journal of Business Research.* [Online]. 69 (10), 4095–4102. Available from: http://dx.doi.org/10.1016/j.jbusres.2016.03.042.

Tsai, C. F., and Lu, Y. H. (2009) "Customer Churn Prediction by Hybrid Neural Networks." *Expert Systems with Applications.* [Online]. 36 (10), 12547–12553. Available from: http://dx.doi.org/10.1016/j.eswa.2009.05.032.

CHAPTER ELEVEN

Marketing Science

ARKETING IS ONE OF THE MOST important functions in asset management. As Sandra Murphy, author of *The Road to AUM*, clarifies, performance on its own is not a competitive differentiation since it is already expected (Murphy, 2018). Just as an automobile company cannot claim mobility of a vehicle as a differentiator (since it is an automobile's basic functionality and hence expected attribute), asset management cannot build a competitive advantage on the basis of performance only. Marketing drives demand for product and services. It understands what customers need and want and develops the best way to communicate the value proposition, gets people interested and excited, and as a consequence, influences demand. AI provides a powerful way to develop and implement marketing strategy. In fact, AI is revolutionizing marketing. In this chapter we discover how to deploy AI to improve marketing in asset management.

WHO UNDERTAKES THIS RESPONSIBILITY?

The head of marketing is responsible for undertaking the AI-centric transformation. The CMO's strategy must align with the corporate strategy and should be consistent with the overall strategy of the firm, customer experience (CX), and sales. This function can create a powerful effect, but conventional marketing is expensive, ineffective, and often unproductive. Companies spend millions, but the return on marketing is often low. At the TSAM (The

Summit of Asset Management) event in Boston, Dominica Ribeiro, head of institutional marketing (North America) of State Street Global Advisors presented the opening keynote titled "Fearless Girl: Strategy Built with a Purpose." The presentation referred to the bronze sculpture that was installed in the financial district of Manhattan and which coincided with State Street Global Advisors' first anniversary of their Gender Diversity Index fund. Placed near the famous Charging Bull, Fearless Girl was deployed to promote awareness for gender equality and the importance of recruiting women in leadership. This is a great example of how low-budget, high-impact marketing can create a powerful advantage. Clearly, State Street determined that gender equality was a major concern. In the era of equal pay and the Women's March, the world was already paying attention to these important issues. Being able to discover such ideas, understand the sentiment and collective consciousness, and take action to create something powerful and viral can be enabled by AI.

HOW TO APPLY AI FOR MARKETING

Marketing planning is composed of five steps:

- Perform assessment;
- Understand your data;
- Develop strategy;
- Plan product portfolio; and
- Execute.

BEGIN WITH ASSESSMENT

Investment management firms are often led by people who specialize in finance and investment management. Marketing is usually not the strong suit of financial people. Even when marketing departments are established or marketing activities are undertaken, sometimes their value is not fully recognized. Here are some of the areas in which significant marketing problems exist:

1. The CMO organization performs an honest assessment of the depth of the firm's understanding of its customers. Many firms remain unclear about who their target customer is. This leads to a mismatch between product offerings and marketing approach. Managers want to target

the institutional market, but their approach to business, brand, and communications is retail style. Within the broad market of retail and institutional, several subsegments exist, and each requires developing a deep understanding of customers. This insight should be taken at the microcosm level of each customer. In other words, investment firms should strive to gain a good understanding of each of their customers, and the customer profile should be comprehensive. The AI technology can help develop those insights. This, obviously, needs to be catered to the product being marketed. One firm can have different products and that means it will have to pursue multiple initiatives to understand a diverse set of customers.

2. The CMO organization analyzes its current process on how it discovers new customers. Identifying, attracting, and onboarding new customers is fundamental for the sustainability of the firm. This continues to be a challenge for many firms. The problem exists on both the retail and the institutional sides. Once marketing develops customer-specific understanding, reaching out to new customers is an area where AI can help tremendously.

3. Communicating the value proposition to customers is key in the asset management business. This is not analogous to stating that the manager has performed over few years. The past performance, while an important consideration, is not an indication for future performance. Communicating beyond the performance includes the unique approach, philosophy, and angle undertaken by the manager. Identifying, helping develop, and communicating the value proposition of the offering is marketing's job. The complexity of the financial products is often overwhelming. The CMO organization measures its ability to develop and communicate the value proposition for the firm.

4. The CMO organization also assesses its process and capability for identifying, clarifying, and communicating the competitive advantage. Communicating the competitive advantage—specifically in terms of the philosophy and the approach of the manager—is an important consideration. Your competitive advantage reflects your strategy but is also influenced by the positioning and strategies of your competitors. A competitive advantage must translate into business results.

5. The next phase of assessment happens when the CMO organization assesses whether the firm is ready to go prime-time—especially if it is targeting the institutional market. The testing for organizational readiness for retail is process-centric, and as long as the process works, you can conclude that the firm is ready, and a marketing strategy can be executed.

With the institutional market, the operational and organizational readiness are configured and customized to the market segment and customers your firm is targeting. This implies that a marketing plan should be tailored to that specific segment, should have consistency, and should be perfectly timed.

6. Besides the customized marketing strategy targeted toward a specific customer segment, building the brand and the brand identity are never-ending pursuits. The CMO organization performs an assessment of the brand, brand recognition, share-of-voice, share-of-mind, credibility, brand personality, and other brand-related factors. The weaknesses and areas of improvement are identified.

7. In some cases, a constant struggle exists between building a brand around the firm or around a person. A firm should be designed to be more than the brand of one or two people. Despite such an aspiration, the fact is that a few individuals often become the face of the firm. They are the ones who are invited to speak at conferences or to be interviewed on Bloomberg or CNBC. Finding that balance is essential to protect the firm and its clients.

 ## KNOW YOUR DATA

Data for marketing in asset management comes from many traditional and nontraditional sources. Depending on the strategy of the firm, you can determine how to develop and deploy marketing capabilities for various segments, but the data sources for various segments may have some similarities. Keep in mind that as we perform data assessment, we are not only seeking customer insights, we are also trying to discover usable patterns for understanding our competitors, partners, emerging environmental factors and trends, and other factors that can influence demand. Additionally, data here implies all types of data including text files, audio, video, and others. Consider the following sources of data:

- **Social media:** Are you capturing sophisticated social media data to understand your customer base (or competitors or others), their behaviors, preferences, and networks?
- **News, articles, coverage:** Are you organizing and collecting content that can be mined to develop insights about customers, partners, competitors, and others?

- **Financial statements and reports:** Significant knowledge can be gained about both institutional clients and retail clients from regulatory filings.
- **Analyst coverage:** Are you studying analyst coverage to develop deeper insights about your clients?
- **Marketing literature:** Are you collecting and organizing the marketing literature from your target customers (and competitors)?
- **Product communications:** Have you captured the product communications from your competitors?
- **Conferences:** Are you tracking which conferences your target clients (institutional) are speaking at and what they are presenting?
- **Interviews:** Are you capturing interviews of your target clients? Have you interviewed target clients about their needs, strategies, challenges, and concerns? Is that data digitized so it becomes minable?
- **RFI/RFP information:** The RFI (request for information) or RFP (request for proposals) questionnaires sent to you from your existing or target institutional client also give you a sense of what is important for your clients. Every request for additional information, every questionnaire sent to you, every request for clarification, every communication from clients becomes minable information. Are you organizing and collecting that data?
- **Market research questionnaires:** Are you using and storing conventional market research tools such as questionnaires, video interviews, and other traditional market research data?
- **Behavioral observations:** In today's data-rich environment, are you collecting data related to human behavior in unrelated situations? For example, knowing how people behave when markets decline rapidly can provide insights about behavioral marketing. Are you conducting such experiments?
- **Architected or simulated environments:** Simulated environments are a powerful way to collect highly actionable information. For example, JP Morgan launched an advertising campaign where they provide a tool that gives various scenarios and you are asked to make different choices in terms of what decisions you would have made in your portfolio under those market or economic conditions. As you participate in a simulated scenario, JP Morgan can learn about you and how you will behave (Morgan, 2018).
- **Customer interactions:** Are you keeping data on all customer interactions with the firm—whether such interactions happened online, over the phone, or in person? Remember that every time a customer uses your online tools, that constitutes as customer interaction, and hence it provides significant usable information.

- **Transactional data:** This is the most often mined data. It is based on the transactions between your firm and the customer and can also be transactional information by your client and a third party.

Scaling and using the above data become the foundational elements of deploying an AI-centric and modern strategy. This is what enables transformation. Your assessment of review of data capabilities is the cornerstone of your intelligent automation–centric asset management marketing plan.

THE AI PLAN FOR ASSET MANAGEMENT MARKETING

The AI plan for asset management marketing is developed for five focus areas:

- Strategic planning;
- Product portfolio management;
- Communications;
- Relationship management; and
- Marketing execution.

PERFORM STRATEGIC PLANNING

Marketing sophisticated products and services to customers requires sophisticated planning. A reactive marketing department stays in a reactionary mode to the needs of the organization—often falling behind the rate of change and always staying in catch-up mode. A proactive marketing department prepares itself for the change and leads the change. Setting the course for success, intelligent automation of marketing research and analysis capabilities is the only way to ensure that the firm can create value during change.

Strategy development looks at the big picture. Two types of mistakes can be made here. The first is that the intelligent automation apparatus for marketing strategy is applied too narrowly. An example of this may be when your firm decides to launch a new product, and marketing begins its strategy development process in response to product launch. It has strategic depth in relation to that one product but not a framework of capabilities that goes beyond a single product. This is not strategy. You must have market analysis, positioning, differentiation, brand, opportunity identification, and customer insights—all set up such that products and services can be developed and launched with the scaffolding provided by the marketing organization. The second mistake happens when you go so broad that you fail to develop deep skills to support your firm's unique needs. These marketing departments develop shallow or a thin veneer of strategic depth and, while they check all the boxes, they lack strategic depth.

Market segmentation and analysis: The market for financial products and services is constantly changing. It is also being affected by major global trends. For example, the Covid-19 pandemic has created new challenges and opened avenues to help clients in various ways. AI provides the most empathetic approach to develop a deeper understanding of customers and for segmenting them in accordance with their needs/wants, and for discovering unique match patterns for existing and future products.

Finding segments to group customers in ways that they differ and can be served in unique ways (for example, product, response to marketing, or actions), marketers can improve their decisions related to positioning, marketing campaigns, communications, and products.

One way to segment customers is by using labeled data. For example, you can use the data obtained from existing customers (survey, feedback, usage, or other type of data) to predict similarities and differences between customers. You can analyze how customers behaved differently in various situations. When markets experienced a hiccup, who panicked, who made calm and calculated moves, and who was indifferent? This does not mean that a firm should only look for classification based on existing labeled data. In many cases expert knowledge is either not available or too expensive to assemble. In other cases getting expert knowledge can be a source of bias. Knowing more about what you already know may not add incremental value. Hence, one way to obtain market segments is to apply unsupervised or semi-supervised learning approaches. Unsupervised learning can enable the search for new niches and identify better matches for customer segments. It can help identify clusters that we do not know exist. It can help discover previously unknown knowledge about customers. The typical methods used are k-means and self-organizing feature maps (SOFM). The process, as explained in previous chapters, is to use input data without knowing the outputs. The algorithm finds interesting patterns based on the input data. It is quite possible that it can find awkward or unexplainable patterns. This search for discovering these segments should become an ongoing exercise.

A marketing science department discovers these patterns and then makes several assessments, such as:

- How can you best explain the segments with business logic or explanation?
- What actions can be taken with the discovered segments?
- How can you use this information for products, services, or other reasons (e.g., brand)?
- Are segments large enough to create value for your business? What is their financial feasibility?
- Who can take the most advantage of the segments?
- Can you use that information for new product development and design?
- Have you considered the social, political, organizational, and other aspects of identifying certain segments? For example, an identified segment, when acted upon, can turn out to be discriminatory toward others.

It is through the prism of marketing research and analysis that we identify opportunities. The patterns of needs and wants when bridged to feasible solutions result in value creation. As we recognize various market segments, the ability to link products and services, explain the segments, and conceptualize solutions helps us develop our strategy.

Our marketing science strategy should include our brand and positioning strategy. AI helps in identifying not only what our brand means for people but also what is the meaning behind and the value of competitors' brands. From colors to image analysis of logos, personality of brand, brand identity, formats and fonts, and other brand features are deciphered with the lens of human perception. How we perceive brands unlocks the mystery of our relationship with them. Different types of data—text, video, images, audio, ethnography, netnography—can be used to develop a better understanding of a brand. The models used are typically natural language processing classification models applied to deciphering the personality, identity, and value of brands. Notice that it can also show the differences between how you (internal management team and employees) perceive the brand vs. how customers and external parties view it.

AI also helps to decipher the best go to market strategy for your firm and products/services. For example, by mining data for previous product launches, the approaches employed, and relative success, you can determine which can be the most effective strategy for you.

In this regard, it is extremely important to recognize that what we discussed above was the "push" part of the marketing strategy. In other words, it is something that we are trying to evaluate, develop, and design. In addition to what we want to accomplish, there are forces that are not in our control. They are the "pull" part of marketing. For example, our clients will be deploying systems to develop insights about us. An institutional investor may deploy an automated system to evaluate the performance, philosophy, approach, people, and methods of managers. How we communicate to the external world can have an effect on how we show up in those systems.

MANAGE PRODUCT PORTFOLIO WITH AI

Your product portfolio is composed of existing products as well as products in the pipeline or your future products. Analyzing this portfolio requires intelligent automation related to how the products are developed, their value proposition and customer benefits, fee structure analysis, and life cycle management. Development of products in accordance with the needs and wants of the identified segments is helpful. What is more helpful is to have clients actively involved in the development of our offerings. Feedback from customers matters. This is true for both active and passive investment management. Every interaction with customers becomes the opportunity to develop your product. We approach marketing automation with design elements that are composed of four interdependent artifacts.

- **Product development manager:** This is an innovation driving portal that links customer feedback with innovation. It also serves as the sandbox for testing new products and services. The artifact uses NLP to extract meaning of needs and wants. It sources, filters, and evaluates new products and can generate ideas for new products (Soukhoroukova et al., 2012). This artifact uses both supervised learning and unsupervised learning to generate innovation. From looking for metaphors to trends, the algorithms explore contexts and relationships between concepts and their non-conscious and conscious connections. Self-generation of product ideas can happen from human need/want exploration or from simulating financial product ideas.
- **Value proposition developer:** AI helps develop the value proposition by studying the benefits offered by competing products as well as by recording and analyzing product-specific communications from competitors. In this artifact, we aim to extract meaningful information about how customers

perceive the value proposition of the offering. To perform this, gather data about customers (retail or institutional). Try to access both non-conscious and conscious data. Non-conscious data is data from activities that we conduct where our primary goal is not to consciously supply data or information—such as playing a game. Conscious data is from activities where we consciously supply data—an example would be writing an article. Use this data to extract people's understanding of risk and reward. Contextualize the analysis by understanding and giving meaning to the risk-reward relationship. For example, you may discover that clients who view ETF as less risky do not care much about fixed income, and they prefer ETF because they feel they have more control over it since they can understand it. Remember the "don't get mad" ad campaign of E-Trade that, it seems, focused on millennials by making them aware of their weak financial position relative to big money while simultaneously giving them hope that they can get there.

- **Fee manager:** This artifact collects information on and analyzes fee structures of competitive products. Run this artifact on data from competitors' pricing and fee structures. Analyze the data to predict what would constitute a reasonable fee for your product. Product features, brand, and other information about competitors can provide the input data. Another version of this could be targeted to the institutional clients where in addition to the product-specific data, there is information on the clients so you can study what you can expect to charge that firm. Just as 4-bedroom house prices may be different in New York City and Phoenix (i.e., location makes all the difference), different institutional clients may pay different fees for the same product depending on how it is sold.

- **Life cycle manager:** This tracks the demand patterns for your products as well as competitors' products. Using various data sources (analyst reports, articles, etc.), this artifact predicts the strength of demand for various asset classes and products.

TRANSFORM YOUR COMMUNICATIONS

To build a strong communications platform, design an AI platform that discovers, measures, updates, evaluates, builds, and recommends communications to engage key stakeholders. This is a broad function since it includes stakeholders such as regulators, society, partners, suppliers, investors, employees, and customers. These days such a platform will help drive communications that add value for all stakeholders, personalize messaging, match signal with targets, and provide thought leadership.

The general platform for that capability performs the following:

- Gathers, analyzes, and synthesizes data.
- Searches and classifies targets on the basis of multidimensional criteria.
- Extracts usable information from communications in the industry.
- Synthesizes information to extract metaphors, cognitive references, trends, and contexts.
- Links messaging signals with messaging receivers' profiles.
- Customizes messaging.

The effect of communications is measured, and communications are directed in a goal-oriented manner for value drivers such as influencing, demand generation, and lead generation.

 ## BUILD RELATIONSHIPS

The CX-centric discussion we had in the previous chapter provides the foundation for this platform. A relationship management platform is critical for institutional relationship management. Reference management and account-based marketing are key components of this platform—however, unlike traditional systems, both aspects have a predictive nature. Use this functionality to determine how and from whom to generate references and predict account conversions.

 ## EXECUTE WITH EXCELLENCE

Build an AI platform that enables you to execute with confidence. For example, budget and talent management, performance management, and goals management can be accomplished effectively with AI. Marketing campaigns, initiatives, and projects should be assessed in accordance with their costs and effect. Your marketing execution platform should be able to give you a good estimate for your marketing plan and also optimize and prioritize the plan for you to maximize the return on investment.

REFERENCES

J.P. Morgan advertisement. (2018). Available from: https://portfolioperspec tives.ft.com/.

Murphy, S. P. (2018) *The Road to AUM: Driving Assets Under Management Through Effective Marketing and Sales.* Noble Ark Ventures.

Soukhoroukova, A., et al. (2012) "Sourcing, Filtering, and Evaluating New Product Ideas: An Empirical Exploration of the Performance of Idea Markets." *Journal of Product Innovation Management.* [Online]. 29 (1), 100–112.

CHAPTER TWELVE

Land that Institutional Investor with AI

ISCOVERING AND ESTABLISHING A LONG-TERM relationship with an institutional customer is the dream of many asset managers. The process is never easy, but it has great benefits. It establishes credibility, brings the right investment, creates a stronger brand, and helps asset managers acquire new professional skills. The ever-increasing requirements to support the institutional clients keep firms on their toes and help them build professional-grade processes. AI has now become fundamental to building, managing, and keeping institutional relationships. We will use the term institutional relationship management science (IRMS) to describe our plan for IRMS automation. In this chapter we show you how to build the platform.

 ## WHO IS RESPONSIBLE FOR IRMS AUTOMATION?

If the firm has recognized that its strategic plan includes attracting institutional clients, then it becomes the responsibility of the entire firm to support that strategic goal. From an automation perspective, the CMO organization can take a lead on these initiatives; however, a cross-functional approach will be necessary to create meaningful results. In smaller firms, the entire management team works to implement IRMS.

IS IRMS YOUR CRM SYSTEM?

IRMS is the deployment of integrated technologies and scientific methods that result in maximizing the ability to attract, maintain, and enhance institutional clients. IRMS is not your run-of-the-mill CRM system. It is not about recording contact history or how many kids the target has. This is not to diminish the value of CRM—as CRM has tremendous value—but merely to point out that IRMS is different than CRM. IRMS is a scientific method and a platform to pursue and close on institutional relationships. This platform technology has six areas of technology solutions that are deployed for maximum result:

KNOW THYSELF: AUTOMATED SELF-DISCOVERY

Start by developing a better understanding of who you are. What parts of your strategy, approach, and philosophy make you different or more appealing? Is it possible that you have the greatest strategy, but you have not been able to communicate it effectively to investors? Trying to develop a self-understanding is not easy. First, who wants to be self-critical or even objective when it comes to analyzing yourself? Second, how can we overcome our own biases? An automated self-discovery module analyzes your firm (and other firms) and enhances your self-awareness as a firm. Here is the process for self-discovery:

- Deploy the algorithms to identify the key metaphors, concepts, ideas, words, and phrases that are yours (and your competitors' and institutional partners').
- Direct other algorithms to identify the contexts in which your products become solutions to some problems. Is it the problem of convenience that your target customer is experiencing? Is it the problem of risk? Is it fear of failing to diversify? Is it getting tired of same old, same old? Your algorithm will create a relationship between your product, the mental models you think people have, and the real-life situations that you are trying to discover. Your own communication style will be the proof of your understanding of your offerings and customers. In addition to your own style, you are also discovering and cataloguing the cognitive maps of competitors and your institutional targets.

AUTOMATED ASSET CLASS ANALYSIS

You deploy this module to enable automated analysis of asset classes. You deploy your algorithms to study asset classes. The goal here is not to reproduce the information that you can easily acquire from data suppliers but to develop new insights about the asset classes.

These new insights can be both empirical facts and qualitative and behavioral insights. They can be captured from narratives and developed to observe the portfolio utility and perception of potential customers. The viewpoints of various target investors expressed should be captured and information about their preferences extracted. Are they expressing interest? Are they showing concerns? Why do they like a certain asset class? Compare that to others' and your own understanding, and try to assess what this investor is missing or how your pitch would tie into the narrative that this investor is pursuing.

AUTOMATED INSTITUTIONAL ANALYSIS

Point your algorithms to collect extreme intelligence on your target institutional investors. You must try to learn everything about them that can be learned before even asking your first questions. Behind every narrative that gets directly communicated to you is another reality. That reality is not shared because what people often disclose is what they want but not what they fear. Those inhibitions and trepidations are strategically placed behind the protective shields of composure. Our job is to not only understand the stated strategies of our target AUM investors but to understand *them*. Point your algorithms to pick up on their speech patterns, their use of words, their sentiment, their use of metaphors, their guidance. Create a personalized profile of each investor (people and firm). Capture their styles, investment preferences, and mental models on how they view the world. Develop the cognitive map that shows their emotional attachments and logical interpretations. Your output is an extensive analysis to determine your investor target's views of asset classes, investment vehicles, operating styles, interests, and others. Have another set of algorithms targeted on what others say about your institutional investor. Whether covered in news media or comments on news stories, all of that content helps in painting a picture by connecting the dots. Extract those stories and narratives for sensemaking. Finally, have a third set of algorithms that are aimed at the competitors of your target. Perform a comparative review of the styles, positions, views, operating styles, and other such factors. Perform the cognitive distance exercise to determine how your target investor is semantically, emotionally, strategically, and in other ways different than the competitors'. Use all that above information for account planning.

 ## AUTOMATED STRUCTURE AND TERMS ANALYSIS

Analyzing structure and terms for institutional offerings is your best friend. If they like you, the discussion will quickly turn to the structure and terms. It helps to understand the terms and structures that are preferred by your investors—as well as the ones used for products, investment vehicles, and asset classes that you are proposing and developing. Information about the existing structures gives you ideas about how to structure your deals. Begin by collecting data sets on structures and terms. Use natural language processing to extract and classify products based on terms and structures. Map the possibilities and then determine the match between the style and preference of the institutional investor and the various structures and terms. Compare them with your competitors' structures and terms.

 ## AUTOMATED FEE ANALYSIS

Fee structures are analyzed in accordance with the products, structures, and terms. Building a reference catalogue for fee structures can be extremely helpful when trying to explain to institutional investors your value proposition and fee structure. Your anticipated fee structures can be studied in comparison to your competitors'. Your automated fee analyst also suggests to you what is a reasonable fee that will increase the likelihood of your winning an institutional client.

 ## AUTOMATED COMMUNICATIONS

Deploy this intelligent module to learn about your communication style, your competitors' communication, and institutional investors' communications. Communications is composed of several areas:

- Understand your own communication styles;
- Develop insights into your competitors' communications;

- Learn about the communications of your target clients;
- Break down communications analysis by:
  - Types of communications—what are various mediums used by you or your competitors?
  - Communications vehicles—what are the specific vehicles used and why?
  - Semantics—what is the semantic composition of messaging?
  - Images and videos—what kind of images and videos, imagery and visual elements are being used and why? What do they symbolize and how do they differ from others?
  - Music—what music is used, and what are the contexts driving the music?
  - Sounds—what are various sounds used in messaging?
  - Location—what types of virtual, physical, or conceptual locations (e.g., places, conferences, or earnings calls) are being used for communications and why?
  - Storylines—what is your main storyline, what is your competitor's storyline, how do they vary by products and markets?
  - Themes—what are the major themes in communications? Try to detect changes in themes and storylines.
  - Rational-emotional breakdown—what is the breakdown of communications between emotions and rational or empirical reasoning? What are the specific elements of emotional messaging and what feelings are they appealing to or what feelings are they expected to trigger? Are there any underlying triggers that are less obvious?
  - Sentiment—what is the sentiment attached to your or your competitor's messaging?
  - Semiotics—what is the symbology used and why?
  - People, celebrities, personalities used in communications—which people or celebrities are being used as spokespeople and why?
  - Tone—what is the overall tone of messaging? Is it a relaxed tone or more aggressive tone?
  - Narratives—what are the main narratives? Narratives are more than the storyline. They have deeper features and represent stories. Computational narratology is an emerging and highly promising area of inquiry in AI.
  - Philosophies: What philosophies or approaches are pursued by your client?
- Your journey to assess the communications is composed of:
  - Algorithms are targeted to extract the above elements.

- With the aid of the above information we can now learn about the product placement and presentation to a client. This happens by algorithmically mapping brand identity and extracting creative elements of a story.
- Measuring the comparative effectiveness of various communications.

 ## UNLEASH THE POWER OF KNOWING

With the above tool set you are ready to turn your institutional investor relationship into a science and transform your approach from a narrow field view to a strategic viewpoint. You can develop deeper relationships and develop a profound understanding of your client.

CHAPTER THIRTEEN

Sales Science

I F MARKETING IS ABOUT MAXIMIZING DEMAND, sales transforms the demand signals into revenue streams. It includes processes such as prospecting, presenting, identifying objections and roadblocks, forecasting, negotiating, and closing. Intelligent automation of the sales process builds on marketing automation.

WHAT IS SALES SCIENCE?

Sales science is the scientific management of sales. As the world shifts to modern technologies, an equal and parallel sensemaking (Weick, 1995; Reynolds, 2015) is needed on the sales/marketing sides. It is the process by which people give meaning to their collective experiences. It has been defined as "the ongoing retrospective development of plausible images that rationalize what people are doing" (Weick et al., 2005). It is a space where plausible stories are shaped and shared, and a collective and coherent meaning develops. In underdeveloped sales approaches, the narratives are usually absent or misaligned between firms and their clients.

New challenges demand the introduction of new technologies. Sensemaking is not about buying some planning software or implementing CRM—it is mostly about extracting and shaping the shared narratives. In sales, it is about creating metacognitive structures about the offerings and aligning them with the perceived benefits of the clients such that a shared meaning develops.

The meaning developed must be contextually connected with the needs and wants of the client.

Since sensemaking emerges from being able to develop a shared sense of meaning, values, stories, narratives, and viewpoints, it must precede sales and marketing execution (Neill et al., 2007) and use both a priori (reasoning, theory) and a posteriori (experience-centric) knowledge to establish that contextual sensemaking. This means that asset management firms must understand the value of analyzing social, behavioral, and cultural aspects as well as the narratology of selling. In essence sales is about sense-giving to clients from social coherence, relatedness, and shared values.

Enhancing interpretive capabilities of clients and systematically developing sensemaking mechanisms shape sales and marketing strategy and are precursors to any marketing strategy (Krush et al., 2013; Neill et al., 2007). The unique nature of financial sales, the importance of trust building, the complexity of the product, the risk, and other factors make the use of simpler models difficult. Hence while models such as value pyramids (Almquist et al., 2019) can help triangulate on value determinants, they are not easily transferable to an asset management client without a socially constructed contextualized awakening.

WHO IS RESPONSIBLE FOR IMPLEMENTING SALES SCIENCE?

Depending upon the size and structure of the firm, the intelligent automation of sales is the responsibility of sales and marketing organizations. The head of sales may report to the CEO. Additionally, sales must not be perceived as a one-time thing. It is a continuous process. Both in retail and institutional sales, executive leaders must play a significant role.

ARE YOU DRIVING THIS IN SALES?

We often refer to certain repulsive salespeople with the stereotype "used car salesman." What is implied in that euphemism is an aversion for the salesperson who tends to place his or her interest above your interest. This person is not doing a fair value exchange; he or she is manipulating you into a transaction. Real sales are different—in fact, I believe they are one of the most noble endeavors in society.

The discussion below is designed for institutional clients but is equally applicable to retail with a slight conceptual readjustment. Here is how to think about strategic sales:

Reframe the organizational memory: Tapping into the organizational declarative, procedural, and emotional memory helps understand the current narratives (Akgün et al., 2014). Declarative memory is about rules and facts, procedural memory is about processes, and emotional memory is about experiences. When it comes to AI, most companies do not have a reference point in their memory, so they tap into their existing experience with financial products. They will view you through the same lens as they see their other suppliers and partners. Working with those three organizational memories can get you in the door. Detaching clients from the old declarative memory, procedural memory, and emotional memory to help them develop new frameworks can unlock tremendous benefits for your firm—but it carries more risk. However, it can be achieved by a systematic introduction of symbols, ontological structures, and experiences.

Create a new narrative: Sensemaking in financial sales includes novel situations, and that type of sensemaking depends on circumstances that are filled with dynamic complexity (Colville et al., 2012). That is where companies need to answer the question, "What is the story?" or even "What is my story?" Colville et al. clarify that this requires higher complexity of thought with simplicity of action—a concept they call Simplexity (Colville et al., 2012). This implies that a new reality needs to be created for clients where the new narrative is not derived from old stories.

Discover the client's identity: Contextualized meaning of who people think they are, their self-image, and how they interpret events and their relationship to technology affect their decisions (Carter and Grover, 2015; Burke and Stets, 2009). Identity can be social, organizational, and corporate (Cornelissen et al., 2007) and is an important consideration during major technology change events in companies (Alvarez, 2008). Yes, you can brag about your technological transformation to your prospects. As AI enters sales, deciphering identity during technology-related change helps guide through complex situations (Stein et al., 2013).

Establish context and extract cues: Even though you would expect financial sales to be based on analytical rigor, sales narratives are equally important. Context gives people cues. Extracting those cues is important to establish what information is relevant and which explanations are more likely to be accepted by people (Stacey et al., 2007). These cues are analogous to points of reference to link ideas to a broader meaning. Like pieces of a puzzle coming together, it is from cues that people develop a sense of what is occurring (Weick, 1995).

Enact the narratives: Narratives and dialogues are sources of enactment. While speaking, narrative accounts are developed, and those narratives help people understand what they think. Narratives are also a source of stability during change (Vaara et al., 2016). Storytelling helps (Gabriel, 2000). Actions themselves represent and are guided by narratives (Gergen and Gergen, 2006). Narratives can be deployed in creative ways to increase human capital (Dumay and Roslender, 2013). Running accounts of what is transpiring in people's worlds give meaning to their realities (Isabella, 1990). How narratives are constructed affects decisions (Abolafia, 2010).

Solidify plausible narrative: The narrative does not have to be accurate, as long as it is plausible. Since change infuses conflicting interests, politics, and multiple shifting identities, accuracy is less desirable than plausibility (Weick, 1995). Plausible does not mean lies or deceitful information. It means tying stories to numbers and numbers to stories. As Currie and Brown state in their article (Currie and Brown, 2003), "In a sense, organizations literally are the narratives that people author in networks of conversations, the intertextuality of which sustains an accumulation of continuous and (sufficiently) consistent story lines that in turn maintain and objectify 'reality'" (Ford, 1999).

Decipher feedback processes: Understand what type of feedback processes are embedded in a firm. Both positive and negative loops should be analyzed to understand how organizations behave (Stacey, 2011).

Create a bold vision: Sensemaking demands that financial sales should be tied to different types of value creation but also to organizational memory contents that include forming new memories. In other words, your client experience is as important as your performance results. You need to constantly supply narratives to clients that address their experience and demonstrate your performance. Some narratives are derived from boldness of vision; others, from familiar stories. These stories—such as iconic stories of Steve Jobs at Apple—build our brands. Having the confidence that you hold the answers to what is important for a client is a powerful way to create change. These bold visions are set in powerful narratives, and such narratives are nurtured and carefully developed over time.

Deploy a portfolio strategy: Just as a portfolio manager creates diversification, it is critically important to simultaneously deploy both strategic and tactical sales (Terho, 2009). Strategic sales, if perceived as high risk, also carry a high reward.

HOW TO BUILD YOUR AI-BASED SALES SYSTEM

In the discussion below I will add to some of the ideas generated by Syam and Sharma, who introduced a comprehensive overview of what an AI technology platform for sales can look like (Syam and Sharma, 2018). They divide the sales process into seven steps of prospecting, pre-approach, approach, presentation, overcoming objections, close, and follow-up. I will explain the action plan for us in accordance with the same classification.

Prospecting

Algorithms can help extract customer behavioral orientation toward products and services. This can be used to generate proper demands estimates and sales forecasts. As identified in the previous chapters, there are several areas from which we can get highly usable data. Your scope for such efforts should include different types of data—structured and unstructured.

Use the data to identify leads and qualify prospects. Instead of chasing clients where there is little hope, your algorithm can help your identify clients with a higher likelihood of closing. Being able to do that early in the game means that you do not go down the rabbit hole where there is no end in sight.

As you build your prospecting capabilities, it is important to factor in that algorithms can help you achieve multidimensional lead generation. Multidimensional lead generation means that the (unsupervised) algorithm may be able to find patterns that you did not know exist. While classification can show you prospect segments based on your prior knowledge, algorithms such as clustering can get you to a new set of highly interesting leads. Algorithms can also suggest cross-selling and upselling opportunities.

Pre-Approach

Pre-approach concentrates on finding entry point to reach clients. These pathways are composed of two parallel activities: (1) identify ways in which you can be introduced to the target clients; and (2) identify which pathways will be best for your sales situation. The first is accomplished by using your firm's CRM data, data from professional social media (such as LinkedIn), and other systems to build an accessibility and approach profile for each client.

Approach

Approach gives us the best way to contact a client. The difference between pre-approach and approach is that while pre-approach gives clues into what is the best link to opening the door to a customer, approach tells us what the best mechanism for the first contact will be. Approach gives us information such as messaging content, delivery, and other such communication content.

Presentation

AI can help us generate presentation and content for our meetings. In the post-Covid-19 world where in-person contact is discouraged and online sales are becoming more common, being able to communicate effectively online is extremely important. Use the customer-specific information—such as customer profile, feedback, and customized value proposition—to generate presentation ideas. Evaluate your presentations to determine how your presentations rate in terms of various communications measures. Determine if you are using the words that close the sale and address multidimensional needs and wants of customers.

Overcoming Objections

AI can help generate questions to better prepare sales organizations. Algorithms can also determine which answers will be effective to address objections.

Closing

Developing a proposal is a critical element of institutional sales. Structuring, terms, and fees are important considerations. We proposed an algorithmic structure and terms analyst product in Chapter 12. Use the output of that product to develop client proposals. Deploy an algorithm to evaluate your proposals and study their effect. Which ones worked? Which ones failed? Can you find patterns in successful vs. unsuccessful proposals? Proposal evaluation can also show you main themes and analyze the narrative in the proposals.

Closing a sale is a complicated process. AI algorithms can help along the way. Specifically, if you have done your homework—as pointed out in Chapter 12—you have sufficient information about the client. You know about the gatekeepers and critics. You know their styles and approaches. You know what will work with them and how to manage them. Use the power of AI algorithms to develop the most effective strategy for managing the closing process.

Follow-Up

Customers should not be forgotten once the sale is complete. Making sure that you continue to assess the strength and depth of the relationship can make all the difference. Client emails, communications, and complaints should be taken seriously. Their feedback should be recorded as data. If they provide verbal feedback, make your best efforts to capture that. Use all of that to perform a constant analysis to determine not just patterns of problems but also patterns of opportunities. Use that to evaluate the depth and strength of the relationship. Even if the switching cost is low—for example, high liquidity position in a mutual fund—a customer may stay with you if the relationship is strong.

 REFERENCES

Abolafia, M. Y. (2010) "Narrative Construction as Sensemaking: How a Central Bank Thinks." *Organization Studies*. [Online]. 31 (3), 349–367.

Akgün, A. E., et al. (2014) "Antecedents and Consequences of Organizations' Technology Sensemaking Capability." *Technological Forecasting and Social Change*. [Online]. 88 (101), 216–231. Available from: http://dx.doi.org/10.1016/j.techfore.2014.07.002.

Almquist, E., et al. (2019) "The B2B Elements of Value." *Harvard Business Review* 96 (3), 18.

Alvarez, R. (2008) "Examining Technology, Structure and Identity During an Enterprise System Implementation." *Information Systems Journal*. [Online]. 18 (2), 203–224.

Burke, P. J., and Stets, J. E. (2009) *Identity Theory*. New York: Oxford University Press.

Carter, M., and Grover, V. (2015) "Theory and Review Me, Myself, and I (T): conceptualizing information technology and its implications." *MIS Quarterly*. [Online]. 39 (4), 931–957.

Colville, I., et al. (2012) "Simplexity: Sensemaking, Organizing and Storytelling for Our Time." *Human Relations*. [Online]. 65 (1), 5–15.

Cornelissen, J. P., et al. (2007) "Social Identity, Organizational Identity and Corporate Identity: Towards an Integrated Understanding of Processes, Patternings and Products." *British Journal of Management*. [Online]. 18 (SUPPL. 1).

Currie, G., and Brown, A. D. (2003) "A Narratological Approach to Understanding Processes of Organizing in a UK Hospital." *Human Relations* [Online]. 56 (5), 563–586.

Dumay, J., and Roslender, R. (2013) "Utilising Narrative to Improve the Relevance of Intellectual Capital." *Journal of Accounting & Organizational Change* [Online]. 9 (3), 248–279.

Ford, J. D. (1999) "Organizational Change as Shifting Conversations." *Journal of Organizational Change Management* 12480–500.

Gabriel, Y. (2000) *Storytelling in Organizations*. [Online]. Available from: http://www.oxfordscholarship.com/view/10.1093/acprof:oso/9780198290957.001.0001/acprof-9780198290957.

Gergen, M. M., and Gergen, K. J. (2006) "Narratives in Action." *Narrative Inquiry*. [Online]. 16 (1), 112–121. Available from: http://www.jbe-platform.com/content/journals/10.1075/ni.16.1.15ger.

Isabella, L. A. (1990) "Evolving Interpretations as a Change Unfolds: How Managers Construe Key Organizational Events." *Academy of Management journal* [Online]. 33 (1), 7–41.

Krush, M. T., et al. (2013) "Enhancing Organizational Sensemaking: An Examination of the Interactive Effects of Sales Capabilities and Marketing Dashboards." *Industrial Marketing Management:*. [Online]. 42 (5), 824–835. Available from http://dx.doi.org/10.1016/j.indmarman.2013.02.017.

Neill, S., et al. (2007) "Developing the Organization's Sensemaking Capability: Precursor to an Adaptive Strategic Marketing Response." *Industrial Marketing Management*. [Online]. 36 (6), 731–744.

Reynolds, N. (2015) "Making Sense of New Technology During Organisational Change." *New Technology, Work and Employment*. [Online]. 30 (2), 145–157.

Stacey, P., et al. (2007) "Making Sense of Stories: The Development of a New Mobile Computer Game." *Proceedings of the Annual Hawaii International Conference on System Sciences*. [Online]. (January 2017).

Stacey, R. D. (2011) *Strategic Management and Organisational Dynamics: The challenge of complexity to ways of thinking about organisations*. 6/e XML Vi. Pearson Learning Solutions.

Stein, M. K., et al. (2013) "Towards an Understanding of Identity and Technology in the Workplace." *Journal of Information Technology*. [Online]. 28 (3), 167–182.

Syam, N. and Sharma, A. (2018) Waiting for a sales renaissance in the fourth industrial revolution: machine learning and artificial intelligence in sales research and practice. *Industrial Marketing Management*. 69 (November 2017), 135–146. Available from: https://doi.org/10.1016/j.indmarman.2017.12.019.

Terho, H. (2009) "A Measure for Companies' Customer Portfolio Management." *Journal of Business-to-Business Marketing*. [Online]. 16 (4), 374–411.

Vaara, E., et al. (2016) "Narratives as Sources of Stability and Change in Organizations." *The Academy of Management Annals*. [Online]. 10 (1), 495–560.

Weick, K. E., et al. (2005) "Organizing and the Process of Sensemaking." *Organization Science*. [Online]. 16 (4), 409–421.

Weick, K. F. (1995) *Sensemaking in Organisations*. Thousand Oaks CA: Sage.

CHAPTER FOURTEEN

Investment: Managing the Returns Loop

W E HAVE DISCUSSED SEVERAL SUPPORT FUNCTIONS in asset management that can benefit from AI—but if Nabisco does not make good cookies or GM does not make good cars, it will not matter how well the support functions perform. Similarly, if your investment operation does not perform, you do not have a business. At the heart of your firm is your investment operation. Build it with care and diligence. This chapter is about helping you envision the modern-era investment function. Of course, how you structure the function will depend on your firm's core strategies and business model. However, I want to provide a general overview so you do not miss out on strategic areas and also because you can evolve into areas that are not part of your existing business model.

While our previous coverage was on the client loop, this chapter is about the returns loop.

WHO IS RESPONSIBLE FOR INVESTMENT MANAGEMENT?

The investment management function is headed by an investment professional who reports to the CEO. Unlike other business and functional areas, the work chain capabilities (data, model, evaluation, deployment, and performance) allocated to this function are greater in terms of both quality and quantity. The peculiar nature of finance machine learning requires a degree of separation with the business and other functional areas.

HOW TO APPROACH BUILDING THE NEW-ERA INVESTMENT FUNCTION?

In a world defined by uncertainty, we strive to predict the future behavior of assets. Through that fog of uncertainty, we try to estimate the difference between expected returns and actual returns and call it risk. We measure volatility by the distribution of returns. We try to extract information from the market to help us understand the behavior of an asset. We also mitigate the risk of the asset by combining it with different assets. We achieve diversification when we find and combine assets that are uncorrelated. We hedge by combining assets that are anticorrelated. With these basic functional combinations, we create complex analytical structures in our trades. We identify market inefficiencies, we try to understand the speed of absorption of information, we look for anomalies—all to give us a competitive edge.

Our two broad areas of constructing investment strategies come from fundamentals and markets. As we think about various approaches to designing our strategic footprint, it helps to understand the various models that are in play today:

Basic Fundamentals: Fundamentals approaches are based on analyzing information disclosed by firms in their financial statements. The traditional methods of fundamentals involve looking at each line item of the financial statement and linking it with an intrinsic valuation estimate that is future focused. The line items themselves can be viewed as drivers of valuation, and based on some assumptions, each is projected to estimate the future performance. Between balance sheets, cash flow statement, and income statement, we get operational insights into the business. From various disclosures and management commentary we learn about the business strategy and risks. Based on those insights, we make projections about the value of the asset. Such estimates include our assumptions about cost of capital, capital structure, and the operational measures (for example, revenues, costs, and A/R).

Business Fundamentals: The basic valuation, while helpful, does not consider several business dynamics. Management commentary and disclosures may not contain sufficient information to give us the picture we need. To gain further insight, we look at various operational information from business. How is the business's marketing? What is the supply chain risk? What is the new product launch pipeline? We extract information from macroeconomics and add dozens of economic indicators to our analysis. With operational considerations and economic analysis, we improve our basic fundamentals analysis and gain insights into the operational frameworks of business.

Competitive Fundamentals: A business is not an isolated system. While projecting future operational performance can be helpful, it does not explain the competitive dynamics in the industry. By understanding the competitive dynamics such as pricing strategies, new market entrants, substitutes, market shares, and technology changes, we can try to expand the business fundamentals. In this case, in addition to the above drivers, our investment targets (stock) were driven by the core business dynamics in which the target company operated.

Basic Market: As we move beyond simply trying to measure the valuation of a firm based on fundamentals and business dynamics—and take the firm into the ocean of the market—new realities reveal themselves. Beta is born. The stock is no longer a lone warrior. Its value is now relative. It is now part of the market and exposed to the sensitivity to the movement of the broader market—measured as beta. Market exposure was sufficient to drive returns. (Note that while CAPM could have been used to estimate the cost of capital in any of the valuations above, I wanted to show the progression of thinking. For instance, Graham's work on valuation in the pre-CAPM time; see Graham and Dodd, 1951.)

Fundamentals with Expectations: An alternative valuation is derived from the expectations analysis where each value driver (you can think of it as each line item from financial statements and the related ratios) is viewed as composed of an intrinsic valuation system adjusted for shareholder expectations. For instance, if market expectations about earnings were higher than what the firm delivered, the stock value may decline even if its earnings rose. This type of valuation, risk, and reward signals were embedded in our behavior. It was assumed that based on the analyst and other communications, investors were forming expectations about each value driver (roughly the line items from the financial statements), and those expectations were driving the market valuations. We have entered the world of behavioral finance.

Factors Market: As various finance researchers recognize, the single factor (market exposure) beta is insufficient to explain the stock risks and returns, so we move into factor investing, or smart betas. Multiple factors—such as size, value, momentum, quality, and volatility—are added to explain risks and returns.

Multi-asset World: As our world expands and portfolio theory helps us discover diversification and hedging, we recognize that it is not enough to gain insights into a single stock's performance (as we had done above). How assets behave with each other is an important consideration. We can now discover the portfolio that maximizes return for a given risk or minimizes risk for a given return. In addition to tracking all the fundamentals information, we now have to track the relative movements of stocks.

Clients: We recognize that our clients are not just recipients of the outcomes of our strategies. They have goals, aspirations, feedback, ideas, preferences, and requirements. We begin focusing on having a multi-portfolio concept of the world where we could customize portfolios in accordance with the needs of individual or classes of customers.

Asset Classes and Alternative Assets: We move beyond the basic equity and debt asset classes and recognize that there are many asset classes, and within each asset class, several types of investment vehicles can exist. We also realize that these vehicles and asset classes have their own fundamental value drivers. We can now easily access foreign markets, and suddenly our horizons expand. Our ability to build portfolios is expanded when we recognize that our newly found large collection of assets can offer us opportunities to diversify our client's portfolios.

Derivatives: To create liquidity and offer additional investment options, we add derivatives to our mix. These products derive their value from the values of the underlying assets. As layers of complexity are added, many new strategies are made possible. We could hedge and create various dynamic portfolios.

Indexes and mix and match: By combining various assets, we create indexes. These passive units acquire their own life.

Market: While a fundamentals-centric mindset keeps us occupied with the peculiar nature of the assets, a new dynamic is brewing. The dynamics of trading itself—it was observed—gives us chances to create value. Using information embedded in the trading itself—bid-ask spreads, order flows, volatility, volumes by times, and many other such factors—we can now look for returns from trading strategies. With typically short holding periods, we can now look at the underlying variables, or even the technical charts of price movements, to make position decisions. The age of big strategy has started and includes value investing, growth investing, momentum, dollar-cost averaging, short-selling, and other strategies.

Quantamental: Combining the two—quantitative and fundamentals strategies—we can now merge strategies from fundamentals and market-centric trading strategies to create new and sophisticated combinations.

Competitors: In the age of big strategy, it is not enough to develop our strategies without considering the strategies of others. This had two components to it: (1) we could observe and re-create strategies of others (the intelligence operation); and (2) we could analyze competitor response from our own strategies and apply a game theoretic perspective (game theory).

Behavioral: The behavioral approach identified in the expectations-based fundamentals theory is not enough. We can identify behavior in a wide spectrum of settings—market behaviors, consumer behaviors, trading behaviors—and the list goes on and on. All the data from fundamentals, such as earnings calls, quarterly and annual filings, and press releases, become the hunting grounds for behavioral mining.

Simulations: We can now add simulations—both simulation of data and strategy—to our toolbox.

Narratives: Finally, all of the above cannot explain how stories take shape and affect our decisions (Shiller, 2017). We needed more than just numbers. We track evolving narratives to help us make better investment decisions.

Many of the above assessments could have been done with regular technologies—but AI's time was coming. The birth of alternative data suddenly gave us the power to put our analysis on steroids. We now possess data that could help us perform better in all of the above. After all, even before AI, everything we were doing was to help us improve our assumptions and estimates. AI has given us exponentially more power to do just that.

The above strategic progression is presented to show you that your business model and strategy can take many shapes—and more so, AI is affecting all those areas. I intentionally broke them down in the above segments to help you realize that both data and strategies are now AI-centric.

Approaches	Machine Learning Applications
Basic fundamentals	Extract information from financial statements.
	Create multidimensional valuation estimates.
Business fundamentals	Automatically observe and quantify operational drivers of a firm.
	Assess the performance potential of a firm based on operational drivers.
Competitive fundamentals	Develop competitive analysis and models.
	Perform automated competitive analysis to understand business and market share dynamics of firms.
Expectations-based fundamentals	Develop deep insights about investor expectations.
	Use AI to analyze analyst reports and other related information to track changes in expectations.
Basic market	Develop better estimates of market risk and cost of capital calculations.
Factors investing	Perform automated factor market analysis.
	Identify new factors.
Asset classes and alternative assets	Collect data on various asset classes.
	Analyze asset behaviors under various conditions.
	Develop a deeper understanding.
Portfolio	Simulate and analyze portfolios.
	Understand various asset behaviors.
	Extract signal, lower noise with ML.
Clients	Analyze and develop portfolios specific to client requirements.
	Build them from the raw materials acquired in above areas.
	Discover and match clients to portfolio.
Indexes	Discover and test various indexes.
	Study the behavior of indexes.
Derivatives	Build valuation models for option pricing and other derivates. Integrate with other strategies.
	Perform analysis in various combinations with other assets. Test.
Market centric	Develop and test strategies based upon market dynamics.
	Discover new strategies (develop new theories to interpret).
	Make trading decisions.
	Act upon trading decisions.
Quantamental	Develop, discover, and test new strategies.
Competitors	Extract various strategies being played out in market.
	Analyze competitor strategies.
	Simulate and study strategies in a competitive environment.

Behavioral	Develop an alternative viewpoint of fundamentals and markets based on behaviors and emotions.
	Design, develop, and discover strategies based on behaviors and emotions.
Simulate	Simulate one or more of the above.
	Generate data.
Narratives	Discover, identify, and explore various narratives.
	Apply computational narratives to assess the stories taking shape.
	Build narratives.

As the above discussion shows, we are now in a different world. Specifically, we need to consider the following:

1. **Building Blocks:** In general, the above approaches could be viewed as the building blocks of today's asset management. In some ways, they are interdependent and reinforce each other.
2. **Reinforce:** The layers in the building blocks reinforce each other, and many are dependent on others.
3. **Integration:** As we move top to bottom, in general, lower layers integrate the effect of the top layers—being able to capture greater value.
4. **Strategic Flexibility:** Having a diverse set of approaches gives us strategic flexibility.
5. **Concentration:** Each layer has its own dynamics but when combined in the last three layers—i.e., quantamental, behavioral, and narrative-based—we get the concentrated power of all. This gives tremendous advantage to firms.
6. **Complexity:** As we move top to bottom, the overall system becomes more complex.
7. **Computational Power, Data, and Machines:** Neither human-centric computation (with classical digital programs) nor traditional statistical methods can enable us to do this type of modeling. Machine learning is the only way to capture this.

THE CORE TOOL SET

As we move from a conceptual design of the investment organization, let us review the type of applications used in AI in finance (Table 14.1). In a literature review (Andriosopoulos et al., 2019) researchers segmented the computational approaches into three categories of optimization models (e.g., linear and non-linear, dynamic, stochastic, fuzzy, multiobjective), data analytics and machine learning and decision analysis decision support systems. They identified the applications and methodologies as (adapted from Andriosopoulos et al., 2019):

Key for acronyms in the table:
ANFIS: adaptive neuro-fuzzy inference system
ANN: artificial neural network
DE: differential evolution
DEA: data envelopment analysis
DL: deep learning
DP: dynamic programming
DST: Dempster-Shafer theory
DT: decision trees
ETF: exchange-traded funds
Forex: foreign exchange
FS: fuzzy systems
GA: genetic algorithm
GO: genetic optimization
GP: genetic programming
LP: linear programming
LR: logistic regression
MCDA: multicriteria decision analysis
MSP: multi-objective stochastic programming
OLS: ordinary least squares
QR: quantile regression
RL: reinforcement learning
SA: sentiment analysis
SOM: self-organizing map
SP: stochastic programming
SURV: survival analysis
SVM: support vector machines
TM: text mining

TABLE 14.1 Applications in Finance

APPLICATIONS	PRODUCTS/AREAS	METHODS
Asset screening and selection	Stocks, funds	DEA, ANN, ANFIS, MCDA, Fuzzy GRA, GA, SVM, GP, fuzzy MCDM, copula models, SA
Capital allocation (mean value extensions)	Different risk measures (e.g., value at risk, skewness, and kurtosis), cardinality-constrained asset allocation, transaction costs and other real features, index tracking portfolio optimization, dynamic portfolio selection	Algorithmic approaches: solutions for complex optimization problems; and modeling formulations: portfolio selection with multiple objectives and goals, stochastic approaches, multiperiod and continuous time models, fuzzy models, robust optimization, network models
Trading	Stocks, forex, equity indices, portfolios, ETF, cryptocurrencies	Rule-based NFIS, RL, ANN, SOM, fuzzy logic, DST, GA, multi-agent system, ANFIS, boosting, GP, SA, online algorithm, SVM, GA, DP, TM, Markov models, ridge regression
Credit risk modeling	Credit scoring and rating, loss given default, loan portfolio management	NN, kernel, classification trees, decision rules, fuzzy and neuro-fuzzy systems, Bayesian models, ensembles, hybrid systems; hazard model, ensembles, credibility theory, mixture model, LR and OLS, SVM, Bayesian, QR, DE, SURV, probit and OLS, copula model, DL; stochastic and dynamic programming, computationally efficient simulation methods, Markov chain models, evolutionary approaches
Asset-liability management		GP, chance constrained programming, RO, SP, multi-objective stochastic programming
Sovereign and corporate debt management		MSP, SP, LP
Venture capital and IPO		Game theory, fuzzy goal programming, SVM, multicriteria analysis, ANFIS, GO, FS, Bayesian inference, Markov chain Monte Carlo

TABLE 14.1 *(Continued)*

APPLICATIONS	PRODUCTS/AREAS	METHODS
Operational and liquidity risk modeling		Extreme value theory, Bayesian inference, Bayesian networks, copula modeling, adaptive fuzzy inference model, fuzzy cognitive maps
Derivatives and volatility modeling		Linear programming, neural networks, wavelets, DL, SVM
Financial fraud detection		Multicriteria analysis, integer programming, TM, stacked generalization, DT, Bayesian classifier, network analysis, graph-based models, random forests, nearest neighbors

WHAT WILL BE THE FUNCTION OF YOUR INVESTMENT LAB?

This book recommends taking the scientific approach to running your firm. Your investment operation functions like a scientific institution. It generates theory and it explains its findings. It discovers strategies but also explains or discovers the theory behind the findings. This spirit of invention, discovery, and innovation is what drives value for your clients and for the firm.

To build that operation, you must allocate proper resources and deploy a transformation plan. Romanticizing machine learning will not get it done. Quant-to-quant love-hate relationships and passive-aggressive interactions will also not get it done.

To win, you must be willing to take the strategic leap. This should come from the entire firm and not just the investment department. AI, in this case, is not your technology option. It is your business model.

MAKE THE DECISIONS

For argument's sake, let's say you argue that you have figured out a winning strategy to pick value stocks and to demonstrate reasonable returns to your investors. The reality is that not only will that strategy be short term, but also it is likely that if it works, then competitors will be able to copy it quickly. The questions you must ask yourself are as follows:

- Based upon the above approaches (or there could be others that I may have not captured), which are you going to layer up in your investment function?
- If you are switching to the scientific approach to manage investments, what areas would you need? This will affect your data and operational costs also.
- Will you outsource some of the capability areas or develop the lab internally?
- If you deploy your AI lab to focus on one area (for example, fundamentals) and your investment operations staff needs to add other areas, how would you do that?
- Can your AI lab produce theory without having the above multi-capability structure?
- Can your AI lab test strategies in a limited setup?
- Can you build and sustain a business model and competitive advantage without having a broader capability footprint?

 ## A NEW WORLD

The asset management business is experiencing major changes. Unlike the old times when the strategic positioning of the firm was shaped by the top-down, dogmatic adherence to the underlying theory and battles raged between various theoretical camps, the new world can be viewed as a bottom-up theory development process. I call it the world of dynamic theory generation.

In this process, the theory manifests and emerges as firms embrace the scientific method. The right solutions for the client are neither dictated nor shoved down the investment lane; instead, they emerge dynamically as the two cognitive elements of human behavior and market behavior are constantly tested and dynamically monitored. Machine learning discovers those patterns, and besides discovering, your job is to explain the underlying theories. In this new world, the role of the asset manager is of an asset scientist and of an empathetic physician. The rest is left to the intelligent machines. We are cautioned by experts not to fall into the trap of either trying to force-fit explanations to data just so that we can feel good about the model or to completely ignore any theoretical foundations and proceed with the discovered observations without having any idea of what is driving such relationships.

THE (UNNECESSARY) DEBATE

Remove the rather unnecessary semantic layer between the two battling camps of modern portfolio theory and behavioral finance, and one would observe that both dominant models are based on cognitive assumptions about humans and markets.

Modern portfolio theory views investors as rational (Miller and Modigliani, 1961), who design their portfolios in accordance with mean-variance portfolio theory (Markowitz, 1952), in an efficient market (Fama, 1969, 1965), and the expected returns are function of nothing else but risks (Sharpe, 1964). Rationality is a cognitive structure, markets can be viewed as socially constructed cognitive structures, while both portfolio designing and understanding expected risks can be viewed as cognitive activities.

The behavioral camp considers investors as normal, more human, thus increasing the distribution of behaviors associated with humans (cognitive states). It claims that markets are not efficient, applies behavioral portfolio theory, and argues that returns follow behavioral asset pricing theory (Shefrin and Statman, 1985, 1994, 2000; Das et al., 2010).

As the theoretical foundations along the two camps solidified in firms, areas of expertise developed along those dimensions. Technological solutions, human resource capabilities, marketing literature, client communications, and performance measures were designed in accordance with the theoretical schools. As the battles became more entrenched, both sides claimed that the other side's models were imperfect. The mediators claimed that they have combined both models and created a balanced viewpoint (Pfiffelmann et al., 2016), and the use of mental accounts to allocate wealth enabled both to coexist (Das et al., 2010).

 MORE BEHAVIORS

The questions about what we do and how we deliver services are two fundamentally different questions. The first question represents our state of belief, knowledge, and understanding of different theoretical concepts that define our approach to help customers.

The second implies how the firm chooses to serve clients—i.e., channel selection, channel allocation of resources, and use of technology.

The adoption of the behavioral model is not only an innovation, it is also an effective response to the existential threat from the commoditization of the non-behavioral models.

The behavioral approach also makes sense since strange and unpredictable events can emerge in our markets, which can be viewed as complex adaptive systems. These erratic behaviors can create bubbles and viral effects in a network. Staying clearheaded is key in those times.

Noise can mean opportunity. Thus, while we cannot escape the rise of behaviorism, designing an infrastructure to understand and model three behaviors—individual customers, groups, and markets—is not easy.

 ## RESEARCH AND INVESTMENT STRATEGY

Some asset managers often claim that fundamentals drive markets, others focus on the trading dynamics. Researchers have recognized that while both claims have supporting evidence—when buyers and sellers react to the fundamentals, they are not reacting to the absolute values determined from the financial statements and disclosures but instead to the expectations they have set about the future performance. Expectations give rise to an element of surprise, and surprise when favorable can bring buyers to the table and when disappointing can push them away.

There are seven parts to the study of investment strategy and research:

- The first part of investment strategy development is based on understanding and modeling the fundamentals of a firm. This is performed in accordance with the investor expectations.
- The second part is to understand the risk factors and their relationships. As such you are not studying risks only as they relate to a certain asset class but as a scientific phenomenon.
- The third part involves understanding specifics of asset classes and subclasses. This area also includes alternatives.
- The fourth part studies the interactions of various variables and asset movements. This also includes understanding and analyzing superstructures and formations of assets (e.g., ETF).
- The fifth part focuses on the combinations of cash flows from existing assets (asset classes) and using derivatives to create new.

- The sixth step focuses on the tax strategies and their effects (wealth side).
- The seventh step is to align other preferences and characteristics sought by the investors.

Together, the above capabilities provide the fundamental platform over which one can dynamically design and study portfolios.

 ## PORTFOLIO

With the above strategic research and investment strategy platform in place, you can now form and study various portfolios. For example, you can simulate and study the performance of various assets and their combinations in accordance with various goal parameters.

Designing the portfolio can be based on configured parameters of a self-guidance model or one more aligned with dynamic goals of the customers. It may achieve active or time-based rebalancing. It can follow the traditional financial model or a more advanced behavioral model.

The key to portfolio design is that customer goals are aligned with the market realities. As the discussion in the previous chapter outlined, understanding customer goals is accomplished via automated empathy compassion marketing. Product and investment selection and asset allocation happen as the behavior of investors is played out against the behavior of markets. This is where automated empathy meets automated expectations.

 ## PERFORMANCE

Performance monitoring is a critical part of ensuring the health of the returns loop. In this, performance is monitored against several standards:

1. External measures;
2. Client measures;
3. Internal measures; and
4. Asset manager measures.

 ## REFERENCES

Andriosopoulos, D., et al. (2019) "Computational Approaches and Data Analytics in Financial Services: A Literature Review." *Journal of the Operational*

Research Society. [Online]. 70 (10), 1581–1599. Available from: https://doi
.org/10.1080/01605682.2019.1595193.

Das, S., et al. (2010) "Portfolio Optimization with Mental Accounts." *Journal of Financial and Quantitative Analysis.* [Online]. 45 (2), 311–334.

Fama, E. F. (1969) "Efficient Capital Markets: A Review of Theory and Empirical Work." *Journal of Finance.* [Online]. 25 (2), 383–417.

Fama, E. F. (1965) "The Behavior of Stock-Market Prices." *The Journal of Business* 38 (1), 34–105.

Graham, B., and Dodd, D. L. (1951) *Security analysis: principles and technique.* New York: McGraw-Hill.

Markowitz, H. M. (1952) "Portfolio Selection." *Journal of Finance* 7 (1), 77–91.

Miller, M. H., and Modigliani, F. (1961) "Dividend Policy, Growth, and the Valuation of Shares." *Journal of Business.* [Online]. 34 (4), 411–433.

Pfiffelmann, M., et al. (2016) "When Behavioral Portfolio Theory meets Markowitz theory." *Economic Modelling.* [Online]. 53419–435.

Sharpe, W. F. (1964) "Capital Asset Prices: A Theory of Market Equilibrium under Conditions of Risk." *Journal of Finance.* [Online]. 19 (3), 425–442.

Shefrin, H. M., and Statman, M. (1994) "Behavioral Capital Asset Pricing Theory." *Journal of Financial and Quantitative Analysis* 29 (3), 323–349.

Shefrin, H. M., and Statman, M. (2000) "Behavioral Portfolio Theory," vol. 35, no. 2 (June):127–151. *Journal of Financial and Quantitative Analysis* 35 (2), 127–151.

Shefrin, H. M., and Statman, M. (1985) "The Disposition to Sell Winners Too Early and Ride Losers Too Long: Theory and Evidence." *Journal of Finance* 40 (3), 777–790.

Shiller, R. J. (2017) "Narratives Economics." *American Economic Review* 107 (4), 967–1004. [Online]. Available from: http://www.nber.org/papers/w23075.

CHAPTER FIFTEEN

Regulatory Compliance and Operations

THERE ARE TWO TOPICS DISCUSSED IN the chapter. The first is about regulatory compliance. The second is about operations.

WHO IS RESPONSIBLE?

The head of regulatory function is responsible for regulatory intelligent automation. The team is placed at the design stage. We are placing operational functions in areas such as reporting and disclosures, institutional support, accounting, and other similar back office under a single discussion umbrella of operations. These activities and functions may be headed by different leaders. Both regulatory compliance and operations intelligent automation are approached from our overall goal of industrial-scale enterprise machine learning.

REGULATORY COMPLIANCE

Regulatory compliance is not just about check-the-box compliance. It is a way of life. It also provides meaningful ways to assess your own performance and provides a comparative basis for others. It is a key component of competitive advantage. A firm that either fails in regulatory compliance or does not adopt ethical standards (such as GIPS) may be viewed as less attractive by investors. Note: some areas of compliance are discussed in Chapter 19.

 ## WHY INTELLIGENT AUTOMATION?

Let us start by evaluating why intelligent automation is the only way forward for asset management firms:

Diversity of regulations: The world of regulations is broad, highly dynamic, and diverse. Regulations come from many sources, are detailed, sometimes conflicting, and regulate different sides of business. The sheer variety and volume of regulations are often unmanageable.

The four requirements: It is a predictive, descriptive, diagnostic, calculative, prescriptive function: in addition to making numerical calculations, regulatory compliance function is diagnostic (identifies and assesses problems), descriptive (describes the problems), predictive (predicts problems), and prescriptive (prescribes solutions).

Requires meticulous planning and implementation: Regulatory management requires comprehensive planning and constant response to emerging and dynamic developments. It also requires flawless execution.

Needs ongoing overview: As requirements change, the execution maps require readjustment. This demands constant vigilance on both ends—strategic response and execution.

It is a cultural phenomenon: Regulatory management is not just a management issue; it is also an organizational and cultural phenomenon. A culture that takes compliance seriously and respects its value is an important asset.

Efficiency increase means money saved: The increase in efficiency of the regulatory process leads to faster implementation and accelerates compliance across the company. This results in both cost savings and cost avoidance.

Effectiveness increase creates ROI: Improving the effectiveness of the regulatory function means that more areas are protected, there are fewer chances of mistakes and errors, higher false negatives and false positives, and programs that are deep in the organizations and that become part of the higher education.

HAVE YOU SCOPED OUT WHAT TO DO?

In the regulatory AI area, it will be necessary to form a cross-functional team. The reg AI team's responsibilities include designing and deploying AI-centric technology for the following objectives:

Single view of regulations: The goal of the technology is to track regulatory developments and changes. This is achieved by accessing regulation data, classifying it into actionable multidimensional themes, segmenting it into execution-centric rules, and identifying overlaps or contradictions across multiple regulations.

Exploring gaps: Based on the above, identify the gaps between where the disparities exist in the existing regulatory plans and frameworks in a firm.

Education: The findings are used to create knowledge areas to educate and inform functions that are affected by specific regulations.

Scenario planning and risk: Scenarios are planned in a simulated environment, and risk assessment is performed continuously.

Prioritizing: Based on impact and relevance, technology prioritizes the regulations and regulatory changes.

Communicating: Communications about regulatory changes and effect are performed using AI. The technology determines who to communicate what and then sends out communications.

Cultural evaluation: Technology constantly assesses the cultural factors in an organization to determine what value the culture places on integrity, compliance, regulations, transparency, and other such factors.

Implementing: Technology can also assess implementation gaps and help develop an implementation plan for workflow, project coordination, and resource identification.

 ## HOW TO DO IT?

1. **Operating/business model analyzer:** Start by building an operating/business model analyzer. Extract both textual and numerical information to develop a dynamic look at business—profile business model elements such as client segments, products, asset classes, distribution channels, pricing, geographies of operations, product structures, and regulatory frameworks and agencies. Expand the basic operating model to include key activities, resources, revenues, costs, and

capital allocations. Extracting business models through text mining is a promising area of AI application (Lee and Hong, 2014). Analyze make vs. buy decision in this area—keeping in mind that making means competitive advantage and being able to perform additional analysis that may not be available to your competitors (see regulations tracker below), and buying implies getting solutions from a party that has economies of scale.

2. **Regulations tracker:** Determine the link between operating/business model elements and regulatory frameworks, changes, and proposed regulations. Deploy a regulatory tracker to capture regulatory developments. This is a data mining and classifying operation. Regulations are classified based on various knowledge areas, themes, and operational requirements. The obtained classifications can be further enhanced by cross referencing, citations, verbs and nouns, specific terms, and named entities.

3. **Impact manager:** Using the information from the operating model analyzer and regulations tracker, the impact manager shows how regulatory changes are affecting or can affect various areas of business. It shows the effect of a regulation on the business in terms of highest to lowest.

4. **Regulatory risk manager:** An automated evaluation of risk is composed of multiple products. The first product calculates risk exposure from having a regulation. This calculates the potential effect of noncompliance in terms of potential losses, fines, and so forth. The output is a directional estimate and not a specific estimate for the firm. Input data includes regulatory developments, business areas affected, and enforcement history by the agencies. The second product takes into account the gaps in a firm's existing regulatory execution. Areas that are wide open for implementation are recognized. This is a two-step process. First, the internally developed framework is compared to the machine-generated comprehensive version. Second, the internal regulatory reporting and performance measurement documents are analyzed to identify areas of improvement.

5. **Assess the effect:** The effect assessment also contains multiple products. One product estimates the probability and effect (dollar) of regulations. The second estimates the increase in risk for the firm.

6. **Understand model effect:** This product helps you determine which business model (business area, asset class, product offering) will be most affected by a particular regulation or a combination of various regulations.

7. **RegTech ecosystem solutions:** In addition to the above, there are various solutions that help in implementing the regulatory program. These solutions should not be approached as one-off. They should be considered as parts of the whole and developed and implemented in a synchronized manner:

   a. KYC (know-your-customers) and AML (anti-money-laundering);
   b. Trade monitoring and surveillance (insider trading, market abuse, misconduct, monitoring personal trading, and others);
   c. Portfolio risk;
   d. Risk management;
   e. Documents and records management;
   f. Tax management;
   g. Regulation-specific applications; and
   h. Basic GRC platforms including risk analytics, risk and control management, workflow, audit, content and document management, metadata, user information, distribution, communications.

8. **Calculations and disclosures:** Both for calculations and disclosures, adding robotic process automation (RPA) along with machine learning can create tremendous value from automation.

9. **Marketing and advertising:** Use NLP to identify compliance gaps in marketing and advertising.

10. **Regulatory filing:** Implement a machine learning solution to assess compliance in regulatory filings. Use a three-tier approach of deterministic, sanity check, and culture check for proper internal controls and quality checks on regulatory filings.

11. **Employee filings:** Use NLP to go over employee disclosures and filings to observe if there are gaps, misstatements, or areas of concern.

12. **Education:** Once gaps are understood, you can apply tools that perform automated learning needs assessments and training requirements.

HOW TO USE TECHNOLOGY FOR GIPS IMPLEMENTATION?

GIPS offers one of the best ways to demonstrate your business's acceptance and pursuance of global ethical standards of disclosures, measuring performance, and strengthening internal controls. It can be a source of competitive advantage. To declare that you are GIPS compliant, you must follow the guidelines and implement the required protocols. The recent version of GIPS (2020) gives even more reason to become GIPS compliant. Adopted by hundreds of companies in dozens of countries, GIPS is one of the most valuable and helpful additions in best practices for the industry.

For efficiency and effectiveness improvement, executives responsible for GIPS implementation processes must consider intelligent automation. The role of automation is not to declare that you are GIPS compliant—since such promulgation needs to be embedded in the standard itself and the technology needs to be approved by some standard-setting body—but instead to support the GIPS implementation. The support part increases the efficiency and effectiveness of implementation, gives a powerful start, helps gain scale, assists in review and audit, and establishes a higher level of confidence.

Recall the three-tier approach that we propose: deterministic calculation (systems that measure and calculate through precise formulas), sanity check (systems that assess the calculated numbers by looking at different variables—a data science–centric solution, and systems that evaluate the human element (culture, seriousness, personality, etc.) related to compliance. Your intelligence automation plan is composed of the following:

Portfolio monitoring: Monitor all portfolios under management from a performance measurement perspective. Use all three approaches of *measure, sanity check,* and *cultural assessment* to evaluate performance and compliant presentation. The *measure* includes both: (1) a calculated performance via hard measure and deterministic formula; and (2) a deterministic validator. Sanity check is different. It is statistical in nature and uses indirect representations to perform a sanity check for accuracy.

Exceptions: Develop a framework for identifying the differences between sanity check and calculated values. Identify outliers. Scan the presentation for compliance. Observe the language usage. Check for cultural or human biases.

Procedures: If performing an audit or due diligence, apply automated discovery of systems, data lineage, and data movement through the enterprise through process-mining technology. If implemented right, the results of the process-mining technology will contain both metadata and transactional information. Use classifiers to observe exceptions or potential errors.

Internal controls: Implement AI for internal controls evaluation. To get some ideas, you can refer to my book titled *Artificial Intelligence for Audit, Forensic Accounting, and Valuation: A Strategic Perspective* (Wiley).

Valuation and accounting: See the operations section below.

▦ BACK AND MIDDLE OFFICE

Valuation: Valuation is a critical task, and GIPS standards provide guidance on valuation principles. Many of the technologies used are deterministic and workflow technologies, but in some areas, AI can be very useful.

Three-tier approach: In all deterministic calculations and reporting, it is helpful to set up secondary sanity check assessments and culture/bias assessments.

Reconciliation, accounting, accruals: I have categorized them together. There are many applications of AI in reconciliation, estimation, accounting, and accruals. Both from an outsourced perspective and internal application, application of machine learning and RPA-centric application yields productivity improvements and error reduction.

Onboarding (retail): For customers, one of the most painful aspects is onboarding. In our desire to learn more about customers, we inundate them with questions. This diminishes positive customer experience and increases the chances of self-bias. Self-bias comes from our belief that our questions are collectively exhaustive to give us a clear picture of our client's goals, aspirations, risks, and problems. Leading with a million questions is not the way to go. We now have the technology to discover aspects of customers that even customers themselves do not know. Through AI, gamification, and behavioral analysis, we can shed light on those questions and gain knowledge about customers from nonconscious data from clients.

Institutional requests management: Reducing operational friction, improving quality and speed of response to requests for information by institutional clients, and making reliable and actionable information accessible go a long way in building deeper relationships. Sharing strategic information with institutional clients also implies anticipating what the asks could be. You can analyze the previous requests, business model of institutional clients, information about the client, regulatory frameworks applicable to the client, and data on the client teams to anticipate and predict what type of information requests you might receive.

As you can observe, AI offers significant opportunities to automate and enhance insights in the regulatory and operational areas. Like everything else in strategic intelligence automation, this area also requires meticulous planning.

CHAPTER SIXTEEN

Supply Chain Science

U NLIKE MANUFACTURING, SOME INVESTMENT MANAGEMENT firms
may not have highly advanced procurement and supply chain functions. Procurement may be viewed as a tactical operation focused on
buying categories such as office supplies and computers. As we become more
advanced in AI, our dependence and reliance on strategic supply chains will
become even greater. Our sourcing of sophisticated data, solutions providers,
outsourcing operations, and advanced hardware will become instrumental for
our success. Strategic excellence comes from building supply chains that have
the following attributes: resilience, rigor, redundancy, reliability, refortification,
and responsiveness.

 ## WHO IS RESPONSIBLE FOR SUPPLY CHAIN SCIENCE?

Asset management firms will need reliable supply of data, hardware, and services and hence need to formalize sourcing and supply chain functions. This
means creating senior supply chain officer positions. This position can report to
the head of data operations. Recall that we recommended a function specializ-
ing in data procurement. The broader supply chain group, however, does more
than procuring data. It is also responsible for all other procurement undertaken
by the firm.

HOW TO THINK ABOUT SUPPLY CHAINS

Supply chains are complex networks. They display complex behavior and are considered as complex adaptive systems (CAS). While CAS are nonlinear systems, many supply chains are modeled as linear systems, and that often creates problems. Failure to model as a nonlinear system diminishes both predictability and resilience of supply chains. One way that helps is to approach them from a risk perspective.

To build the supply chain management capabilities, we suggest viewing it as supply chain risk management (SCRM). Our reason for that is because the nature of investment management requires us to depend on reliable sources of data and services. AI is revolutionizing SCRM, and significant research is taking place in this area (Baryannis et al., 2019).

Supply chain theory has also been approached as networks and complex adaptive systems (Carter et al., 2015). The nodes of the network can be viewed as profit maximization agents that interact with each other. In those interactions, money, data, goods, and information are exchanged and transferred among agents. Supply chains are composed of both physical and informational supply chains. Since supply chains are relative to a product and service—from an investment management perspective data becomes the central driver of the data supply chain. The farther away you are from the center, the harder it becomes to have a good view of the supply chain since physical distance or cultural distance or other factors diminish the visible horizon of the planning agents.

Other researchers had set the agenda for analyzing supply chains (Choi et al., 2001). *Internal mechanisms*, a planning construct, includes agents, schemas, self-organization, emergence, network connectivity, and network dimensionality. Connectivity refers to the complexity of the relationships in the network. For example, connectivity can be measured by the number of relationships where a higher number of relationships can lead to an increase in the overall complexity. Dimensionality is inverse to complexity in the sense that it decreases as complexity increases since it refers to the autonomy of agents. Autonomy is recognized by how much influence each agent has on another agent. When the number of links increases, it implies the autonomy declines. The decisions of one entity or agent affect the decisions of others.

Wilson and Hearnshaw compared supply chain networks with other networks, such as social, biological, neurological, ecological (Hearnshaw and Wilson, 2013). They identified three common properties: a short characteristic path length, a high clustering coefficient, and the existence of a power law connectivity distribution. *Short characteristic path length* measures the average distance between two nodes—which in a supply chain could be viewed as the shortest distance to move data (or anything else) between two randomly selected firms. The *power law distribution* represents configurations with a small number of high connection nodes and a large number of nodes with a low number of connections. Think of them as major hubs with high density, connected to smaller networks, which are connected to even smaller networks. This configuration makes the network robust—since failure of smaller networks does not spread into larger hubs and even failure of larger hubs does not necessarily affect other hubs. Therefore, the system can function even with larger failures. Third, the *clustering coefficient* measures the likelihood that links exist between two or more nodes that stem from the same node. This gives the degree to which they cluster together. Just as these three measures can be applied in any type of network, they can also be applied in supply chains.

What matters most is the resilience of supply chains. For that, Mari et al. provided a mathematical model (Mari et al., 2015). They first highlighted the problem of not being able to model a nonlinear system with widely prevalent linear tools in supply chain analysis. Resilience must be defined and measured. Prone to disruptions, supply chains behave erratically when disruptions transpire. Supply chain resilience is measured by accessibility, robustness, flexibility, and responsiveness.

- Accessibility refers to being able to participate in the supply chain after an unfavorable event has transpired. This means the firm can respond to market demand after a major event.
- Robustness refers to being able to deploy contingency plans when disruptions happen.
- Flexibility implies being able to reconfigure and shift production between various suppliers when needed.
- Responsiveness implies being able to respond to demand, market, and customer changes.

The difference between accessibility and responsiveness is that while accessibility only refers to existing demand, responsiveness also includes changes in demand patterns. One way to model statistical mechanics of complex networks is by random graph modeling.

Supply chains have a variety of structures—organizational, technological, financial, informational, topological—and therefore, structural dynamics of a system should not be ignored (Ivanov et al., 2010). Authors clarify that adaptive supply chains with powerful dynamics can often produce incoherence and inconsistency. Thus, rapidly evolving structural dynamic implies robust plans need to be created rapidly. Mathematical modeling research generally focuses on three methods: optimization, simulation, and heuristics.

- Optimization focuses on discovering the best and most efficient supply chain.
- Simulation imitates a system's behavior.
- Heuristics are intelligent rules that can lead to good solutions.

Consequently, supply chain can change its behavior, improve, evolve, and adapt to changes.

Other researchers acknowledge that supply chains are networks and argue that global supply chains today are interconnected with complex relationships (Pathak et al., 2007). While managers must consider several factors, two of the most important factors are related to the structural ambiguities of their interconnected supply chains and the need to adapt to change. Pathak et al. provided several examples where companies optimized their supply chain decisions by using neural networks and agent-based models (with ant-foraging algorithms). *Interconnectedness* and *dynamic learning* help model the supply chains as complex systems. The other challenge, Pathak et al. argue, is to figure out how to be adaptive in behavior.

How Does That Translate into an Action Plan for AI?

- Start by understanding the supply chain data that you have available. Look for data in your accounting systems, purchasing systems, HR records, and other areas where you can find the data (Fan et al., 2015).
- Build an AI application that models your data (and other purchases) supply chain. Ask data suppliers to provide you with the sources (if they can). Create models of supply chain to study the risks.
- Model potential data losses, supply chain disruptions, costs, timeliness, and reliability of the supply chain.
- Develop an AI-based system that can assess supplier capabilities. You can use RFI and RFP information from your sourcing programs to model that.
- Generate plans for alternative supply options if data used in your critical studies is interrupted. Consider developing an alternative supply base or generating data internally.

– Estimate connectivity and dimensionality in the data supply chain.
– Analyze path length between critical suppliers in your supply chain.

Recap

Using AI to improve your supply chain offers a great opportunity to manage risk and ensure that your strategic data keeps flowing. With sourcing and supply chain automation you can:

1. **automate work**—AI automates work;
2. **enable insights**—AI enables analytics and provides new insights;
3. **improve operational precisions and accuracy**—AI helps at becoming more proficient, accurate, and precise;
4. **enable prediction**—AI enables better prediction ability; and
5. **do a preemptive intervention**—AI enables preemptive intervention, thus improving the odds of success.

REFERENCES

Baryannis, G., et al. (2019) "Supply Chain Risk Management and Artificial Intelligence: State of the Art and Future Research Directions." *International Journal of Production Research*. [Online]. 57 (7), 2179–2202. Available from: https://doi.org/10.1080/00207543.2018.1530476.

Carter, C. R., et al. (2015) "Toward the Theory of the Supply Chain." *Journal of Supply Chain Management*. [Online]. 51 (2).

Choi, T. Y., et al. (2001) "Supply Networks and Complex Adaptive Systems: Control versus Emergence." *Journal of Operations Management*. [Online]. 19 (3), 351–366.

Fan, Y., et al. (2015) "Supply Chain Risk Management in the Era of Big Data." International Conference of Design; User Experience; and Usability. Springer; Cham. [Online]. (August), 283–294.

Hearnshaw, E. J. S., and Wilson, M. M. J. (2013) "A Complex Network Approach to Supply Chain Network Theory." *International Journal of Operations and Production Management*. [Online]. 33 (4), 442–469.

Ivanov, D., et al. (2010) "A Multi-Structural Framework for Adaptive Supply Chain Planning and Operations Control with Structure Dynamics Considerations." *European Journal of Operational Research*. [Online]. 200 (2), 409–420. Available from: http://dx.doi.org/10.1016/j.ejor.2009.01.002.

Mari, S. I., et al. (2015) "Complex Network Theory–Based Approach for Designing Resilient Supply Chain Networks." *International Journal of Logistics Systems and Management*. [Online]. 21 (3), 365–384.

Pathak, S. D., et al. (2007) "Complexity and Adaptivity in Supply Networks: Building Supply Network Theory Using a Complex Adaptive Systems Perspective." *Decision Sciences*. [Online]. 38 (4), 547–580.

CHAPTER SEVENTEEN

Corporate Social Responsibility

W ITH ESG (ENVIRONMENTAL, SOCIAL, AND CORPORATE governance) becoming popular, social responsibility is more than an investment strategy. It has now become a way of life to operate a business. As AI and machine learning have become pervasive in business, their effect is being felt in the CSR (corporate social responsibility) arena. If done right, AI can be used to improve the effectiveness and efficiency of the CSR programs. AI in CSR is a three-step process that consists of:

- Understanding the CSR processes in the firm;
- Determining the failure points; and
- Applying AI technology for automation and insights.

CSR WOES: CAN PROCESSES EXPLAIN THEM?

Having ethics, sustainability, a multi-stakeholder model, and corporate social responsibility programs is one thing; making them effective, another. In general there is consensus that these programs help the firm, the world, the society, the environment, and human civilization (Dhiman, 2008). However, these programs are not without critics. Many of those criticisms are not discussed in the corporate world. We tend to focus on the good news, while ignoring the bad.

The criticism is mostly about the underlying processes of CSR. Automation offers one way to improve the processes and hence close the gap.

Visser defines CSR as "the way in which business consistently creates shared value in society through economic development, good governance, stakeholder responsiveness and environmental improvement. Put another way, CSR is an integrated, systemic approach by business that builds, rather than erodes or destroys, economic, social, human and natural capital" (Visser, 2011, p. 7). He acknowledges that traditional CSR has not been successful. Segmenting CSR's history into five ages of greed, philanthropy, marketing, management, and responsibility, Visser argues that each age corresponds to a stage of CSR, which includes defensive, charitable, promotional, strategic, and systemic, respectively. Visser adds that while we have more CSR than before, we have not been able to make significant progress, "Be it the gap between rich and poor, deforestation, biodiversity loss, carbon emissions or corruption—shows that things are still getting worse, not better" (Visser, 2011, p. 127).

Visser proposes a solution: CSR 2.0. Based on five principles of creativity (think outside the box), scalability (achieve scale), responsiveness (harness cross-sector relationships to drive change), glocality (think global, act local), and circularity (sustainable use of resources), he shows how CSR can be improved.

 ## WHAT ARE THE CRITICISMS OF CSR?

The criticism of CSR generally shows up in the following three broad categories:

1. Measurement issues: Failure to measure, or measuring the wrong things, or measuring that is inconclusive or irrelevant;
2. Behavioral issues: Management behavior that intentionally dissuades or deters the CSR program from achieving its full potential; and
3. Strategic and organizational: Inability to properly integrate CSR into business strategy or vice versa, communicating the CSR program, getting organizational support, and other similar organizational issues.

 ## MEASUREMENT ISSUES

There are two major issues related to measurement:

Value: The value issue is related to what constitutes "value" and whether the value contribution of CSR should be measured in economic terms or is it more than that, and includes other factors such as social justice (Harrison and Wicks, 2013; Ferrero-Ferrero et al., 2016). On the opposite side it is hard to measure the effect of CSR on shareholder value—for example, specifically what parts of CSR create shareholder value or competitive advantage (Hillman and Keim, 2001) or whether the program creates shareholder value at all (Nguyen et al., 2017). Other criticisms question whether CSR programs justify their costs (Sprinkle and Maines, 2010), and whether value destruction, (i.e., the reverse of value creation) should also be measured (aka CSI, corporate social irresponsibility; Price and Sun, 2017). We know such a number is not reported by firms.

Measurement methods for CSR have disappointed—for instance, the inability of ratings systems to accurately measure CSR performance (Chatterji et al., 2009)—and have created more doubts about CSR initiatives. Many concerns—such as whether CSR programs enhance a firm's value (Khan et al., 2016) or the relationship between financial performance and CSR—are not resolved (Wang and Sarkis, 2017). Thus, financial performance, which can be viewed as an umbrella term for other financial measures such as cost of capital, risk spreads, profits, free cash flows, and so forth, also remains inconclusive about the effect of CSR (Menz, 2010; Cortez, 2011).

The distance between CSR "actions" and "claims" draws consumer skepticism (Yoon et al., 2006) and leads to consumer backlash (Skarmeas and Leonidou, 2013). Many popular measurement and reporting systems, such as the triple bottom line (TBL), have been contrasted and compared to other methods (Vanclay, 2004) and the need for new measurement systems has been pointed out (Perrini and Tencati, 2006). Other researchers plead that reporting empirically can be a mistake since TBL is subjective and does not provide a comparative standard (Norman and MacDonald, 2004).

Materiality: The second problem of measurement is that stakeholder priorities and concerns are major inputs to the design and development of CSR programs (Edgley et al., 2015). Researchers argue that such assessments are based on subjective data and that materiality becomes relative to management agendas and constrained by their knowledge and wisdom (Nishant et al., 2016). Survey questions can be framed and biased and therefore lack sincerity. Since there is no standard for how to perform materiality, different firms reach different strategies and conclusions (Eccles and Serafeim, 2013). Nonfinancial measures are often ignored (Wadhwa, 2017).

BEHAVIORAL AND ROLE ISSUES

In many cases managerial behaviors and roles become the greatest obstacle to the success of the program. Misalignment of incentives can drive such behaviors. Managers may take actions to block or subvert CSR.

"Agency conflict" continues to be an impediment (Cennamo et al., 2009). Of course, the programs can be biased. Managers can have conflicts of interest, and they may carry incentives beyond the most obvious goal of maximizing shareholder value. CSR programs can grant managers tremendous authority to compromise shareholder value. From an agency concept, it is suspected that CSR can convolute the focus on shareholder value creation that can lead to the dilution of the power of owners. This does not stop at managers and in fact extends to consultants as well—as Norman and MacDonald plead that the same people who invent the accounting standards for CSR are also the ones who make lots of money implementing such reporting programs in companies (Norman and MacDonald, 2004).

CSR programs have been denounced as unauthentic, deceitful, self-serving, and promotional (Visser, 2011). Critics say that CSR has become a tool to do less bad rather than more good, thereby protecting the downside vs. creating an upside.

 ## STRATEGIC AND ORGANIZATIONAL ISSUES

Negligence or incompetence drives strategic and organizational issues and not intentional deceit. This line of criticism points to the need to build CSR into corporate strategy (Galbreath, 2009). Integrating CSR and company strategy can lead to competitive advantage (Porter and Kramer, 2006).

Organizations fail to make a distinction between business for sustainability and sustainable (Wikstrom, 2010). CSR programs are often derailed due to factors such as lacking support from business units, centralized teams losing touch with reality, and short-lived executive support (Browne and Nuttall, 2013).

Former US secretary of labor Robert Reich pleaded that managers should focus on value creation and leave the CSR responsibility to the government (Reich, 2007). This argument of *legitimacy and role* is often countered by others who argue that government is inefficient and lacks the financial resources and discipline to make a difference—and hence only businesses can create a positive result (Pava, 2008) and that government failures should not be conceived as market failures (Desrochers, 2010).

▓ HOW TO APPLY AI IN CSR?

Fix the Measurement Processes

Step 1: Deploy AI for value measurement and discovery. Measure the key processes of value measurement and discovery by automating for total stakeholder value calculation. Calculate stakeholder value in economic as well as in social and environment terms. You can reduce the human bias factor by using internal and external data to develop an independent assessment of actions and effects. This makes it possible to evaluate the synergy between shareholder and stakeholder value (Tantalo and Priem, 2014).

Step 2: Automate materiality assessment. With AI, the materiality assessment process can be improved by using rigorous, objective, and empirical criteria. You can algorithmically determine the most important elements for stakeholders and then test them against the sample of direct input from stakeholders. Such an exercise can also give voice to the stakeholders who are legitimate but may lack the power to influence the firm. This is achieved by using data from stakeholders and determining the preference structures, perceptions, and CSR demands of customers. For example, using a preference-determining mathematical model known as analytical hierarchy process, which is often used to solve multi-criteria decision-making (MCDM) problems, Calabrese et al. (Calabrese et al., 2016) applied a fuzzy quantitative assessment in sustainability management to quantitatively determine preference structures. Using salience and risk as two dimensions, Whitehead (Whitehead, 2017) also focused on prioritizing sustainability indicators quantitatively. Failure modes and effects analysis have also been applied to develop materiality assessment (Hsu et al., 2013). AI monitors and provides constant feedback, which helps in prioritizing and in performing risk assessment on an ongoing basis.

Step 3: Measure performance. Direct the algorithm to track the performance of the CSR program. Identify the variables that affect the performance. Make sure to use various features such as regulatory standards, global standards, and internally set goals as inputs to determine the success and effect.

Step 3: Automate to fix the behavioral issues. In this case we deploy AI to develop incentive systems that are aligned with the interests of the shareholders as well as other stakeholders. A machine learning–based system creates transparency and reduces human bias. Instead of humans developing and managing the incentives, we allow algorithms to independently monitor and align the incentives. Just as materiality assessment can be independently managed by technology, programs that lack substance can also be identified.

This would be done on similar patterns as AI being applied to combat corruption and financial statement fraud (Ravisankar et al., 2011; Lin et al., 2015; Kim et al., 2016), thwart management fraud (Pai et al., 2011), and improve internal controls (Boskou et al., 2018).

Automate the strategy and organizational issues: Implement algorithms to evaluate, design, and monitor the linkage between the strategy of a firm and its CSR strategy. Establishing that link is critical to creating value (Porter and Kramer, 2006). This is a learning algorithm that tracks the key dimensions of a firm's business strategy and its CSR program and continuously evaluates the relationships between them. Organizational commitment and communications can also be tracked and program success determined.

CSR MUST NOT BE FORGOTTEN

The central theme of this book is that all parts of an investment management business should be automated and that automation should be done in a strategic and planned manner. The advances in technology, therefore, must also help improve the underlying processes of managing a CSR program. For decades CSR has promised the world a better future. AI can provide the inflection point to lift the performance curve of CSR upward. The time of AI could be the time of CSR.

ESG INVESTMENT

Claiming to start an ESG-focused fund is easy. Defining the standards in accordance with which the fund will operate is much harder. What makes it extremely difficult is that you must deliver reasonable returns to the investors.

Some researchers argue that there is no evidence that ESG-compliant firms deliver better returns. Despite such skepticism, a strong movement has taken shape within investment circles. This movement is about using the power of capital to create meaningful social value.

While the environmental part of ESG is well understood, the social and governance parts remain somewhat obscure and ambiguous. They are addressed in this section.

If ESG fund managers do not pay attention to social concerns, then they are not doing justice to their fund. If they do, there could be other ramifications. For example, a fund manager may believe that a certain social issue is related to the distribution of power in society while her investors may feel otherwise. If she creates goals that are too ideologically driven, she may lose investors or may not find good investment opportunities. Both can be detrimental for the fund.

Without more elaborate frameworks, asset managers tend to lean upon some obvious areas such as diversity, human rights, consumer protection, and animal welfare—but even within those areas, significant positional differences exist. The United Nations has established the sustainability agenda with 17 goals. But these are cookie-cutter approaches, and knowing the goals does not mean they can be easily transferable to fund management. You need to address three areas to clarify your social and governance focus:

1. The question of value driver inclusion: This is where funds determine what constitutes a social or governance concern and what does not. It can also be viewed as determining which *social value driver* to include and which to exclude. For example, would exposing animals to clinical testing be considered a concern about animal welfare? Would running clinical trials in impoverished areas—where populations may not really understand what they are getting into—constitute human rights violations? Would capturing personal information of digital technology users be considered a human rights issue?
2. The question of definition: This is close to the first question, but it captures a different perspective. While the first addresses which broad areas to include, this problem addresses how to define a value driver once a decision is made to include one. For example, if you have selected weapons manufacturing as a (negative) *social value driver,* does all weapons manufacturing violate human rights or does only selling weapons to countries that violate human rights constitute a violation? This helps define the variables.
3. The question of measurement: Once variables are defined, the next question is how to measure the social impact. Would the measurement be against an absolute standard or would there be a relative standard?

Once the above questions are addressed, the fund must figure out how to deliver return above and beyond your investors' expected cost of capital (return expectation).

This means that answers to the above three questions should somehow be linked with returns—and that means answering various *strategy and goals of fund* questions.

To clarify the strategy, one needs to address the ESG approach. For example: Is the fund operating with the goal of behavior modification for a target firm or is it trying to reprimand offenders? Will the firm establish internal goals or abide by external goals? And most importantly, how does the ESG-enabled strategy translate into a competitive advantage?

The solution to solving the three problems and determining the returns relationship lies in artificial intelligence.

 ## HOW CAN AI HELP?

A firm can use machine learning to define and customize its ESG investment strategy. The way to conceptualize the model is to think about two processes—the social (or governance) value discovery process and the final machine learning model development process (see Figure 17.1 for a *social* process example). The social and governance process begins by outlining and clarifying the fund's strategy. The tasks of identifying value drivers, variables, and measurements follow the strategy clarification part. Based on the measures, a fund establishes the link between its financial performance and the drivers, variables, and measurements.

The process of establishing a link between the financial performance (returns generation) is derived from identifying those investment targets that conform to the drivers, variables, and measurements. For example, assume that a fund wants to establish workplace equality as a social value driver. It defines it as equal pay for women and workplace diversity. It establishes measures such as actual pay statistics and number of lawsuits or complaints filed against a company to evaluate the firm's performance. Based on these criteria, a set of target firms is then identified. These firms can be the candidates for inclusion in the portfolio. The portfolio is simulated to study its performance under various market conditions and with different assets. Once the testing (or backtesting) prevails, you can then fully automate the process. An automated process will scan and collect data in accordance with your specified variables and measures and prepare it for processing. The algorithms will identify the assets that meet your requirements and constantly simulate the portfolio return to give you the best possible portfolio options. Additionally, for the existing portfolio, you can manage both the risk of an asset from a financial performance perspective as well as the risk from the ESG perspective.

This enables dynamic fund management. The word *dynamic* refers to having the ability to constantly evaluate the link between social value creation and returns. This strategy can work for both passive and active investment styles.

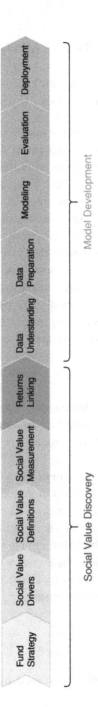

Fund Strategy · Social Value Drivers · Social Value Definitions · Social Value Measurement · Returns Linking · Data Understanding · Data Preparation · Modeling · Evaluation · Deployment

Social Value Discovery

Model Development

YOU MUST AVOID THESE MISTAKES

To secure solid returns and keep your ESG a strong contributor to value, you must avoid the following five mistakes:

Do not go with a cookie-cutter approach or insincerity: Investors are smart, and they will be able to assess whether you are being insincere about your true motivations for embracing an ESG policy. Whatever your strategy is, live up to it. Do not make promises that you cannot fulfill. Your investors will be able to judge the insincerity associated with the cookie-cutter approach. Make social value creation a competitive advantage for your firm. This means you must develop a customized framework.

Do not move forward without the 5th step: Make sure to link returns to your social value drivers, variables, and measures. Whatever you undertake in social value creation, you must be able to defend it. Make sure to have a clear and defensible framework that unmistakably defines what value creation means for your portfolio.

Do not proceed without properly understanding the data and algorithms: What data you select and which algorithms you use can also become a source of bias for your analysis. Establish a clear strategy on how to deal with bias.

Make sure to test your strategies: Establish protocols for testing your strategies. Use proper backtesting so that your model can work in active and live settings. Good investment strategies often come to die on the altars of overfitting.

AI itself can be a tool of oppression: One of your critical evaluations needs to be whether your target investments (firms) are using AI to create or destroy social value. These days AI is the top agenda item for most firms—and it can be used to do good or bad—and your knowledge of how your target firms are using AI can make all the difference. For example, AI is being used by some oppressive governments to track legitimate dissent or profile minorities. Companies that enable governments to have such technologies can be held accountable.

 ## SUMMARY STEPS

Based on the above, here are the five steps to **put a solid ESG strategy in your portfolio:**

1. **Understand your strategy;** identify your environmental, social, and governance value drivers, variables, and measures.
2. **Establish a hot link with returns.** Study how to qualify assets to be included in your ESG strategy. Test, test, and test. Do not use a cookie-cutter approach.
3. **Establish best practices for data management and preprocessing.** Implement data management and preprocessing as formal capabilities as recommended in this book.
4. Understand how to make several models work together. This means you will need multiple models to work in cohesion to **get a synchronized value-creation framework implemented.**
5. Factors that affect your portfolio will constantly change and evolve. **Know and proactively manage when change happens.** It can happen when the underlying distributions have changed—or the set of features you used to define the social or governance context have been altered.

REFERENCES

Boskou, G., et al. (2018) "Assessing Internal Audit with Text Mining." *Journal of Information and Knowledge Management*. [Online]. 17 (2), 1–22.

Browne, J., and Nuttall, R. (2013) "Beyond Corporate Social Responsibility: Integrated External Engagement." *McKinsey & Co.* (March), 1–11.

Calabrese, A., et al. (2016) "A Fuzzy Analytic Hierarchy Process Method to Support Materiality Assessment in Sustainability Reporting." *Journal of Cleaner Production*. [Online]. 121248–264.

Cennamo, C., et al. (2009) "Does Stakeholder Management have a Dark Side?" *Journal of Business Ethics*. [Online]. 89491–507.

Chatterji, A. K., et al. (2009) "How Well Do Social Ratings Actually Measure Corporate Social Responsibility?" *Journal of Economics and Management Strategy*. 18 (1), 125–169.

Cortez, M. A. A. (2011) "Do Markets Care about Social and Environmental Performance? Evidence from the Tokyo Stock Exchange." *Journal of International Business Research*. 10 (2), 15–23.

Desrochers, P. (2010) *The Environmental Responsibility of Business Is to Increase Its Profits (by creating value within the bounds of private property rights)*. [Online] 19 (1), 161–204.

Dhiman, S. (2008) "Products, People, and Planet: The Triple Bottom-Line Sustainability Imperative." *Journal of Global Issues*. 2 (2), 51–58.

Eccles, R. G., and Serafeim, G. (2013) "The Performance Frontier: Innovating for a Sustainable Strategy." *Harvard Business Review* (May), 50–60.

Edgley, C., et al. (2015) "The Adoption of the Materiality Concept in Social and Environmental Reporting Assurance: A field Study Approach." *The British Accounting Review*. [Online]. 47 (1), 1–18.

Ferrero-Ferrero, I., et al. (2016) "The Effect of Environmental, Social and Governance Consistency on Economic Results." *Sustainability*. [Online]. 8 (1005), 1–16.

Galbreath, J. (2009) "Building Corporate Social Responsibility into Strategy." *European Business Review*." 21 (2), 109–127.

Harrison, J. S., and Wicks, A. C. (2013) "Stakeholder Theory, Value, and Firm Performance." *Business Ethics Quarterly*. [Online]. 1 (January), 97–124.

Hillman, A. J., and Keim, G. D. (2001) "Shareholder Value, Stakeholder and Social Issues: What's the Bottom Line?" *Strategic Management Journal*. 22 (2), 125–139.

Hsu, C., et al. (2013) "Materiality Analysis Model in Sustainability Reporting: a Case Study at Lite-On Technology Corporation." *Journal of Cleaner Production*. [Online]. 57142–151.

Khan, M., et al. (2016) "Corporate Sustainability: First Evidence on Materiality." *The Accounting Review*. [Online]. 91 (6), 1697–1724.

Kim, Y. J., et al. (2016) *Detecting Financial Misstatements with Fraud Intention Using Multi-Class Cost-Sensitive Learning*. [Online]. 6232–43.

Li, Y. (2017) "Deep Reinforcement Learning: An Overview." 1–70.

Lin, C., et al. (2015) "Detecting the Financial Statement Fraud: The Analysis of the Differences between Data Mining Techniques and Experts' Judgments." *Knowledge-Based Systems*. [Online]. 89459–470. Available from: http://dx.doi.org/10.1016/j.knosys.2015.08.011.

Menz, K. (2010) "Corporate Social Responsibility: Is it Rewarded by the Corporate Bond Market? A Critical Note." *Journal of Business Ethics*. [Online] 96117–134.

Nguyen, P., et al. (2017) "Does Corporate Social Responsibility Create Shareholder Value? The Importance of Long-Term Investors." *Journal of Banking and Finance*. [Online]. 01–21.

Nishant, R., et al. (2016) "Sustainability and Differentiation: Understanding Materiality from the Context of Indian firms." *Journal of Business Research* [Online]. 69 (5), 1892–1897.

Norman, W., and MacDonald, C. (2004) "Getting to The Bottom of 'Triple Bottom Line.'" *Harvard Busines Review*. 14 (2), 243–262.

Pai, P., et al. (2011) "Knowledge-Based Systems: A Support Vector Machine–Based Model for Detecting Top Management Fraud." *Knowledge-Based Systems*. [Online]. 24 (2), 314–321.

Pava, M. L. (2008) "Why Corporations Should Not Abandon Social Responsibility." *Journal of Business Ethics*. [Online] 83805–812.

Perrini, F., and Tencati, A. (2006) "Sustainability and Stakeholder Management: The Need for New Corporate Performance Evaluation and Reporting Systems." *Business Strategy and the Environment* 15296–308.

Porter, M. E., and Kramer, M. R. (2006) "Strategy and Society: The Link Between Competitive Advantage and Corporate Social Responsibility." *Harvard Business Review*. December 78–92.

Price, J. M., and Sun, W. (2017) "Doing Good and Doing Bad: The Impact of Corporate Social Responsibility and Irresponsibility on Firm Performance." *Journal of Business Research*. [Online]. 80 (July 2015), 82–97.

Ravisankar, P., et al. (2011) "Detection of Financial Statement Fraud and Feature Selection Using Data Mining Techniques." *Decision Support Systems* [Online]. 50 (2), 491–500. Available from: http://dx.doi.org/10.1016/j.dss.2010.11.006.

Reich, R. (2007) *Supercapitalism: The Transformation of Business, Democracy, and Everyday Life*. New York: Alfred A. Knopf.

Silver, D., et al. (2016) "Mastering the Game of Go with Deep Neural Networks and Tree Search." *Nature*. [Online]. 529 (7585), 484–489.

Skarmeas, D., and Leonidou, C. N. (2013) "When Consumers Doubt, Watch Out! The Role of CSR Skepticism." *Journal of Business Research*. [Online]. 66 (10), 1831–1838. Available from: http://dx.doi.org/10.1016/j.jbusres.2013.02.004.

Sohrabi, S., et al. (2017) *State Projection via AI Planning*. 4611–4617.

Sprinkle, G. B., and Maines, L. A. (2010) "The Benefits and Costs of Corporate Social Responsibility." *Business Horizons*. [Online]. 53445–453.

Tantalo, C., and Priem, R. (2014) "Value Creation through Stakeholder Synergy." *Strategic Management Journal*. [Online]. (October 2014).

Vanclay, F. (2004) "The Triple Bottom Line and Impact Assessment: How Do TBL, EIA, SIA, SEA, and EMS Relate to Each Other? What is the Triple Bottom Line?" *Journal of Environmental Assessment Policy and Management*. 6 (3), 265–288.

Visser, W. (2011) *The Age of Responsibility: CSR 2.0 and the New DNA of Business*. John Wiley & Sons.

Wadhwa, P. (2017) "Non-Financial Reporting: Corporate Social Responsibility, Executives and Materiality." *International Journal of Research in Commerce & Management*, 854–57.

Wang, Z., and Sarkis, J. (2017) "Corporate Social Responsibility Governance, Outcomes, and Financial Performance." *Journal of Cleaner Production*. [Online]. 1621607–1616.

Whitehead, J. (2017) "Prioritizing Sustainability Indicators: Using Materiality Analysis to Guide Sustainability Assessment and Strategy." *Business Strategy and the Environment*. [Online]. 26 (August 2016), 399–412.

Wikstrom, P.-A. (2010) "Sustainability and Organizational Activities—Three Approaches." *Sustainability Development*. 107(18), 99–107.

Yoon, Y., et al. (2006) "The Effect of Corporate Social Responsibility (CSR) Activities on Companies with Bad Reputations." *Journal of Consumer Psychology*. 16 (4), 377–390.

CHAPTER EIGHTEEN

AI Organization and Project Management

I N PART 1 AND PART 2, WE RECOGNIZED that the AI transformation is not merely an extension of the classical era digital revolution. The underlying competitive dynamics, economics, business strategies, business models, and processes are all changing. A new reality of *how to run business* is emerging. In Part 1 and Part 2 we covered how to create a competitive advantage in the AI era. In this chapter we will first discuss what an AI-era organization looks like and then show how to build one. Second, we will cover the AI-related change management. Third, we will describe how to manage an AI project.

THE NEW ASSET MANAGEMENT ORGANIZATION

Recently, a third dimension has been added to the age-old debate about where asset management CEOs should come from—investment or sales. The third dimension is of technology. In a recent article titled "Who Deserves to Be a CEO?" George Wilbanks, a former Russell Reynolds Associates recruiter who now runs Wilbanks Partners, commented, "In every CEO search I've recently worked on, the boards all want someone with a broader background: technology, human capital, operations, strategy experience" (Segal, 2019). On that theme, Debra Brown, a senior member of Russell Reynolds' investment management practice added, "It's likely to happen: a CEO or another senior executive coming from tech." We can already observe the signs of evolution. Asset management firms are recognizing that with nearly all business processes being automated, the boundaries between technology and asset management are collapsing. The two are becoming one.

However, bringing in a tech executive without changing the underlying organizational structure will not show results. We observed that scenario playing out in several department stores, in the retail sector, where firms hired top executives from Amazon and other e-retailers, but their business performance did not improve.

A new type of organizational structure will be essential to make this work. Based on the AIAI's model, we suggest the following organizational setup in legacy asset management firms that are looking to transform to the AI era.

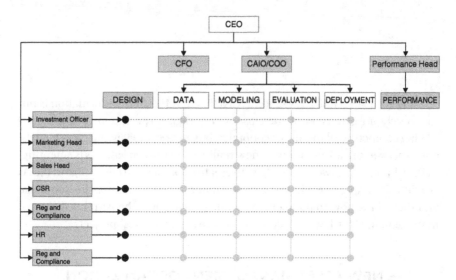

In this structure, we have the traditional functional business organizations reporting to the CEO; however, their primary function is for design and strategy. We also have the investment and risk management functions reporting to the CEO. In addition, the CFO, CAIO/COO, and performance head report to the CEO.

The CAIO/COO is a new role that does not exist in firms today. Essentially, the entire operational responsibility of delivering on the strategies of business/functional and investment leaders resides with this. It is building the assembly line for automation and machine learning. Four areas of data, modeling, evaluation, and deployment report to the CAIO/COO.

Since the design teams directly report to the functional heads, the overall strategies are developed and designed at that level. The performance head from the CEO office takes an integrated strategy outlook and evaluates the collective (whole vs. the parts) of the firm. The handover of work process happens when design teams finish their SADALs and pass them to the data team. Data teams are part of the CAIO/COO office. They enhance SADALs to analyze the data options and pass on to the modeling (model development) team. That is where algorithms are developed and passed on to the evaluation team. Once models are evaluated, they are then deployed by the deployment team. The deployment team is headed by what is the traditional CIO (chief information officer) role today.

 ## WHY A CAIO/COO ROLE?

We are collapsing the roles of COO and CAIO into one. This will end the confusion between various roles and responsibilities that exist today. Today, every functional head is hiring his or her own data science team. Chapter 1 explained that it is creating AI artifact proliferation and hence increasing the total cost of ownership. It is also increasing complexity and adding layers of failure. A CAIO-led organization is needed to build business capabilities for industrial-scale enterprise machine learning.

Since we have argued that machine learning and AI are the most important drivers of value going forward, the leadership for this area cannot be viewed narrowly as only technical. In legacy firms, you often hear statements such as "He is a technical person; you can't have him in the client-facing role" or that "she is technical and will not get the business strategy." Whatever the reasoning behind such statements was in the old era, I can assure you they are not applicable in the new era. The Silicon Valley tech sector has shown us that tech people are savvy businesspeople.

Since going forward, business will be about technology and technology about business, there is no point in having the COO and CAIO or CIO (information) or CDO (data) or CTO (technology) as different positions. I understand this will be a shock for some people, but take a step back and think. If your entire business strategy rests on your AI strategy, and your AI strategy is built to support your business strategy, then, from an operational perspective you must not treat these as two different functions. All your business strategy will be executed and operationalized from your work automation. And that is why your COO and CAIO should be the same person.

WHAT IS CHANGING?

The modern-era investment management organization has several changes:

- Functional heads and design: Functional heads are responsible for design (Chapter 3). They build strategies, and their strategies are integrated and vetted by the performance organization (Chapter 8). However, in our suggested approach, functional heads do not have their little department-based data science teams. They work with the internal COO/CAIO teams to implement and manage their AI automation. This brings execution discipline, reduces cost of implementation, and introduces best practices. This also means that one organization deals with the external AI suppliers and AI consultants.
- The CIO (investment) is in the same position. The investment or portfolio strategy and design work undertaken by the CIO is passed on to the industrial-scale enterprise machine learning (ISEML) assembly line.
- CIO (information), CDO (data), and CTO (technology) are collapsed under the CAIO/COO. This will also end the ongoing rivalry between the CIO and CDO offices (Samuels, 2015). The closest a CIO role can come to is the head of deployment. The head of deployment can be called CIO. That role is responsible for infrastructure, hardware, production environments, security and privacy, and other traditional IT responsibilities.
- The primary function of the CAIO/COO organization is to build and maintain an industrial-scale assembly line for enterprise machine learning. CAIO/COO organizations improve the productivity (how quickly), effectiveness (how capable), collaboration (machine-to-machine and human-to-machine interaction), adaptability (how adaptable solutions and systems are), and self-awareness (metacognition).
- The performance organization has a dotted-line reporting relationship to the board.

 HOW TO GET THERE?

You can do it yourself or engage a consulting firm to transition you to the industrial-scale enterprise machine learning firm. The process to transition is complex and requires realignment of several moving parts:

Selecting the CAIO/COO: The CAIO/COO selection part will be integral to the success of the investment management firm. You will be seeking a person who offers a strong background in both AI and business. In addition to leadership skills, this person will need strong management and professional services background to provide excellent customer service to the functional departments. The traditional CIO (information) is probably not the best candidate for this role. Someone with reasonably good machine learning background and a solid understanding of business will be a good match.

Consolidating the various data science talent: The second step will be to move the data science talent spread all over the firm to a central organization. This will require an assessment of the skill sets of professionals. Based on the skill sets they can be reassigned to data, modeling, evaluation, or deployment areas.

New hiring: Many new types of talent will be needed. In some cases, professional training will be needed to upskill the existing workforce.

Building the industrial-scale assembly line: The assembly line is not just a linear mechanism of work transfer; it also requires work processes to be conducted efficiently. This means the work transfer across various organizations should happen smoothly.

Implementing best practices: The new organization is supported by best practices. These best practices determine how work gets done. For example, at the design stage, the SADAL document becomes the document that details the work stream that follows design.

Incentive system design: The new organization will need to redesign the incentive systems. The measurement of incentives will be undertaken by the performance organization.

Performance organization: A carefully designed performance organization will serve as a strategy management function. Its design was discussed in Chapter 8.

Cross training: Cross training will be critical—not just between AI and business teams but also between AI and IT teams. Note that AI or data science people are not necessarily from an IT background. It is a mistake to assume that people with an IT background will understand AI or can develop or design AI systems. AI / data science professionals are uniquely skilled in data science–related subject areas, such as data preprocessing, algorithms, learning techniques, and optimizing algorithms. They may have professional or academic backgrounds in data science, cognitive science, neuroscience, statistics/mathematics, artificial intelligence, or other engineering or science fields. Typically, these professionals have a doctorate-level education.

The second category of professionals for the new era are the business leaders who understand artificial intelligence to drive change and innovation in their firms—and this book is an attempt to create that professional category. These professionals lead and drive change. They can be functional heads who move their businesses forward and become the project owners of solutions.

ISSUES OF THE NEW ORGANIZATION

The following two areas must be considered to build the new-era investment management function:

Leadership Roles for the Legacy vs. Traditional

The rise of an automation-centric transformation is challenging the traditional approaches to functional roles and style of management. Machines do not require the bureaucratic structures needed to manage human-centered organizations. Automation will also eliminate the existing function-specific silos that exist in companies. Additionally, legacy leaders unwilling to change may be replaced with leaders with a strong understanding of the dynamics of the new era. Many organizations have hired a director or VP-level person who is responsible for innovation or *future of work*–type transformations. This is not the right way to transform. These people usually have no budget, no teams, no ability to influence traditional departments, no background in AI, and no ability to achieve their goals. Others who do have background in AI are either too technical or get lost under the layers of bureaucracy. Experience from the 1980s (ERP systems) and from the late 1990s (the Internet revolution), shows that this is the wrong way to lead the transformation. You cannot jump into a transformation half-heartedly and with a half-baked plan. AI is not a photo-op or a PR stunt. Despite what you are being told, it is not hype. It is a real change phenomenon with massive power. Every person in the company must transform. Every leader must develop critical skills to lead the AI revolution. Every VP or functional head must have a comprehensive AI transformation plan. Every area of the organization must dare to imagine a future where the power of AI will be unleashed to create powerful value for shareholders.

For such a transformation to happen, CEOs must lead their organizations with an AI-centric strategic transformation mindset. The worst thing you can do is to view AI from the "use case" perspective. Unfortunately, many consulting firms are doing exactly that—and many machine learning platform sales teams are also approaching AI sales from that perspective. A use case–centric mindset is non-strategic, and it can never lead to the creation of competitive advantage. Strategy must lead the use cases and not the other way around.

Remember: you are designing systems from data and not for data. This is a profound difference.

PhDs vs. MBAs Struggle

As is clear, the new organization will be composed of data scientists and AI people. Many legacy (non-tech) companies have been structured around business graduates. In many firms, technologists are often stereotyped or labeled as lacking people skills, business acumen, and management and leadership traits. Such a categorization is unjust, misleading, and problematic. As we transition to a new-era company, CEOs and HR must help create conditions to facilitate science-oriented (PhDs) people becoming part of the culture. In many sophisticated asset management firms this is not an issue. In others, some work may be needed.

Science vs. Pseudoscience

One of the biggest changes that will be needed is to transition to data-centric decision-making. Replacing the gut feel with science might be challenging in non-investment functions. This is where new training will be needed. Additionally, there are also areas in which we believe we are being scientific, but it is really pseudoscience. For example, many consulting firms survey executives from different companies and based on those surveys declare what their companies should embrace and do. You should not plan your company's future based on executive surveys. First, these surveys may not have been conducted in a scientific manner and may be structured with bias. Second, they may contain bias in the responses. Third, they may only show the limits of what your peers and competitors are thinking—who may not have the breakthrough thinking that you need.

Investment into AI

Clearly, rebuilding capabilities will require new investment. CEOs and boards should recognize that making that investment will be necessary for sustainability of the business. AI is changing the business world. Embracing the change is not enough—you must lead the change. The investment needed may turn out to be more than the investments made in the ERP or CRM systems, or Internet-based transformations. But there is no choice. It is an existential requirement.

CHANGE MANAGEMENT

The transformation also requires a sophisticated change management initiative. Specifically, there are three areas of concern from a change management perspective: unemployment, work planning, and reskilling.

Fear of Unemployment

Leaders and teams will be concerned about AI. You must address the major concern: would automation lead to job loss? This is a valid concern. There is no doubt that many jobs will be eliminated. Leaders must not misguide their people by giving false narratives. Many leaders mislead when they claim that AI will not replace human work and that it will only save time and effort so humans can work on more interesting things. While this is also true, it is not the full story. Human work will be automated, and jobs will be eliminated. The idea is to retrain people to make them valuable for the firm in the AI economy.

Work Planning

A renewed focus on work planning will be necessary to drive innovation. Begin by looking at all the major work streams by functions. Identify the tasks in accordance with value creation goals. Knowing what will be automated when is part of the work planning. We will need function-by-function and job-by-job detailed planning about what work processes, tasks, and jobs will be automated—and eliminated. A corporate registry of AI artifacts should be maintained to know what has been automated. Think of it as keeping track of your digital workforce.

Reskilling

The massive intensity and magnitude of change requires constant retraining. Both business and IT professionals need to be retrained. The retraining goes beyond learning about machine learning, as it requires understanding that business strategy is changing. Executives can benefit from training on how to lead in the AI economy.

 ## MANAGING AI PROJECTS

There are seven steps of project planning and leadership for AI:

1. **Cognitive transformation strategy:** This part of the plan defines the transformation mission, approach, and vision for the future. This is undertaken by the design and performance organizations, and it is led by the CEO.
2. **Cognitive business plan:** This is an enterprise plan that links strategy to execution. It is developed by business units and functions. This is managed by the design, performance, and CAIO organizations.
3. **Cognitive transformation plan:** The business plan is used to develop the use cases, and those use cases are prioritized and developed in accordance with the strategic priorities and operational bandwidth of firms. Projects are arranged based upon experience, value, complexity, and customer need.
4. **Cognitive transformation tech plan:** The tech plan is for the CAIO office. It includes plans about all the four steps of data, modeling, evaluation, and deployment.
5. **Cognitive governance plan:** AI has introduced several challenges in governance. They are covered in detail in the next chapter. In this step, firms develop a comprehensive AI governance plan.

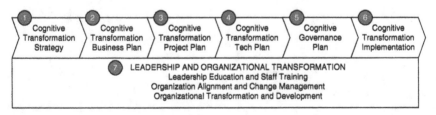

FIGURE 18.1 AI Organizational Planning

6. **Cognitive transformation implementation:** This is managed by the CAIO organization, and it includes detailed design of the technical resources (hardware, architecture, security, tech stack, etc.). AI artifacts are developed and implemented in this part of the project.

7. **Leadership and organizational transformation:** In this step, firms design and implement plans for leadership and staff education, organizational alignment, change management, retraining, reskilling, and organizational development.

REFERENCES

Samuels, M. (2015) "Chief Data and Digital Officers Rise to Threaten the CIO." *ComputerWeekly.com.* (February), 15–18. [Online]. Available from: https://www.computerweekly.com/feature/Chief-Data-and-Digital-Officers-rise-to-threaten-the-CIO.

Segal, J. (2019) "Who Deserves to Be a CEO?" *Institutional Investor.* [Online]. Available from: https://www.institutionalinvestor.com/article/b1d30ytq6qmwth/Who-Deserves-to-Be-a-CEO.

CHAPTER NINETEEN

Governance and Ethics

G OVERNANCE AND ETHICS ARE IMPORTANT CONSIDERATIONS in the AI era. The changing nature of business necessitates addressing governance and ethics issues. We will look at the following:

1. Corporate governance with AI;
2. Governance of AI; and
3. Ethics.

Notice the difference between governance with AI and governance of AI. One deals with implementing corporate governance with AI and the other with governing AI itself.

CORPORATE GOVERNANCE WITH AI

Your automation plan for corporate governance is composed of eight areas of capability building: forming and running effective boards, implementing executive checks and balances, internal controls, risk management, regulatory compliance, culture of accountability and transparency, protecting clients, and environment, social, and governance (ESG). Since ESG was covered in detail in the CSR chapter, we will only introduce that as a capability area.

1. Effective board

The history of problems in corporate governance is a living testament of board failures. With failed boards, we observe obliviousness on one end and hypocritical and disingenuous activity on the other. In the former we see an outright negligence stemming from laziness or indifference; in the latter a façade of deception. The good news is that thanks to AI, today we have several methods and capabilities at our disposal to make sure that we recruit and help manage effective boards. Here is how to deploy your AI tool set for board management:

a. **Select the board:** Deploy this tool to analyze publicly available data to select board members. The system analyzes the backgrounds of potential board members and classifies them in areas of capabilities. A separate algorithm can break down the governance needs of the organization. This could be done by mining board documents, publicly available information, and other data in a firm to assess what the firm's real needs are. When combined, these two AI artifacts can give you best matches for your board members. Such an assessment can be an ongoing feature and can be applied to the existing boards as well.

b. **Independence:** Evaluating independence has two parts to it: pre-board membership independence evaluation and post-board member evaluation. In other words, independence is not a static concept. People's business and personal relationships evolve. A classification algorithm can classify board members into various groupings that can show potential conflicts. A separate unsupervised algorithm works behind the scenes and captures various unknown or unsuspected potential relationships. The data for both comes from public sources.

c. **Conflict of interest:** Conflict of interest goes beyond independence and captures conflicts in decision-making. To do that, start by designing a simple natural language processing (NLP)–based utility that first creates a dictionary of keywords from the decision-making process, ensuring that named entity recognition (NER) can extract entities. Then using public data, deploy a separate algorithm to explore if the decision-maker and the NER may have any conflict of interest.

d. **Personality:** Deploy your algorithm to assess and measure the personality of people. There are many ways to do that. One way to assess is for the algorithm to analyze the written communications of the management team and the board members to search for words that signify integrity, ethics, values, and personality. This approach has been deployed to study the fraud risk from linguistic and vocal patterns of earnings calls (Throckmorton et al., 2015) as well as from documents (Management's discussion and analysis, or MD&A, section of the 10-K form; Humpherys et al., 2011). Humpherys et al. also discovered that "fraudulent disclosures use more activation language, words, imagery, pleasantness, group references, and less lexical diversity than nonfraudulent ones. Writers of fraudulent disclosures may write more to appear credible while communicating less in actual content."

e. **Diversity:** We are not only seeking diversity from an ethnic or gender perspective but also by making sure that we have diversity of opinion. Implement an algorithm to discover if you are experiencing groupthink in your board. Groupthink is dangerous (Janis, 1971)—especially in the investment world—and we now have new technologies that help ensure that board members and management teams don't fall victim to that. This too comes from NLP.

f. **Effectiveness:** Measure the effectiveness of the board to govern the firm. One way to do that is to develop some quantitative and qualitative measures and have your algorithm track for those. To assess that, use data from board minutes. The goal is to track what was the contribution of the board members. Identifying themes from data mining is one way to extract the strategic themes (Kobayashi et al., 2018).

g. **Communication:** Analyze the communications to and from the board and classify that to study the cultural, ethical, business, and other attributes (Kobayashi et al., 2018).

h. **Role played in internal audit:** This is one of the most critical areas. Audit comes with its own requirements from board members. Boards are tasked with the oversight responsibility for internal controls (COSO, 2013). That is where you can direct an algorithm to track that boards are performing their oversight responsibility. You can also look at the independence to assess that board members are independent of the audit firm.

i. **ESG:** Please refer to Chapter 17, where we covered the topic of ESG in detail.

2. **Right checks and balances**

a. **Compensation:** Compensation assessment is automated to assess whether it is fair and competitive. If the firm has access to such data, you can deploy an algorithm (supervised, regression) to calculate and suggest that.

b. **Conflict of interest and strategic consistency:** Assess whether your firm is making decisions in the best interest of clients. Design and implement an AI artifact to ensure that the best interests of clients are considered. This artifact will vary by firms. It is based on your strategy. Typically, this would work for fundamentals-centric strategies. Data related to your strategy is used to predict if your investment is consistent with your declared strategy.

3. **Internal controls**
   a. **Review controls:** Significant technology potential exists in automating the internal controls assessment. Please refer to my book on AI in Audit (Wiley).

4. **Risk management**

   Enterprise risk management: Enterprise risk management with AI is a broad topic, and an entire book can be dedicated to that. The important points about enterprise risk management and AI are:

   a. AI provides an avenue to assess atheoretical risk assessment—that means risks that you are not looking for since there is no theoretical framework to look for them. Typical risk evaluations are based on a hypothesis developed to support an existing theory. With AI, you can explore the unknown unknowns (things you don't know that you don't know).

   b. Several useful applications are being developed for risk management. With proper data and resources, you can deploy many powerful capabilities in-house. For example, market risk, credit risk, RegTech, and reputational and operational risks can be addressed using AI (Aziz and Dowling, 2019). Trading-centric compliance risks can be managed proactively.

   c. A robust enterprise risk management AI strategy is critical for a modern-day asset management operation.

5. **Regulatory management and compliance**

   Like many other areas in governance, RegTech adoption is also chaotic, all over the map, and tactical. Strategy is often absent or underdeveloped. Arner et al. give an excellent description of what is transpiring: "RegTech to date has focused on the digitization of manual reporting and compliance processes. This offers tremendous cost savings to the financial services industry and regulators. However, the potential of RegTech is far greater—it has the potential to enable a nearly real-time and proportionate regulatory regime that identifies and addresses risk while facilitating more efficient regulatory compliance." (Arner et al., 2017). Our approach to automated and strategic RegTech is as follows:

   a. Intelligence on legislation and regulation: Develop and deploy a regulatory intelligence tracker that collects intelligence on both legislative and regulatory developments. This tracker uses data supplied from dedicated regulatory and legislative data providers, and also uses your own data collected from public sources. The goal of this utility is to keep you posted on important developments. There are three steps to designing this. First is a web-scraping engine that pulls and consolidates data from various relevant websites. Second, the data is classified by content. Third, analyses are performed to extract important details. The analyses track the opportunities and risks to your organization. The tracker also analyzes support and sentiment related to the sentiment, the segments of the population where they are coming from, and how they are being perceived.

b. Automated communicator: An intelligent influencer utility is designed for social media platforms. It can communicate a company's position related to a certain legislative development. This can also track interactions and crowdsourced responses to understand the implications and momentum behind various legislations.

c. Analyze the existing regulations: Using NLP, analyze the existing regulations and assess for overlap and contradictions. If the firm has a global footprint, make sure to include regulations from other countries and global standards. This exercise helps produce an index of regulations based on multidimensional attributes. In other words, instead of a linear way of looking at regulations, you can compare and contrast regulations from different angles. For example, by client types, structures, asset classes, geographies, agencies, channels, clients, and products.

d. Use robotic process automation for implementing regulatory protocols that require specific measurements. Then validate their accuracy using machine learning–centric validation. RPA will consolidate in a deterministic way and give you the totals and the balances—but a sanity check for their relative accuracy can be undertaken by machine learning. With a smart selection of features, you can assess whether the numbers being reported by your RPA bot make sense or not.

e. Deploying a strategy: Analyze the regulatory framework of your firm in comparison to weaknesses and strengths. Are there areas in which your framework is weak? There are two parts to it. First, implement an artifact to determine if the framework itself is comprehensive and robust. Use NLP to assess against a broad spectrum of regulatory data to determine if your framework is paying enough attention to a certain regulation. Second, observe the implementation of the regulatory frameworks in the firm. You can use corporate data (emails, communications, and others) to see frequency of mentions about a specific regulation. This gives you a measure of share-of-corporate-mind by various regulations. In other words, it helps you determine what regulations people are most knowledgeable about. Obviously, these are organizational behavior measures—but we believe they must accompany the more standard measures. In general, we advocate an approach where any mathematically (deductively) measured calculation that is required by regulations should be combined with (1) a sanity check measure that is inferred from variables that are indirectly related to what is being deductively measured; and (2) a cultural and organizational measure that shows the share-of-mind and organizational consciousness about a certain regulation. This approach is not that different from how audit works—except it is automated. A human can study the results to assess for reasonability. We advocate exploring the framework by the principal regulatory objectives: financial stability, prudential safety and soundness, consumer protection and market integrity, and market competition and development (Arner et al., 2017).

f. Integrated RegTech: Implementing RegTech piecemeal as point systems—for example, in investing and trading (Wall, 2018)—will not lead to a robust system. We discussed the concepts of collaborative and adaptive AI in Chapter 3. With metacognition, an integrated perspective of AI can give you greater control and a more robust framework for supervision.

g. Simulate risk: RegTech should be approached from an enterprise risk management perspective (Choi et al., 2016). Simulating enterprise risk (Sohrabi et al., 2018) and assessing enterprise risk in virtual organizations (Chen et al., 2010) using AI are game changers. Deploy simulations to perform regulatory review and generate failure scenarios and assess vulnerability.

h. Audit trail: Develop a utility that uses metadata to analyze the use of systems—for example, by who, when, where, for what purpose. Use process mining to extract processes, and then feed that data to a classifier that can classify that in terms of risk. Follow up in areas where the system shows suspicious activity. Use a combination of the metadata and transactional data to assess the level of change that will be necessary to support a regulatory change. Tie that into a qualitative and quantitative assessment of regulatory change effect using traditional methods.

i. Compliance testing: Perform compliance testing in both simulated environments and real environments. Once again, use the method of: (1) calculating deductive measurements; (2) validating by sanity checks; and (3) assessing cultural and organizational elements. The idea is to be able to do that monitoring 24-7.

6. **Culture of accountability**

    MIT Sloan launched a study to measure and compare cultures across various companies (Sull et al., 2019). Known as Culture 500, MIT researchers used NLP to evaluate values such as agility, collaboration, attention to customers, diversity, execution, innovation, integrity, performance, and respect. They used Glassdoor data from evaluations authored by employees or former employees of companies. The patterns discovered were classified into cultural categories. To make it work they trained the algorithm by developing custom hand-coded features. This is an example of how algorithms can be deployed to assess the culture of a firm.

    Employee behavior in organizations can be predicted by deploying machine learning and data mining textual information such as emails (Straub et al., 2016). A separate analysis of an organization can also show power flows, influence, and informal social interactions (Fire and Puzis, 2016).

7. **Protect rights and interests of shareholders/clients**

    a. Shareholder communications: Analyze your shareholder communications to understand your own biases. Develop insights into your style and speech patterns. Identify if you are using the best ways to communicate.

    b. Voting: Develop insights into your voting styles. Do you use a criterion? Why? The goal of the AI artifact in this case is twofold: (1) Help you identify voting patterns across the industry; (2) Give you the research necessary to show if your voting has been consistent with your stated strategies and values.

8. **ESG**

    Please refer to Chapter 17, where we covered the topic of ESG in detail.

 ## GOVERNANCE OF AI

The biggest elephant in the room is not how to use AI to govern but instead how to govern AI. Throughout this book we emphasized the need for AI. We showed hundreds of applications of AI and gave you a vision for an AI-centered design of

GOVERNANCE FRAMEWORK

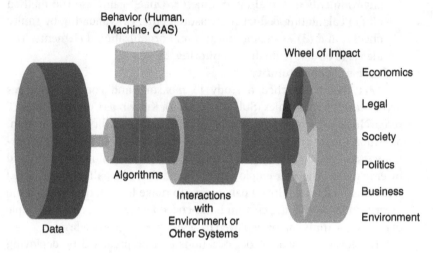

FIGURE 19.1 The AIAI Governance Framework

your firm. The obvious problem is how to police the police. In other words, how to govern AI. This problem has invited significant debate. Many large tech firms have tried to establish boards and repeatedly failed. We believe that fintech and asset management firms should have their own AI governance committees in their boards and that global standards should be established for AI governance.

In 2016 I developed a model which is now the American Institute of AI's official model for AI governance (Figure 19.1). It has the following three main parts:

The nature and functionality of technology: The nature of technology is composed of data, data distributions, and algorithms. This part focuses on the functionality of the artifact. Specifically, it determines the application's performance in accordance with its goals. It also measures whether the artifact is stable and safe for human use and consumption (Figure 19.2). Safety means that the artifact cannot harm humans or their interests. Stability means that the application will perform in accordance with its goals throughout its lifetime. In other words, the artifact cannot evolve to a state that is inconsistent with its goals. Both safety and stability are analyzed in two ways: transparency (knowledge that the artifact is safe and stable) and accountability (ability to demonstrate that the artifact is safe and stable). In addition, mechanisms are

ARTIFACT SAFETY AND STABILITY MODEL

safe	processes and products to evaluate safety I know it is safe	processes and products to create safety-centric transparency I can show it is safe
stable	processes and products to evaluate stability I know it is stable	processes and products to create stability-centric transparency I can show it is stable
	accountability	transparency

—Stable means artifacts can only perform within the strict confinements of their goals

—Safe means the stated goals of the artifacts are legal and beneficial for humankind

—Accountability means establishing clear responsibility with users, designers, and developers

—Transparency means being able to explain

FIGURE 19.2 AIAI Safety and Stability Model

put in place to track that data distributions underlying the artifact's training are consistent with what the artifact was trained on, the algorithms are still relevant and optimized, and the solution is optimized in terms of ensuring that the features used are collectively exhaustive and no new features have been identified that can make the current solution less valuable and useful. We also track the relationship between the problem-solution mapping to make sure that the solution approach is still relevant. Finally, what transpires in the mind of the machine is sometimes hard to determine. In deep learning systems, for example, at the current state of the technology, we are sometimes unable to explain what goes on in the mind of a neural network and hence while we can see the inputs and impressive outputs, we are unable to explain why the machine made its decision. This could mean that in those areas in which you must explain why a machine made a certain decision, such a system may not be a good solution. Although I believe that, even in those areas, using the deep learning solution as a sounding board (under human decision authority), or as producing knowledge for which theory needs to be established, is not a bad idea. Scientists are working to create explainable AI (XAI), which will eliminate such constraints (Doran et al., 2017; Wang et al., 2019). AIAI defines governance as the actions and processes by which stable and safe AI artifacts develop and persist (Figure 19.1). This applies to both products and services. Notice this definition includes the role played by the users, designers, enablers, and developers of artificial intelligence.

The two elements of safety and stability are not afterthoughts, as they must be considered right at the inception of AI system design. In summary, the interaction of the two dimensions of safety and stability with the two dimensions of accountability and transparency give us four focus areas of being able to know and demonstrate safety and stability.

The social dynamics of technology: Machines work in collaboration with other machines and interact with humans. That means that machine-to-machine interaction and machine-to-human interaction are important considerations from a risk and governance perspective. The governance part of artificial intelligence is not only related to capturing the cognitive aspects of a machine, it must include the behavioral and social dynamics of machines. These social dynamics can unfold in many ways. The ability to understand the interaction of multiple AI artifacts as a society (for example, swarm or ant colony) is pivotal to govern multi-agent systems (Aydin and Fellows, 2017, 2018). In addition, attempting to understand and govern (to some level) the social dynamics is also important because the configurations of machine and human interaction is a complex adaptive system (CAS). CAS is a system where understanding the parts does not necessarily imply one understands the whole. These are nonlinear dynamical systems where complexity results from being a dynamic network of interactions between intelligent machines and humans. Such systems are adaptive, as they have self-organizing and emergent properties.

The effect of technology on human systems: The third dimension of AI governance is how it affects human systems. The effect of machine actions is an important consideration. How machines behave can affect our social, economic, and political decisions, frameworks and institutions, organizations, and culture. In other words, what a machine thinks is one question, whereas what a machine does is another question. The consequences of the thinking and the actions of the machine requires exploration. The wheel of impact provides a mechanism of determining the impact or the consequences of the technology on various human processes including economics, politics, legal, society, business, and environment.

FRAMING THE ETHICAL PROBLEMS FROM A PRAGMATIC VIEWPOINT

Will the introduction of intelligent machines change our existing frameworks of ethics? How to implement ethical frameworks for machines?

These two questions form the basis of fundamental analysis on these topics and are some of the most important considerations for the new era of intelligent automation. While the prospects and the promise of new technologies and the AI era are certainly the most exciting parts of the transformation, from a governance perspective we must address the following issues:

- We must ask what ethics mean in the context of intelligent automation. Machines, even intelligent, do not seem to have intent. They are deployed in accordance with human intent. How can you associate ethics with machines when they do not possess intent?
- How should we audit machines from an ethical perspective? What role do human intent and ethics play in that audit?
- The introduction of intelligent automation has greatly changed the risk characteristics of business. New and unprecedented risks are now introduced in modern business. For example, flash crash in financial markets, where markets lose significant value within minutes, has been attributed to autonomous and automated trading. What are the ethics when no single company or firm does something unethical, but the combined effect of crowdsourced intelligence of machines and humans creates a catastrophe?
- We must also be aware of a new type of highly potent risk that is taking shape due to intelligent systems. This is not a typical inherent risk, since it is not inherent in a business function or process; instead it is intentionally induced and injected in the business by an adversary. Analogous to traditional cybersecurity risk where a malign-intentioned adversary attempts to harm the enterprise, this new risk is a cousin of that. What makes it different from the cybersecurity risk is that it does not have to penetrate the firewall of a firm, and that means we do not have protections against it. I have termed it as the ex-asymmetric risk where "ex" signifies that risk generally emanates outside the firewall. In this attack, the adversary strategically attacks the profit-generating or goal-achieving potential of a firm. Such attacks can be targeted to disseminate false and misleading information

about the products and services of a firm that can lead to fear and adverse reaction by various stakeholders. As such attacks spread virally on social media, they can wreak havoc on the value of a firm. They are often enabled by coordinated actions by armies of bots. Intervention to dispel or quell the allegation, or to present the facts about the veracity of the claims, often arrive too late.

SOME OBVIOUS ETHICAL ISSUES

Some recent and obvious examples of ethical violations of AI systems include profiling, sexism, discrimination, prejudice, and bigotry. Many other not so obvious problems include:

- **Risk of exploitation and manipulation:** With the power to process huge amounts of data about humans, machines can develop deep profiles. Such profiles can be used to create anger and conflict in society. For example, during elections, fake news and targeted campaigning can be used to arouse rage and hateful sentiments across populations.
- **Risk of overreliance on autonomous technology:** We can sometimes become so dependent on technology that we miss out on signals we receive from our instincts.
- **Risk of unemployment, wealth redistribution:** Automation is creating a major risk of unemployment. The financial sector is shedding hundreds of thousands of jobs (Kelly, 2019). As the wealth concentration happens, it can lead to rapid social disintegration.
- **Risk of corruption:** AI can also enable criminals and fraudsters to commit fraud and corruption by using more powerful technology.
- **Militarization risks:** Last but not least, the risks specific to the military include the race to arm and irresponsible weaponization with AI.

HUMANS AND AI

As we introduce more powerful AI technologies, we must consider the following effects:

- **Dignity:** Human dignity and self-image may be negatively affected when humans feel that they are being placed in a subservient position to a machine. For example, when a human is interviewed by a robot and not selected, or when a person loses his or her job to a robot. In human interactions, we are generally cognizant of how to express difficult messages without hurting human dignity—but machines do not have such empathy. For instance, when a machine hangs up on you, it does it with an abrupt a message, "Please try your call later." A human, before hanging up, would explain the reason or at the very least apologize for why he or she was unable to help you. Also, view the interaction from a human perspective. Let's say even if a machine offers an apology, how would you react knowing that it is not coming from someone who might actually feel your pain?

- **Privacy:** The ability of machines to process massive data is both highly intrusive and can lead to the invasion of privacy. Setting up standards about fair, permissible, and transparent use of data will go a long way toward AI ethics.
- **Safety:** Safety of AI systems remains a critical issue. For example, accidents of autonomous cars have raised concerns about their viability. It is likely that the problems in recent Boeing 737 MAX crashes resulted from malfunction in autonomous control systems (Pasztor and Tangel, 2019).
- **Relationships:** AI affects how we build and manage our relationships. For example, dating applications use algorithms to match people. Do we risk going so far that we will lose the basic human instinct of in-person human-to-human social interaction?
- **Trigger irrationality:** AI can be deployed to hijack human emotions and rationality by invoking sentiments via extremely personalized campaigns.
- **Values:** AI can be used to redefine social values and create an alternative system of values that could be inconsistent with the long-held shared and established values of human civilization. Perception engineering can fracture the existing bonds and relationships between social groups.
- **Cyber:** In recent years we have seen large-scale cyberattacks. Their sophistication is increasing.
- **Power:** Lastly, AI can give too much control to government agencies over individuals and companies.

ETHICS CHARTER

We advocate that every asset management firm should consider adding references to AI in their corporate values, governance frameworks, and ethics charter. The American Institute of Artificial Intelligence has created the following ethics charter, which can be adopted by your firm:

- **Human benefit:** We will strive to maintain the supremacy of humans over machines. We will ensure that technology and science benefit humankind. We will not use, design, or enable artificial intelligence technology in areas that will increase human suffering, diminish human dignity and privacy, or enhance human exploitation.
- **Human protection:** We will protect humans and human institutions from the misuse of technology in social, political, and economic areas of human life.
- **Better world:** We will strive to maintain the supremacy of natural life-forms over machines. We will help create a better world with AI. A better world ensures that natural lifeforms thrive, and both intelligent and less-intelligent natural lifeforms can coexist in a safe and healthy environment safe from artificial lifeforms.
- **Confidentiality:** We will protect and respect the confidentiality of the proprietary data and algorithms of our employers and our internal and external clients.
- **Law:** We will abide by the laws of all the countries in which we operate.
- **Bias:** We will make our best efforts to ensure that the artifacts we design, and work with, will not be biased toward anyone on the basis of religion, gender, ethnicity, color of skin, race, heritage, sexual preferences, and other such factors.
- **Learn:** We will constantly enhance our skills to become and stay relevant and valuable for our employer and clients.
- **Ethics:** We will maintain the highest professional standards and ethics.

In addition to having the framework, AI can be used to measure and assess the application and abidance of ethics in your firm. Adhering to ethics can also have a large positive effect on your investment strategy and brand.

 ## REFERENCES

Arner, D. W., et al. (2017) "FinTech, RegTech, and the Reconceptualization of Financial Regulation." *Northwestern Journal of International Law and Business*. 37(3), 373–415.

Aydin, M. E., and Fellows, R. (2017) *A reinforcement learning algorithm for building collaboration in multi-agent systems.* [Online]. Available from: http://arxiv.org/abs/1711.10574.

Aydin, M. E., and Fellows, R. (2018) "Building Collaboration in Multi-Agent Systems Using Reinforcement Learning." *Lecture Notes in Computer Science (including subseries Lecture Notes in Artificial Intelligence and Lecture Notes in Bioinformatics).* [Online]. 11056 LNAI201–212.

Aziz, S., and Dowling, M. (2019) "Machine Learning and AI for Risk Management," in Theo Lynn et al. (eds.) *Disrupting Finance, Fintech and Strategy in the 21st Century.* Palgrave Macmillan. p. 33.

Chen, H., et al. (2010) "Virtual Enterprise Risk Management Using Artificial Intelligence." *Mathematical Problems in Engineering.* [Online]. 2010 (Volume 2010, Article ID 572404).

Choi, Y., et al. (2016) "Optimizing Enterprise Risk Management: A Literature Review and Critical Analysis of the Work of Wu and Olson." *Annals of Operations Research.* [Online]. 237(1–2), 281–300.

COSO (2013) *Internal Control - Integrated Framework.* [Online]. Available from: https://www.coso.org/Documents/990025P-Executive-Summary-final-may20.pdf. Available from: https://www.coso.org/Documents/990025P-Executive-Summary-final-may20.pdf.

Doran, D., et al. (2017) *What Does Explainable AI Really Mean? A New Conceptualization of Perspectives.* [Online]. Available from: https://arxiv.org/abs/1710.00794.

Fire, M., and Puzis, R. (2016) "Organization Mining Using Online Social Networks." *Networks and Spatial Economics.* [Online]. 16 (2), 545–578.

Humpherys, S. L., et al. (2011) "Identification of Fraudulent Financial Statements Using Linguistic Credibility Analysis." *Decision Support Systems.* [Online]. 50(3), 585–594.

Janis, I. (1971) "Groupthink." *Psychology Today.* 84–90.

Kelly, J. (2019) *Wells Fargo Predicts That Robots Will Steal 200,000 Banking Jobs Within The Next 10 Years* [Online]. Available from: https://www.forbes.com/sites/jackkelly/2019/10/08/wells-fargo-predicts-that-robots-will-steal-200000-banking-jobs-within-the-next-10-years/#db949ad68d78.

Kobayashi, V. B., et al. (2018) *Text Mining in Organizational Research.* Vol. 21. [Online].

Pasztor, A., and Tangel, A. (2019) "Investigators Believe Boeing 737 MAX Stall-Prevention Feature Activated in Ethiopian Crash." *The Wall Street Journal.* 29 March. [Online]. Available from: https://www.wsj.com/articles/

investigators-believe-737-max-stall-prevention-feature-activated-in-ethio
pian-crash-11553836204.

Sohrabi, S., et al. (2018) "An AI Planning Solution to Scenario Generation for Enterprise Risk Management." *32nd AAAI Conference on Artificial Intelligence, AAAI 2018*. (i), 160–167.

Straub, K. M., et al. (2016) *Data Mining Academic Emails to Model Employee Behaviors and Analyze Organizational Structure*. [Online]. Available from: https://vtechworks.lib.vt.edu/bitstream/handle/10919/71320/Straub_KM _T_2016.pdf;sequence=1.

Sull, D., et al. (2019) *Measuring culture in leading comapnies* [Online]. Available from: https://sloanreview.mit.edu/projects/measuring-culture-in-leading-companies/.

Throckmorton, C. S., et al. (2015) "Financial Fraud Detection Using Vocal, Linguistic and Financial Cues." *Decision Support Systems*. [Online]. 7478–87. Available from: http://dx.doi.org/10.1016/j.dss.2015.04.006.

Wall, L. D. (2018) "Some Financial Regulatory Implications of Artificial Intelligence." *Journal of Economics and Business*. [Online]. 100 (November 2017), 55–63. Available from: https://doi.org/10.1016/j.jeconbus.2018.05.003.

Wang, D., et al. (2019) "Designing Theory-Driven User-Centric Explainable AI." *CHI 2019 Glasgow Scotland May 4–9*. Paper 6011–15.

CHAPTER TWENTY

Adaptation and Emergence

THIS BOOK IS ABOUT BUILDING A hypermodern investment management firm. Isn't every asset management or investment management firm already modern? After all, for decades companies in the financial sector have invested in digital transformation. CEOs have bragged about their digital capabilities, and many companies in recent years have announced automation projects.

Giant firms manage trillions of dollars and are meticulously segmented into functional departments, each with their own department heads, business plans, and organizational targets. Powerful program management offices and centers of excellence are carefully embedded in day-to-day operations. Process-by-process charts of operations and best practices are recorded, observed, and followed. Clearly, everything that points to being modern is already there. Then why challenge the status quo? Why rock the boat that seems to be floating fine? Why tinker around with this well-oiled machine?

The reality is that they are anything but well-oiled machines. In fact, our obsession with finding cause and effect–centered relationships and architecting our functions and businesses as layers of cogs of well-oiled machines continues to fail us. Our siloed functions and their interdependencies have disappointed us on so many occasions. From strategic weaknesses to tactical miscalculations, from catastrophic failures to systemic meltdowns, we have seen our firms falter and cave every time markets hiccup. At other times, we have observed our companies to be part of the problem.

Consider the possibility that all we know, all we have done, all our plans, and all our current ways of doing things suddenly become irrelevant. For a moment, entertain the idea that the forces that shape business change to a point where business is barely recognizable. Imagine that the underlying frames and models which we relied on for centuries become irrelevant. In this book, we are making that assumption. We want to present investment management from a completely different perspective.

Our reasons for making those assumptions are simple. We live in a world where goals and data can be connected without human thoughts or actions. In this world, data shapes our reality and not the opposite. In the hypermodern world, we do not divide our business into segments and parts, or study causal relationships between processes, or structure our business designs first and then create systems. In this world, data creates our business. Data gives structure to our business and business models. Data determines what products we will develop and to whom we will market. Data gives us strategies. This bottom-up approach implies that the top-down human-centric strategy and strategic design become irrelevant. A new model and a new reality take shape. This reality is built bottom-up from knowing, understanding, and using data—such that it is efficiently consumed by intelligent machines to perform work. In this new model, we no longer deploy machines for data, we deploy machines from data.

The distinction between a hypermodern and a modern asset, wealth, or investment management firm is significant. A hypermodern asset management firm is designed bottom-up in response to the data a firm has. It establishes processes in response to its strategic goals and the data. In other words, unlike yesterday's firms that first establish processes and then try to organize and analyze data around them, the process is reversed. An organization sets a goal and then first establishes what data it has (and can have) and how can it create value from that data. The processes are established on top of that.

THE REVOLUTION IS REAL

The artificial intelligence revolution is sweeping across the globe. Pick any newspaper or magazine, go to any major news site, or explore business or government strategy–related documents and you are likely to see a reference to artificial intelligence. This sudden emergence of artificial intelligence is redefining how business is conducted. In some ways it is revising the fundamental assumptions on which our economies are built. This new era is not just about automation. It is about conducting business in a completely different way. It is about new business models. It is about powerful and unexpected innovation.

Artificial intelligence is not a new technology. However, its widespread adoption and application are a new phenomenon. The AI era is not determined by when the technology was developed but instead when it became mainstream and widely adopted. The wide adoption of the AI technology is evident from its use in products and services that range from mobile phone–based personal assistants to autonomous cars. Take the example of digital assistants, like Siri, that you can direct to perform various jobs for you. As you give verbal commands, the assistant complies and performs in accordance with your directive—but while doing so, it also learns about your accent, speech pattern, and voice. The applications that it works with also learn about your habits—for example, a GPS-based map application learns about your commuting habits.

For products and services to learn and accumulate experience is different than the products or services working together as a system or automation. The digital revolution was about computer automation, but such automation was limited to systems that processed data based on programming code that specifically directed the program to do what needed to get done. If various paths in the logic of the program were available, programmers used if-then statements to guide the program to take the right logical path. There was no learning involved. There was no experience accumulation. There was no mechanism to predict new pathways or identify new and unknown solutions. Imagine writing a program with if-then statements to drive a car. With all the possibilities that can happen while driving, it will be nearly impossible to identify every situation and line by line write code to direct the computer to drive. But with machine learning, you are not directing the computer to pick the right choice based on if-then instructions but instead teaching the computer to learn itself from data. This distinction is important because it separates the digital era from the artificial intelligence era. In the digital era we achieved automation, while in the artificial intelligence era we are targeting for intelligent automation.

The demands of this new era are understood far better by fintech startups and some state players than by the traditional big banks, many governments, and investors in general. For many large banks, investment managers, and finance firms, the vision for automation is limited to having robotic process automation (RPA) teams trying to automate simple repeatable processes or their quant department experimenting with machine learning. If the potential and goals of the intelligent automation were so limited, then it is not much of a revolution. The application of AI models for investment evaluation, opportunity identification, and portfolio and risk management has been going on for decades; however, it is highly proprietary, and often closely held by small teams. The knowledge, while used for the benefit of the firm, does not necessarily become shared knowledge or used across the firm. Generally small and siloed teams of quants or researchers who develop such solutions continue to have the know-how and benefit from the technology.

But the world is changing. Artificial intelligence–based automation is emerging as a powerful force. The walls of legacy companies are collapsing as fast-paced innovative competitors nibble at profits from all angles. The legacy firms are concerned about their survival, and while they know, one would hope, that their survival depends on their ability to become centers of excellence for intelligent automation, they are not sure how to do it.

In this book I introduced to you the intelligent automation world from the strategic point of view. I showed you how to rebuild your entire operation. I know that your transformation will not happen overnight. I know that you will not pick everything in this book and start implementing it at once. The real point of the book was to give everyone involved in asset management a way to think differently and a plan to build a modern firm.

I hope you recognized that it is not enough to apply artificial intelligence in some limited capability area of a firm. In fact, it is counterproductive to deploy AI solutions in one functional area or department and ignore others. A good analogy for that concept comes from a manufacturing supply chain. If you increase the efficiency of some parts of a supply chain but not others, it will lead to bottlenecks, and the performance of the total supply chain will not improve. Similarly, if you approach artificial intelligence on a piecemeal basis, it will not lead to the creation of a powerful company or give your firm a competitive advantage. Your firm's total automation strategy is what will enable you to compete effectively in the new era.

COMPLEX ADAPTIVE SYSTEMS

We live in a complex world. In fact, we can describe our world as composed of billions of human agents and trillions of machines who interact with each other on an ongoing basis. Individually they can be viewed as parts, microsegments, or micro-modules. When they interact, they form a dynamic system. Scientists call these systems complex adaptive systems (CAS). Complex adaptive systems cannot be explained through linear, cause-and-effect relationships. Predicting them is even harder. The knowledge of individual parts does not aggregate into the knowledge of the whole, as the whole displays properties that could be significantly different than the parts or even a linear, cause-and-effect based understanding of the assembly of the parts. They tend to be stable, and that implies that while they interact with the external environment, they resist systemwide change—at least up to a certain point. But change is imminent, and as change happens it attempts to destabilize or alter the state of the CAS. Few interactions have limited power, but when they combine, their force consolidates and CAS transition occurs—something that scientists call emergence.

To function well in CAS, it will be helpful to have some level of awareness about our role and interaction in this system. AI offers you one way to develop your state of awareness about the complexity that surrounds us. More importantly, it gives us some level of feedback to understand if emergence is happening. Without AI, we will soon deplete our ability to understand our reality. Building, pursuing, and executing profitable strategies will become impossible We must move fast.

OUR CORONAVIRUS MELTDOWN PREDICTION

This is exactly how we understood and predicted the coronavirus-related meltdown. If human consciousness, both at individual level and collective level, can be viewed as a complex adaptive system, then the information about the lethality of coronavirus would have to fight some internal battles with all the other distractions we had to struggle with. This fight implies that information exchanges are taking place across agents, and some pattern of that information exchange may lead the system to the point where it will transition to a new state. This new state is the state of collective consciousness, which will lead to viewing the coronavirus threat as a real threat to our economy, our health, our financial well-being. That is the point where a collective awareness and socially constructed reality will emerge, and that will push us to act. That is when we will start selling, close our positions, rebalance our portfolios, or make other bets. That happened around mid-March of 2020. It is as if there was an incubation period of social awareness, as if the markets were trying to make sense out of it, and the learning period for the world was about 20 days when the size of awareness was doubling.

Perhaps it gives us a clue about how human civilization, given the current communication technologies, processes information. This included the greatest investors, the best asset managers, the leading experts. Market performance is a testament to the fact that few had seen what coronavirus really was: a devastating blow to the global economy. Our failure to value the risk properly shows that communications technology has not really improved. Clearly, coronavirus was not a black swan event. It was not something that we could not have predicted or imagined. Once we paid attention to the news, the reasoning was simple, crisp, and clear.

This places us in a dilemma. What good is all the news if we are unable to make sense out of it? Humans are social animals, and we like stories. Stories affect our consciousness (for example, earnings calls are familiar stories), but coronavirus in February of 2020 was not. It was a foreign story to us.

Listening to stories is an important attribute of our ability to achieve investment success. In fact, it can be argued that it is one of the most important variables. It goes beyond the fundamentals that are taught to us. It goes beyond the empirical explanations. It enters the realm of sensemaking, and that is one of the areas where artificial intelligence is making tremendous progress. One of the most interesting stories of modern times is of AI itself. That story, in some ways, is the story of metacognition, since it entails the stories of all other stories we can hear, see, imagine, and feel. It is the story of our evolving into "more."

Index

Page numbers followed by *f* or *t* refer to figures or tables